EDUCATIONAL FACILITIES
New Concepts in Architecture & Design

現代建築集成／教育施設

序文

本書が取り上げるのは1989年以降に完成した多くの教育施設の中から、建築としても計画プログラムの面からも興味深く、見事なデザインとして地域に定着した優れた学校である。

"教育施設"といえば、ここに取り上げた規定された学校ばかりではなく、社会教育施設も含めるべきかもしれない。生涯の各時期(ライフステージ)における人間のための学習の施設という視点に立てば、それら近年特に増えてきた生涯学習のための諸施設と、規定された学校に区別を設けることさえ問題であり、それらとの連携は益々深まってゆくことが予想される。しかし、この巻の内容は、幼稚園、小学校、中学校、高校、大学、専門学校といった従来の規定された学校に限定した。

近年そうした規定された学校、特に公立の小、中、高等学校が建築家の手によって設計され、実現してき始めたのは喜ばしいことである。標準的な柱間に合わせて全体の間取りがつくられ、それが設計業者によって実施図に移し変えられ、現実化するという手順が自動化していた公共施設のひとつであった学校が変わってきた。特にこの数年の変化には著しいものがあるように思われる。取り上げた29の作品の多くも、決して潤沢とはいえない建設コストや設計費といった委託条件の中で、建築家が全力を挙げて教育の環境がいかにあるべきかという課題に取り組んだ結果である。

また、こうした従来の定型を破った学校建築の出現は突然起こったのではなく、その背景には文部省による80年代に始められた多目的スペースへの面積割増しや、屋外環境やクラブハウスへの資金的な補助制度の充実などがあったことを見逃すことはできない。また、そうした制度を整備する動きをつくり出した、行動的な計画研究者の力も忘れることはできない。自治体の具体的な学校建設と関わり続け、追跡調査するといった地道な長年の努力がその過程にあったのである。

学校とはひとりの人間の生にとって、幼少年期から青年の時代にかけての長い時間をそこで過ごし、それぞれが生涯にわたって固有の記憶を抱き続けている建築のひとつである。学校に通った者にとっては一時的に利用する施設というより、住まいと同じ居住施設であるといった性格を持っている。また周囲の地域に住む人々にとっては地区の生活や余暇の活動と深い関係を伴って記憶に残っている。そうした意味で、学校の施設のデザインは重要である。決しておざなりに処理されてはならないものだ。その町のなかの佇まい、運動場や校舎の配置、教室や廊下の雰囲気、さらには窓や階段の細部のディテールの端々から、知らず知らずのうちに人は多くの影響を受け、多くの事柄を学んでいる。その空間を日々利用する過程で、学ぶということの楽しさ、その歓びを感覚することができる。生長の時期に得たそうした歓びの経験は生涯引き継がれてゆく。施設のデザインそのも

のも重要な精神的な教育の一環なのである。

それゆえに、近年学校環境に社会の目が注がれ、こうした事柄に自覚的な地方の教育委員会や熱意ある学校が全国的に現われ始めたことは実に嬉しい事柄である。また一部であるにせよ、優れた学校建築の計画者の誘導によって、建築家の設計による、計画の面でも建築的にも優れた学校が日本全国に相次いで実現し始めたことは、学校が誰にとっても身近な施設であるだけに希望が持てる。それは建築が機能を果たすと同時に、人の心に訴える文化であることが社会的にも認められる第一歩であろうと思われるからである。

本書に収録された、ここ5年間に実現した学校を見るといくつかの事柄に気付く。第一に、興味深い教育の環境をつくり出している小学校、中学校の多くが、日本全土に散らばった、地方の小さな町の学校としてつくられていることである。それらは地形の変化を利用して、固有の佇まいが自然環境の中に繰り広げられ、魅力を持った生活の場所として設計されている。

第二に様々な学習形態に見合う、自由度の高い教室の設計が考えられていることである。多彩な行動を誘発するラウンジやコーナーの場所が心を込めて設計されている。また教室から教室へ至る移行の空間を、自然に接して気分の転換が図れるような場所として設定しているのも見られる。設計者が積極的に性格の異なった多様な場を学校の内部につくり出そうという努力が感じられる。

第三に地域の公共施設の核として学校が考えられ始めている傾向である。都心部では貴重なオープンスペースを確保する公園や防災拠点であったり、都市の景観をつくる重要な要素であったりする。また小さな村では、文化センターの役割も果たし、地域の人々の心の拠り所ともなっている。つまり教育施設が都市施設や町の中核の施設として、教育という機能を単に果たすだけのものではあり得なくなっていることである。そこに公共に開かれた建築としての格調や魅力も求められているのだと思う。

本書に見られる29の学校はいずれも個性と特色を持ち、まったく画一的ではない。学ぶものは自分たちの学校という意識をそれぞれに持ち、固有の空間の記憶とそこでの出来事を心に刻み付けるに違いない。こうした建築としても優れた学校が日本各地に次々と生み出されることを、これから期待せずにはいられない。そして本書の写真と図面から"教育施設"の可能性と新しい傾向を感じ取っていただきたい。

富永讓
富永讓＋フォルムシステム設計研究所代表

Foreword

This monograph introduces a selection of educational facilities built after 1989 that are of value in terms of architecture and planning and that have well rooted in their respective communities as an outstanding design work.
"Educational facilities" should perhaps include those for continued social education. When viewed as a facility that provides people with an opportunity of learning at different stages of life, it may not be appropriate to distinguish facilities for continued education from what we generally know as schools. Such facilities are increasing in number in recent years, and the link between these two types of facilities is expected to grow stronger. Despite our awareness of such trend, this volume introduces only those in accordance with the traditional definition of school; that is, kindergarten, elementary, junior and senior high schools, universities and technical colleges.
That schools, particularly public schools, are being designed and constructed by professional architects is a very welcoming phenomenon. Instead of automatically conforming to regulatory standard of spatial span which in turn defines the overall floor plan, public schools are undergoing changes in their architectural designs and plans. The trend appears to be particularly marked in the past few years. Most of the 29 works introduced in this volume are proof of sincere efforts by architects who are tackling with the task of pursuing how an ideal educational environment should be while being challenged by restrictions such as insufficient budget of construction and design costs.

Emergence of non-stereotype school buildings is not a chance occurrence. We should not overlook the fact that the Ministry of Education launched in the 1980s programs that allowed allocation of larger area for multi-purpose spaces or that enhanced financial aids for constructing better outdoor environment and club rooms. We should also remember that there were pioneer researchers and plan-makers who paved the road and nurtured the climate for such movements. These people had committed themselves for many years to the actual process of building schools implemented by the local governments, and continued untiring efforts of following up the outcome.
School is a place where people spend much of their time from the childhood to the adolescence and of which memories they cherish for the rest of their life. School in its nature is not a facility offered for temporary use but is more like a place where one lives his/her life. At the same time, school as hardware is closely linked with the daily life and leisure activities of the community residents.
In that sense, the architectural design of school bears significance; it should not be slighted. The appearance viewed in relation with the neighborhood, layout of the playground and the classroom buildings, atmosphere in the classrooms or corridors, details of the windows and stairs ... all these factors have subliminal influences and people learn much without realizing it. As we spend our time in school from day to day, we feel the joy and pleasure of learning. The precious sensation of joy of learning experienced in the early years will remain cherished in

our hearts for the rest of our life. Architectural design of school is, in that sense, a very important element of mental education.

We find it an encouraging trend that our society is paying much attention to school environment, developing awareness among those involved in education such as local school boards throughout Japan. Although still limited in number, new schools are being constructed under the leadership of innovative plan-makers. Considering that a school is something very essential and familiar to everyone, the new trend in school construction brings us a favorable outlook for the future. It certainly is a first step for the society toward recognizing that architecture has its functions but is a part of our culture at the same time.

An overview of school buildings constructed in the past five years gives us some insights.

Firstly, many of the elementary schools and junior high schools with unique environment are being built in small local cities throughout Japan. These schools are tactfully designed to utilize the topographical features, creating an attractive place of learning and living amid the natural environment.

Secondly, new school buildings are designed with a high degree of freedom to allow diversity to the mode of education. Lounges and nooks stimulate children's imaginative activities, and spaces connecting classrooms are in many cases created as a place of relaxation where children can refresh their minds through close contact with the nature. Through such diversified designs, architects' positive efforts and enthusiasm to create spaces with variety of features and characters within school can be felt.

Thirdly, there seems to be emerging a new trend to regard schools as the core of community activities. In urban areas, schools function also as a precious open space that can be used as a park, an emergency refuge or an important element of the urban scene. In small villages, on the other hand, schools are the cultural center of the community. Schools are no longer a space that functions merely as a place of education. They must be architecture with refined style and charm and they must be open to the public as well.

The 29 works carried in this volume are schools with their own unique characters and features; none conforms to stereotype. Children will surely register the space and the form in their memory, as well as the time spent there. It is our sincere wish that future school buildings will bear such architectural significance as well. We also wish our readers to discover the new possibilities and trends of future "school facilities" from the photographs and drawings contained in this volume.

Yuzuru Tominaga
Representative, Yuzuru Tominaga & Form System Institute

目次／CONTENTS

幼稚園　Kindergartens	9
小学校　Elementary Schools	27
中学校／高等学校　Junior and Senior High Schools	67
複合施設　Combined Facilities	117
大学　Universities / Colleges	149
専門学校　Technical Colleges	203
インデックス　Index	217

EDUCATIONAL FACILITIES
New Concepts in Architecture & Design

Copyright©1994 MEISEI PUBLICATIONS

All rights reserved.
No part on this publication may be reproduced or used in any form or by any means graphic, electronic, mechanical, recording, taping, or information storage and retrieval systems without written permission of the publisher.

ISBN4-87246-293-9 C3052 P16000E
First Edition Jun. 1994
MEISEI PUBLICATIONS

#203, 3-11-1 Kanda Jinbo-cho, Chiyoda-ku, TOKYO 101 Japan
Phone. 03-5276-1941 Facsimile. 03-5276-1966

幼稚園　KINDERGARTENS

あいく幼稚園, ANNEX
AIKU KINDERGARTEN

岩本秀三設計事務所
HIDEMI IWAMOTO ARCHITECT & ASSOCIATES

グラウンドに張り出した保育室外観　Nursery overhanging the playground

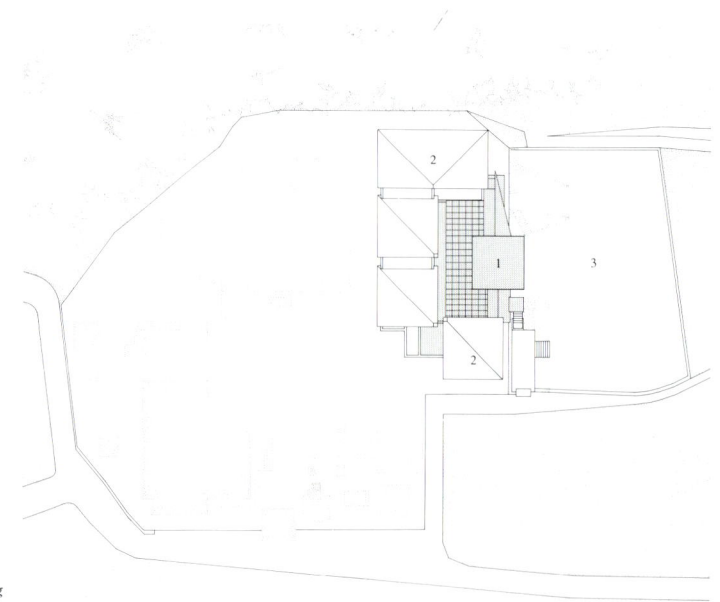

1　増築部分　Extension
2　既存部分　Existing building
3　グラウンド　Playground

Site plan　1:1000

保育室 南側外観　South facade of the nursery

オープンスペースから保育室入口と南側出入口を見る　Looking at the entrance to the nursery and the exit on the south in the open space

オープンスペース　Open space

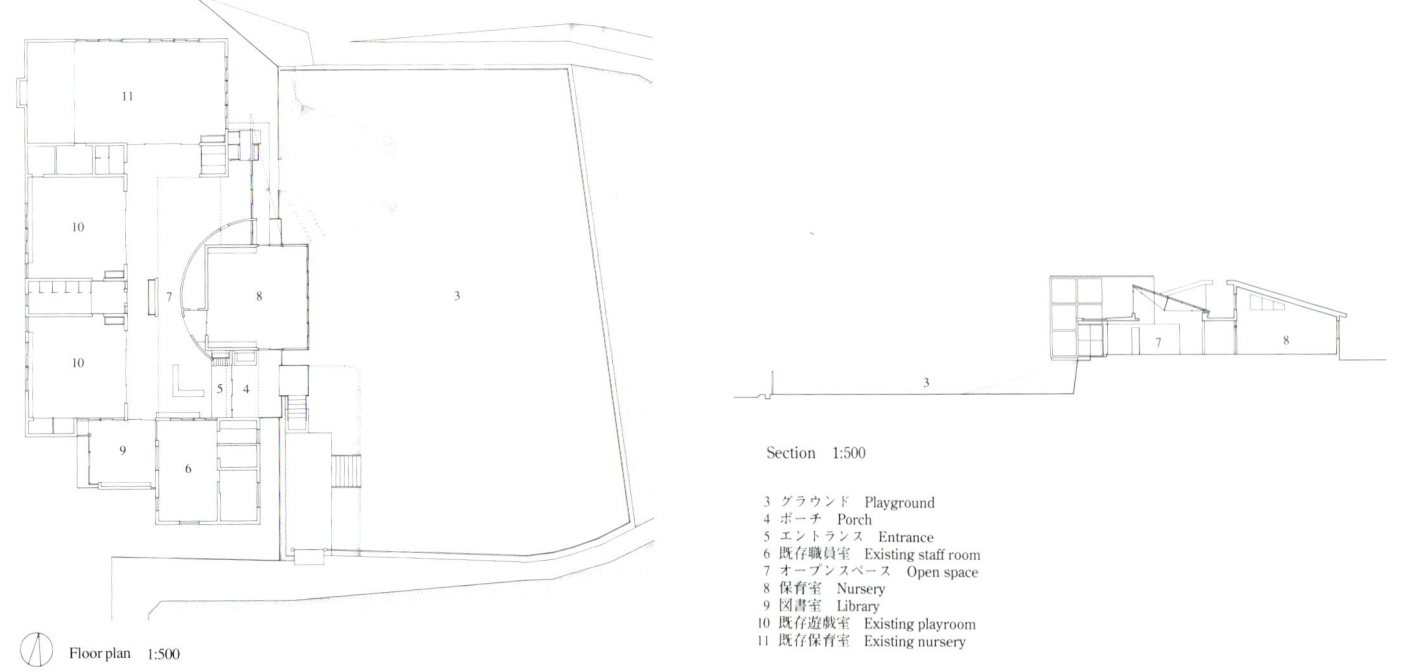

Floor plan 1:500

Section 1:500

3 グラウンド　Playground
4 ポーチ　Porch
5 エントランス　Entrance
6 既存職員室　Existing staff room
7 オープンスペース　Open space
8 保育室　Nursery
9 図書室　Library
10 既存遊戯室　Existing playroom
11 既存保育室　Existing nursery

南東側外観 白い増築部分の両サイドは既存の園舎　Looking from the southeast; existing buildings on both sides of the white-colored extension

既存園舎は、東に向かって開いたコの字型プランで諸室はすべて室内から一段下がった開放廊下でつながれていた。全体は、コの字の中庭に一粒の種を植えるように置いた保育室と既存園舎との相関関係によって成立させた。それまで外気に開放されていたエントランスホールは図書室に再生すると同時に、既存園舎と新たな保育室との隙間全面に張った床をかつての開放廊下にも廻らすことで新旧の境界を曖昧につなげることを意図し、同時にこの増築をきっかけとして、建築全体にまったく新しい建築空間を表出させようとした。

The existing buildings were arranged in U shape opening on the east and connected with open corridors one step below the level of classrooms. The nursery is newly added, situated in the courtyard to harmonize with the existing buildings. The former entrance hall is remodeled into a library. The flooring that covers the space between the existing buildings and the new nursery is repeated into the former open corridors in order to bring certain degree of integrity. The intention was to create an entirely new architectural space by the addition of the annex.

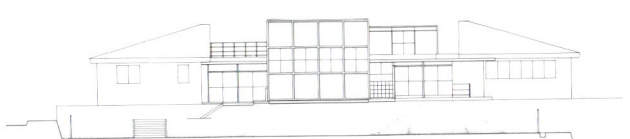

East elevation　1:500

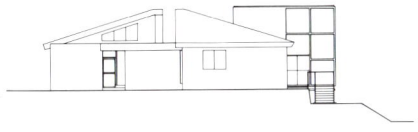

South elevation　1:500

所在地　　広島県安浦町
設計　　　岩本秀三設計事務所
施工　　　井本建設
竣工　　　1993年2月
敷地面積　1,595.51m²
建築面積　494.12m²　増築：146.97m²
延床面積　475.42m²　増築：131.76m²
階数　　　地上1階　増築：地上1階
構造　　　鉄筋コンクリート造　増築：鉄骨造
撮影　　　新建築社

Location:　Yasuura-town, Hiroshima
Architect:　Hidemi Iwamoto Architect & Associates
General contractor:　Imoto Kensetsu Co.,Ltd.
Completion date:　February 1993
Site area:　17,173.91sq.ft.
Building area:　5,318.66sq.ft.　extension: 1,581.97sq.ft.
Total floor area:　5,117.37sq.ft.　extension: 1,418.25sq.ft.
Number of floor:　1 floor above ground
extension: 1 floor above ground
Structure:　Reinforced concrete structure
extension: steel structure
Photographer:　Shinkenchiku-sha・Co.,Ltd.

板橋さざなみ幼稚園 アネックス
ITABASHI SAZANAMI KINDERGARTEN ANNEX

遠藤建築スタジオ　遠藤吉生
Yoshitaka Endo　ENDO ARCHITECT STUDIO

南側外観　South facade

デッキ Deck

保育室 Nursery

1階 トイレ　1st floor, lavatory

南側テラス　South terrace

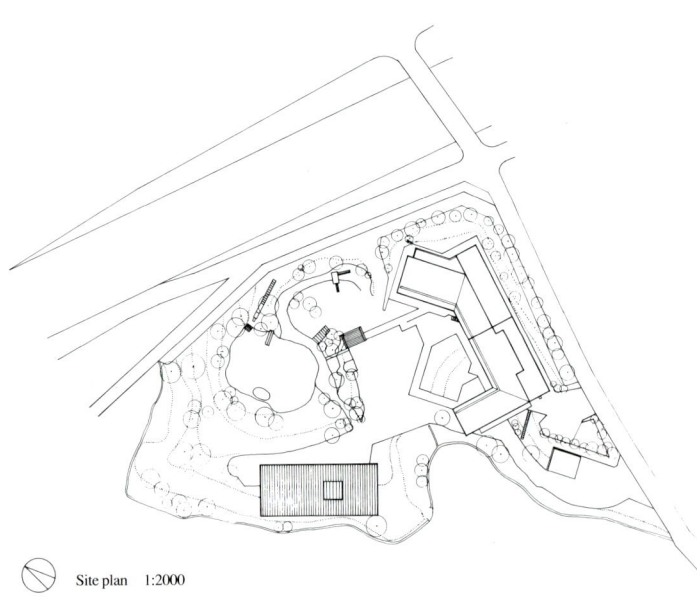

Site plan　1:2000

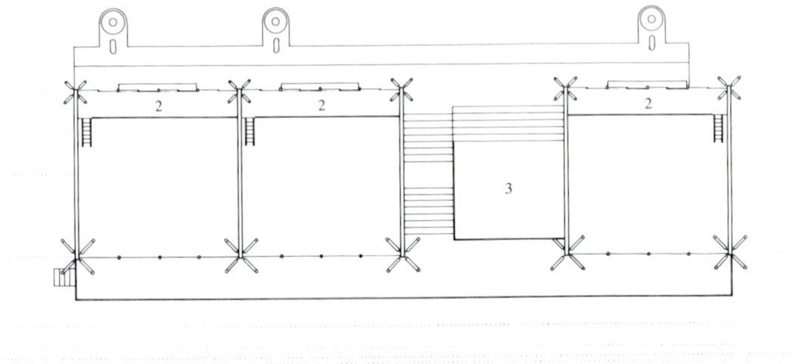

1　保育室　Nursery
2　ロフト　Loft
3　デッキ　Deck

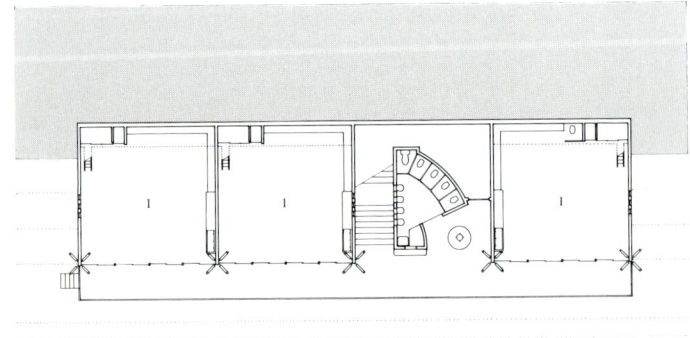

Upper floor plan

1st floor plan　1:400

北側外観 夜景　North facade at night

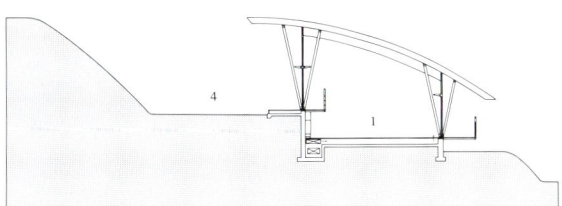

Section 1:400

1　保育室　Nursery
4　前庭　Front yard

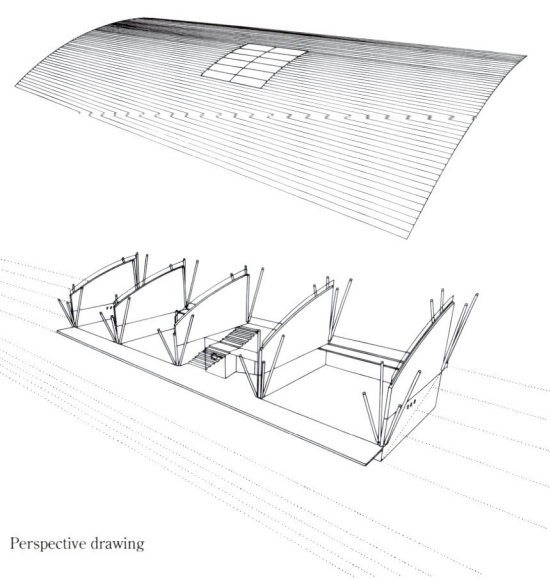

Perspective drawing

子供たちが自然の中で生活することにより、自然や風土に対する意識と感覚を培うことを目標としている。保育室は2面を全面開口とし、斜面方向の景観のダイナミズムの中に存在している。保育室以外はすべて外気に開放されており、室内と同等な比重を持つ重要な場所となっている。ひとつはオープンデッキで多目的スペースとして利用される。もうひとつは廊下や階段で、本来の目的以外の行為や遊びが発生しやすい場所であり、道草的な行為が誘発されることを期待している。

The concept is to foster in children the awareness of and affection for nature and the climate by offering a space surrounded by nature. The nursery opens on two sides, and is situated in a dynamically sloping terrain. The open-air spaces play an equally important role as the inside: the open deck is used as a multi-purpose space while the open corridors and stairs allure children as a non-ordinary space. Playfulness rather than utility is the design motif here.

所在地　　広島県東広島市
設計　　　遠藤建築スタジオ　遠藤吉生
施工　　　日興
竣工　　　1993年3月
敷地面積　8,276.21m²
建築面積　353.05m²
延床面積　287.10m²
階数　　　地上2階
構造　　　鉄骨造、鉄筋コンクリート造
撮影　　　新建築社

Location:　Higashihiroshima-city, Hiroshima
Architect:　Yoshitaka Endo　Endo Architect Studio
General contractor:　Nikko Co.,Ltd.
Completion date:　March 1993
Site area:　89,084.30sq.ft.
Building area:　3,800.19sq.ft.
Total floor area:　3,090.32sq.ft.
Number of floors:　2 floors above ground
Structure:　Steel structure and reinforced concrete structure
Photographer:　Shinkenchiku-sha・Co.,Ltd.

OPEN-AIR KINDERGARTEN

宮本佳明+アトリエ第5建築界
KATSUHIRO MIYAMOTO + ATELIER CINQUIÉME

北西側より遊戯室を見る　Looking at the playroom from the northwest

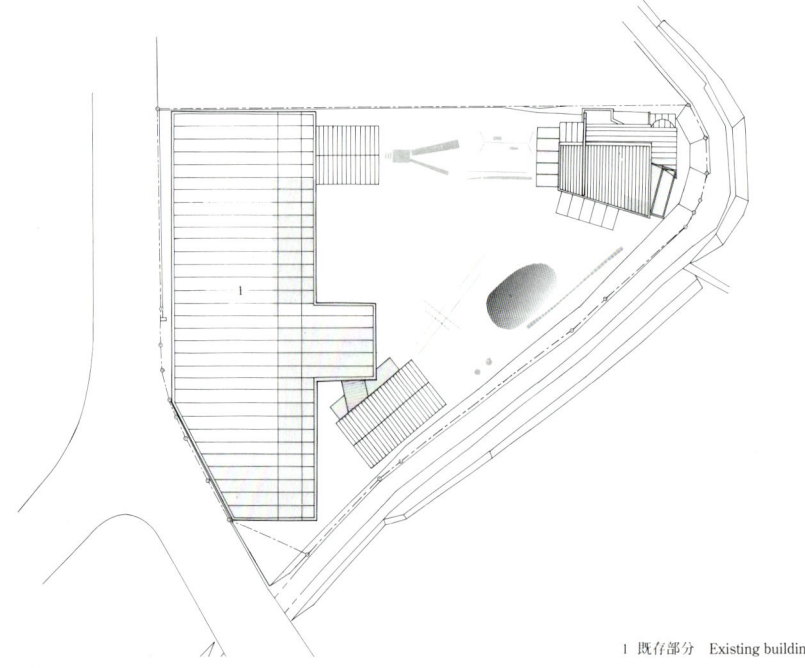

1　既存部分　Existing building

Site plan　1:600

遊戯室　Playroom

北西側外観　Northwest facade

北西側外観　跳ね上げ戸を閉鎖した状態　Northwest facade with the trap doors closed

南東側外観　Southeast facade

階段室　Staircase

地階 母の会室　Mothers' Club meets in the basement

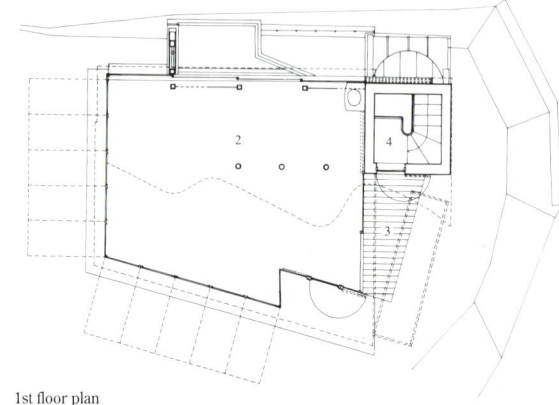
1st floor plan

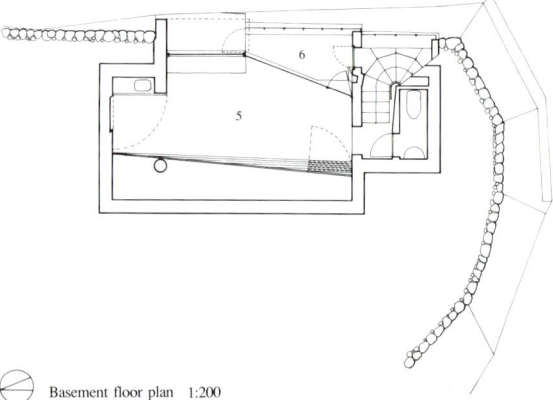
Basement floor plan 1:200

2　遊戯室　Playroom
3　濡れ縁　Open veranda
4　階段室　Staircase
5　母の会室　Mothers' Club
6　坪庭　Tsuboniwa garden

南西側外観 夜景　Southwest facade at night

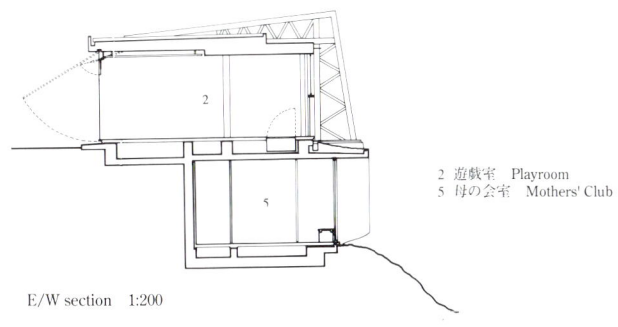

2　遊戯室　Playroom
5　母の会室　Mothers' Club

E/W section　1:200

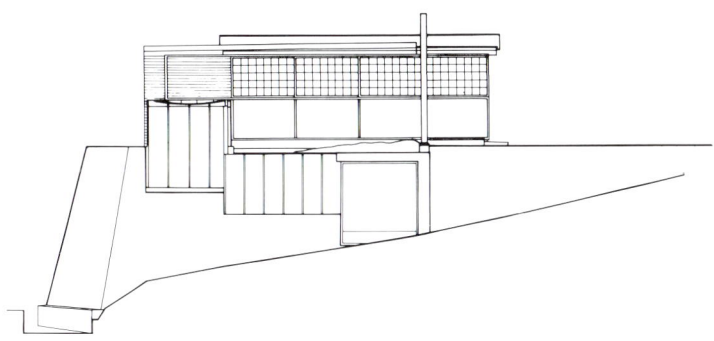

East elevation　1:200

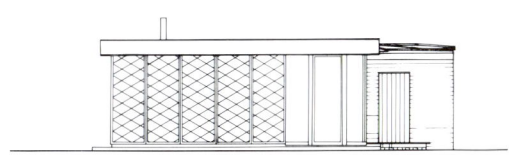

West elevation　1:200

遊戯室はそれ自体が空間的な遊具である。四方を巡る建具は普段はすべて開かれており、全体として"あずまや"のような形をしている。特に跳ね上げ戸は園児だけが自然に飛び込んでくる高さに持ち上げられており、園庭との間に緩いフィルターとして作用する。一方で"母の会"の部屋は、雑木林に面した古い石積み擁壁をカットして開口を設けた上で地下室として扱い、園庭の喧噪からは隔絶された落ち着いた空間となっている。

The playroom is an element of play in itself. The fittings on four sides are opened during the day, creating a space similar to that of an "arbor". In particular, the trap doors are swung open to a height that allows only children to jump in and out of the room, acting as loose partitions separating the inside from the outside. The room for "Mothers' Club", on the other hand, is located underground by cutting out an opening in an old retention wall of stone masonry facing a thicket as a quiet and serene space isolated from the clamor of the playground.

所在地　　兵庫県宝塚市
設計　　　宮本佳明＋アトリエ第5建築界
施工　　　中武建設工業
竣工　　　1992年10月
敷地面積　1,067.78m²
建築面積　44.91m²
延床面積　72.81m²
階数　　　地上1階、地下1階
構造　　　鉄骨造、鉄筋コンクリート造
撮影　　　生田将人

Location:　Takarazuka-city, Hyogo
Architect:　Katsuhiro Miyamoto + Atelier Cinquiéme
General contractor:　Nakatake Construction & Industry Co.,Ltd.
Completion date:　October 1992
Site area:　11,493.48sq.ft.
Building area:　483.41sq.ft.
Total floor area:　783.72sq.ft.
Number of floors:　1 floor above ground, 1 floor below ground
Structure:　Steel structure and reinforced concrete structure
Photographer:　Masato Ikuta

東金市立嶺南幼稚園
REINAN PUBLIC KINDERGARTEN

篠原聡子＋空間研究所
SATOKO SHINOHARA + SPATIAL DESIGN STUDIO

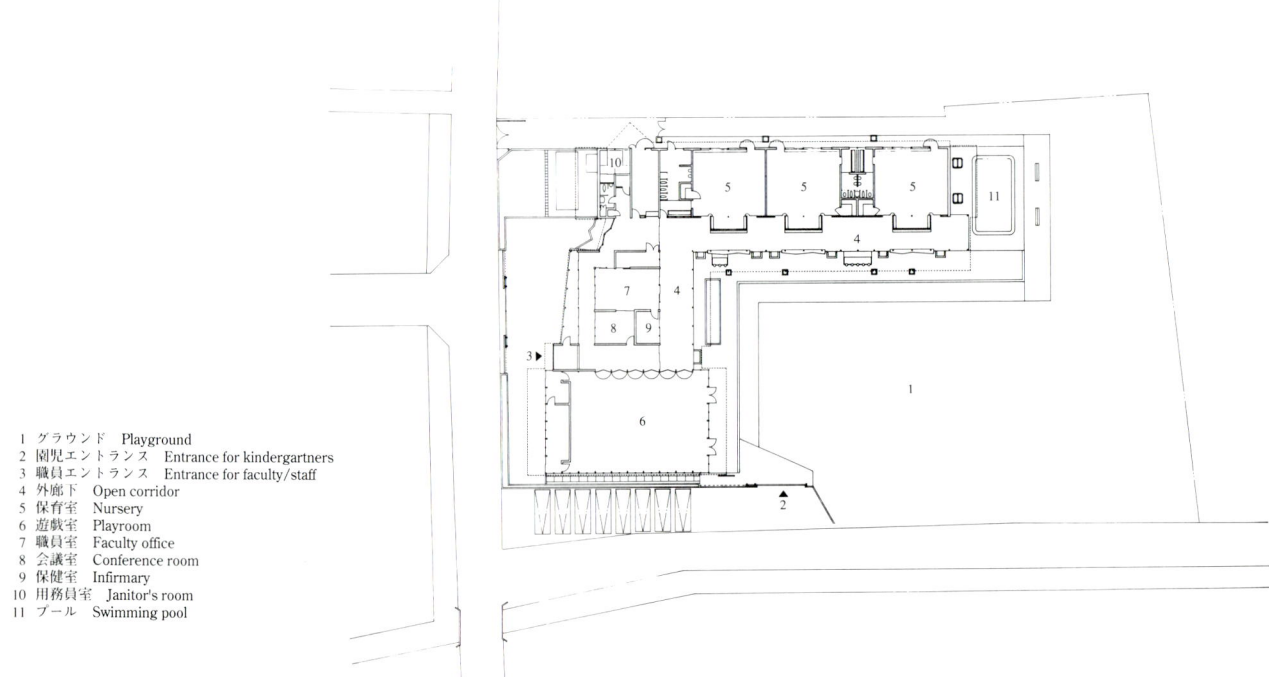

グラウンドから保育棟を見る　Looking at the nursery from the playground

1　グラウンド　Playground
2　園児エントランス　Entrance for kindergartners
3　職員エントランス　Entrance for faculty/staff
4　外廊下　Open corridor
5　保育室　Nursery
6　遊戯室　Playroom
7　職員室　Faculty office
8　会議室　Conference room
9　保健室　Infirmary
10　用務員室　Janitor's room
11　プール　Swimming pool

Site plan + 1st floor plan　1:800

北側外観　North facade

保育室棟東側屋根部分　Nursery roof on the east

保育室前吹放し廊下　Open corridor in front of the nursery

保育室前吹放し廊下　Open corridor in front of the nursery

North elevation　1:500

保育室　Nursery

保育室　Nursery

Section　1:500

5　保育室　Nursery
10　用務員室　Janitor's room

遊戯室棟 西側外観　West facade of the playroom

遊戯室　Playroom

波と鯨の背を思わせる屋根のラインは、九十九里の海岸線の後退によってこの敷地が陸になったという遠い記憶とつながっている。保育室棟と管理棟を形成するウェーブラインは家並みのようにも見え、遊戯室棟となっているホェールシェイプと周辺の田園風景との仲立ちの役割を果たしている。異なる形態の3つの棟は吹放しの廊下によって緩やかに結ばれ、子供たちの想像力を刺激しつつ、彼らの縦横無尽な行動を十分に許容し得る構成となっている。

The roof lines suggestive of waves and the back of a whale remind us of the ancient memory that the site was once the Kujukuri Beach. The wavy roof line over the nursery and administrative wing also suggests a street scene, linking the whale-shaped playroom with the rural landscape in the background. The three wings in different shapes are loosely connected by open corridors, letting children to freely move around and stimulating their imaginations.

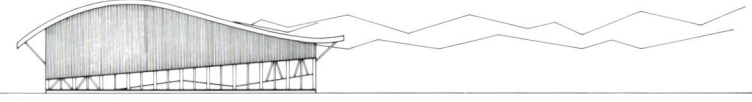

South elevation　1:500

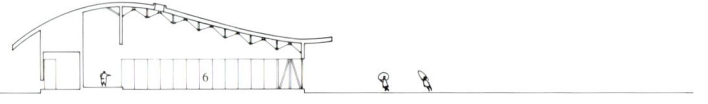

Section　1:500
6　遊戯室　Playroom

所在地　　千葉県東金市
設計　　　篠原聡子＋空間研究所
施工　　　旭工業
竣工　　　1993年2月
敷地面積　3,220.40m²
建築面積　881.60m²
延床面積　685.30m²
階数　　　地上1階
構造　　　木造
撮影　　　小林研二／22-24,25上,26　　柴田泰夫／25下

Location: Togane-city, Chiba
Architect: Satoko Shinohara + Spatial Design Studio
General contractor: Asahi Construction
Completion date: February 1993
Site area: 34,664.06sq.ft.
Building area: 9,489.45sq.ft.
Total floor area: 7,376.50sq.ft.
Number of floor: 1 floor above ground
Structure: Timber construction
Photographer: Kenji Kobayashi / 22-24, 25: top, 26
Yasuo Shibata / 25: bottom

小学校　Elementary Schools

出石町立弘道小学校
KODO ELEMENTARY SCHOOL

Team Zoo いるか設計集団＋神戸大学 重村研究室
TEAM ZOO ATELIER IRUKA CO.,LTD. + KOBE UNIVERSITY SHIGEMURA INSTITUTE

南側より建築群を見る　Looking at the buildings from south

南西側よりサブグラウンドを囲む低学年棟を見る　Looking at the lower graders' wing enclosing the auxiliary playground from southwest

S/N section　1:1400

E/W section　1:1400

1　教室　Classroom
2　音楽室　Music room
3　図工室　Art/craft room
4　体育館　Gymnasium
5　メディアセンター　Media Center

左に高学年棟、右は中学年棟　The upper graders' wing on the left, the middle graders' wing on the right

ランチルーム屋上より体育館・管理棟を見る　右下はサブグラウンド　Looking at the gymnasium/administration wing from the rooftop of the lunchroom; the auxiliary playground below right

低学年棟の教室よりワークスペースを見る　Looking at the work space from a classroom in the lower graders' wing

低学年棟の教室　中央にワークスペース　Classroom in the lower graders' wing, the work space in the middle

高学年棟下階の吹抜ワークスペース　Work space in the light-well below the upper grader classrooms

高学年棟1階ワークスペースの一角に設けられたたたみコーナー
Tatami space in one corner of the work space on the 1st floor of the upper graders' wing

体育館への階段を見下ろす　Looking down at the stairs to the gymnasium

1	教室　Classroom
2	音楽室　Music room
3	図工室　Art/craft room
4	体育館　Gymnasium
5	メディアセンター　Media Center
6	低学年棟　Lower graders' wing
7	中学年棟　Middle graders' wing
8	高学年棟　Upper graders' wing
9	体育館・管理棟　Gymnasium/administration wing
10	ワークスペース　Work space
11	理科室　Science lab.
12	グラウンド　Playground
13	サブグラウンド　Auxiliary playground
14	屋外ステージ　Outdoor stage
15	自然学習園　Nature-watching garden
16	職員室　Faculty office
17	校長室　Principal's office
18	保健室　Infirmary
19	児童会室　Student Council room
20	ラウンジ　Lounge
21	ランチルーム　Lunchroom
22	時計塔　Clock tower
23	家庭科室　Home economics room
24	プール　Swimming pool
25	教材開発室　R&D lab. for teaching material
26	ミーティングルーム　Meeting room

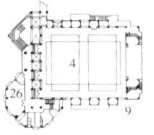

2nd floor plan

体育館・管理棟2階の体育館　Gymnasium on the 2nd floor of the gymnasium/administration wing

Site plan + 1st floor plan　1:2400

出石町は美しい城下町である。敷地は山の中腹であったため、土地造成を最小限に抑えるとともに自然に溶け込むように、全階が接地性を持つようにした。新しい教育を目指して、オープンクラスター配置を行い、1学年2クラスがひとつの多目的スペースを共有しているとともに、学校の中心となるメディアセンターやランチルームは、多様な教育の場としても多学年交流の場としても使われるよう計画した。何よりも豊かな教育の場として、計画的に自然環境を残し、その中に棟と棟をつなぐ半屋外や屋外空間、屋上テラスや低学生サブグラウンドを設けている。

Izushi is a beautiful castle town. The site is situated and the midslope of a mountain, land improvement is kept minimum and all the floors are planned to connect with the ground to close linkage with the surrounding nature. The classrooms are arranged in an open-cluster system, aiming at education with innovative concepts. Two home-room classes of the same grade share a multi-purpose space, while the media center and the lunchroom function also as a forum for inter-grade activities. Surrounded by verdurous nature which is left intact to the maximum extent possible, the semi-open and open-air spaces which connect the separate wings with the rooftop terrace and the auxiliary playground for the lower grades provide unlimited sources of imagination for the children.

所在地　兵庫県出石町
設計　Team Zoo いるか設計集団
　　　＋神戸大学 重村研究室
施工　川嶋工務店・川見建設・徳網建設JV.
竣工　1991年5月
敷地面積　37,690.00m²
建築面積　4,070.92m²
延床面積　4,846.02m²
階数　地上2階
構造　木造、一部鉄筋コンクリート造、鉄骨造
撮影　彰国社　中川敦玲/28-29,32下
　　　新建築社/30-31,32上,33-34

Location: Izushi-town, Hyogo
Architect: Team Zoo Atelier Iruka Co.,Ltd.
+ Kobe University Shigemura Institute
General contractor: Joint venture of Kawashima, Kawami and Tokuami
Completion date: May 1991
Site area: 405,691.39sq.ft.
Building area: 43,818.98sq.ft.
Total floor area: 52,162.07sq.ft.
Number of floors: 2 floors above ground
Structure: Timber construction, reinforced concrete structure and steel structure
Photographer: Nobuaki Nakagawa The Shokokusha Publishing Co.,Ltd. / 28-29, 32: bottom
Shinkenchiku-sha・Co.,Ltd. / 30-31, 32: top, 33-34

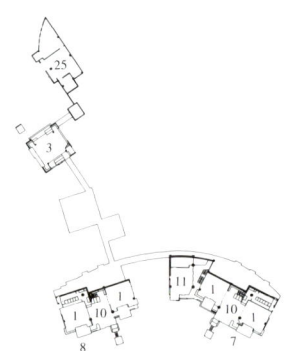

Basement floor plan

稲城市立城山小学校
SHIROYAMA ELEMENTARY SCHOOL

船越徹＋アルコム
TOHRU FUNAKOSHI + ARCOM R&D, ARCHITECTS

南側アプローチ　奥に朱色のスクールウォール　South approach, the vermillion wall in the back

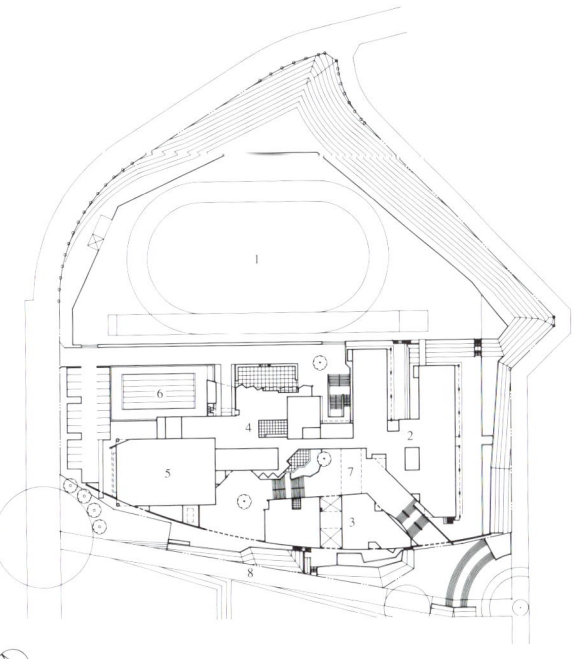

1　グラウンド　Playground
2　普通教室棟　Classroom wing
3　特別教室棟　Special classroom wing
4　管理棟　Administration wing
5　体育館棟　Gymnasium
6　プール　Swimming pool
7　モール　Mall
8　歩行者専用道路　Pavement

Site plan　1:2600

北側アプローチ　North approach

モールの最上部より南東側を見る　Looking southeast from the top of the mall

特別教室棟の間に設けられたスペース　Open space connecting the special classroom wing ▶

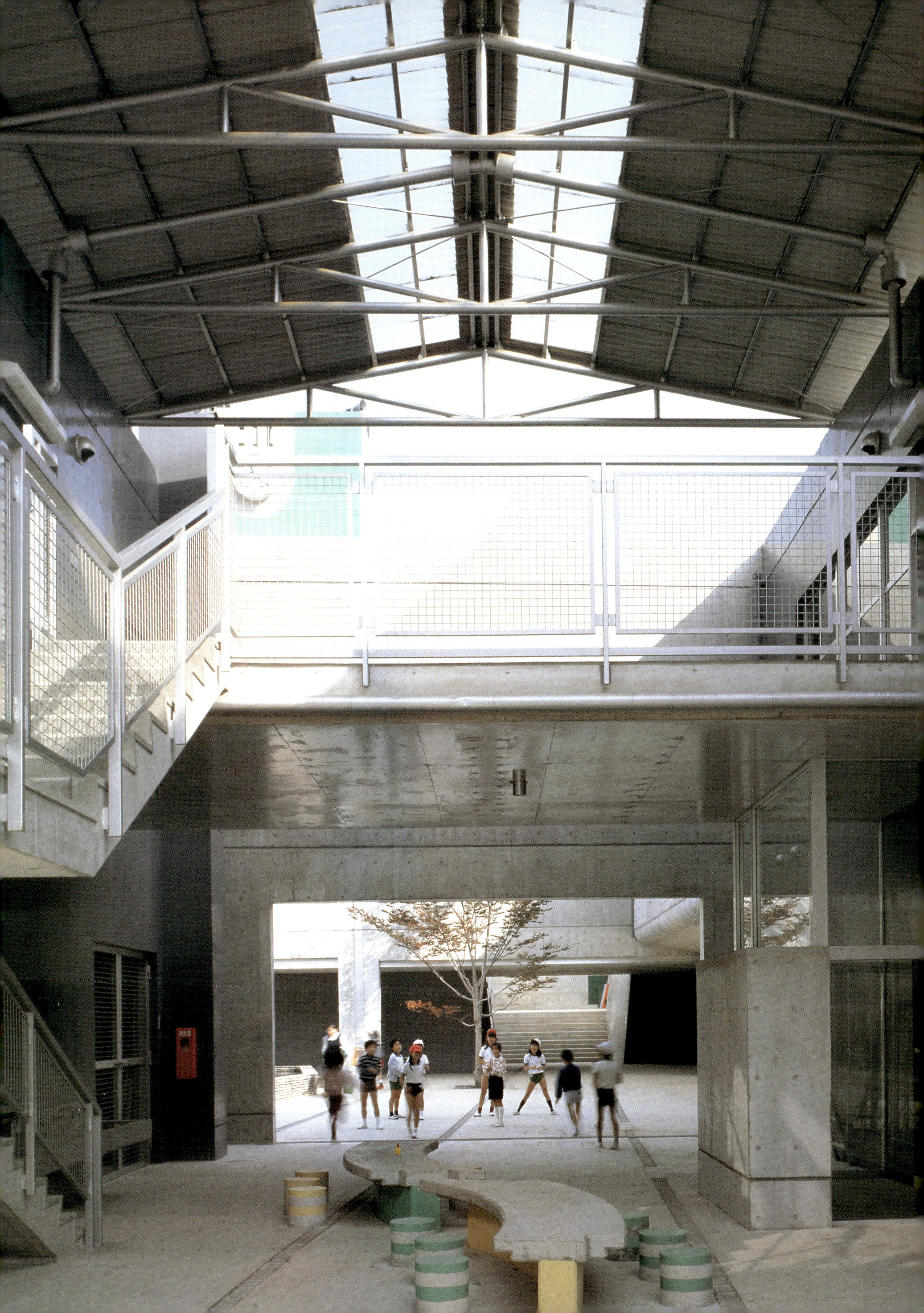

普通教室棟1階ホール　左にエントランス　The 1st floor hall in the classroom wing; the entrance on the left

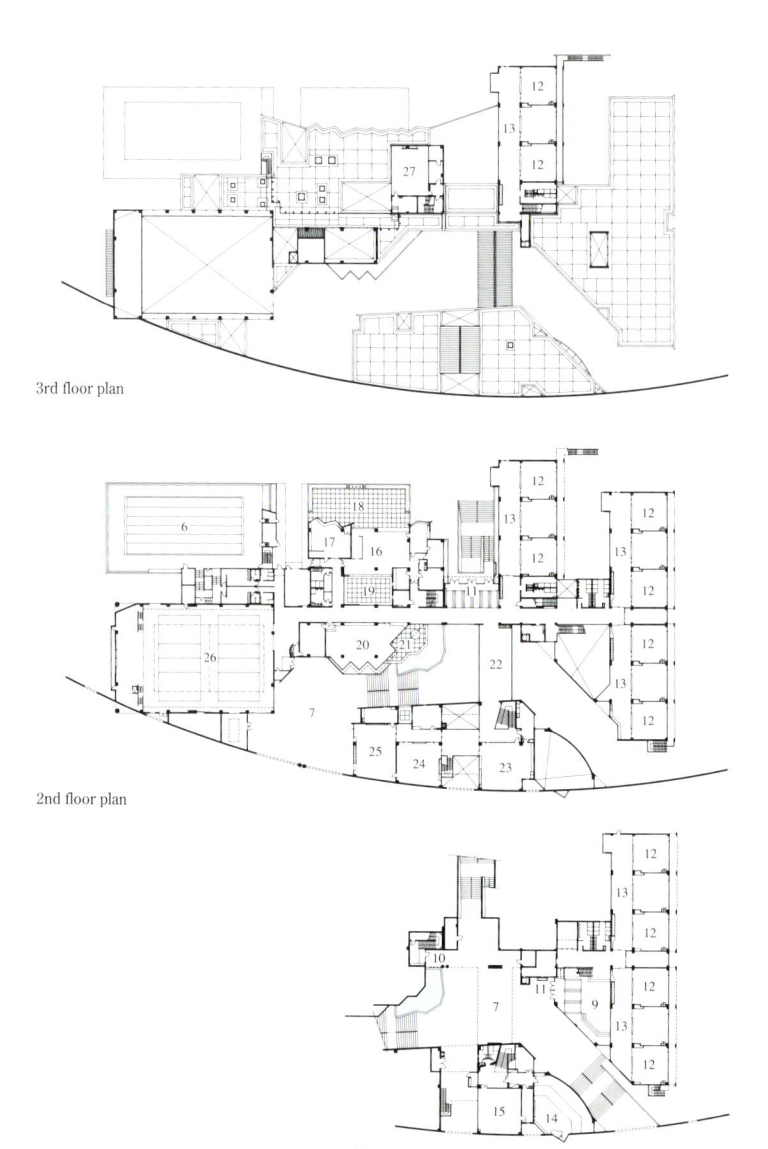

3rd floor plan

2nd floor plan

6　プール　Swimming pool
7　モール　Mall
9　ホール　Hall
10　職員・外来エントランス　Entrance for faculty and visitors
11　エントランス　Entrance
12　教室　Classroom
13　多目的スペース　Multi-purpose space
14　音楽室　Music room
15　視聴覚室　Audio-visual room
16　職員室　Faculty office
17　保健室　Infirmary
18　前庭　Front yard
19　中庭　Courtyard
20　図書室　Library
21　テラス　Terrace
22　渡り廊下（食堂）　Corridor (lunchroom)
23　家庭科室　Home economics room
24　図工室　Art/craft room
25　理科室　Science lab.
26　体育館　Gymnasium
27　特別活動室　Special activities room

1st floor plan　1:1600

教室および多目的スペース　Classrooms and the multi-purpose space

図書室　Library

音楽室　Music room

渡り廊下（食堂）　Corridor (lunchroom)

鳥瞰　Bird's-eye view

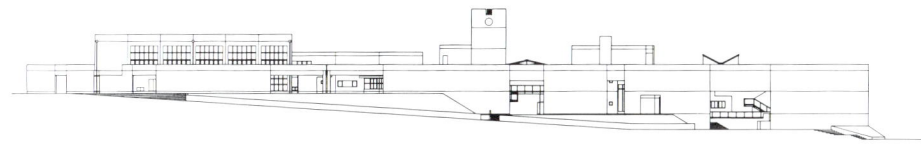

West elevation 1:1300

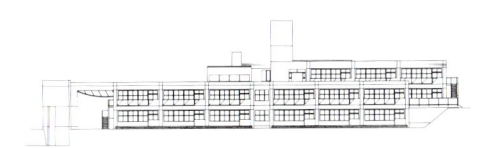

South elevation 1:1300

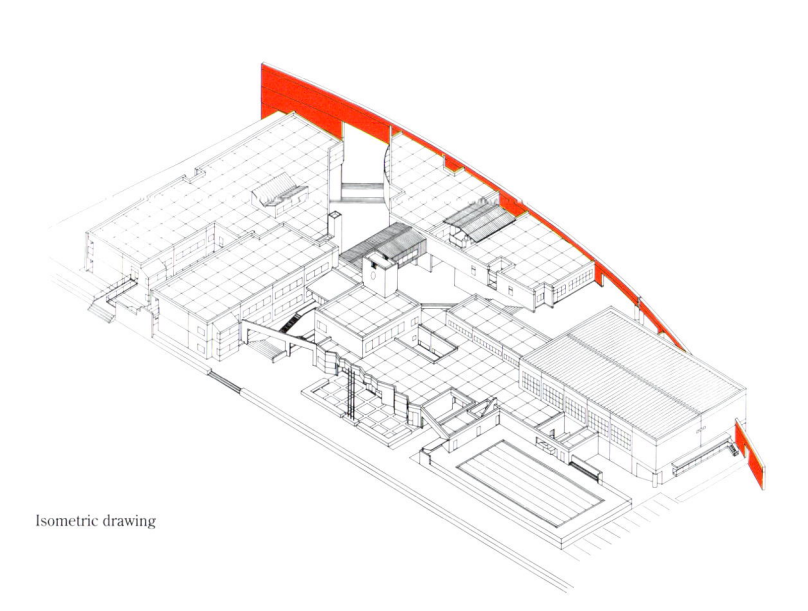

Isometric drawing

小学校と街との空間領域を明確化するために、円弧半径220mの緩やかな、長さ150mというスクール・ウォールを作った。これは都営住宅と対峙し、歩専道を緊張感あるものとしている。特別教室棟と管理棟との間に設けたモールは、スクール・ウォールと相関し、外からのアプローチとなっている。モールは学校内に引き込まれた街路であると同時に、包み込まれた学校の中心的空間でもある。また、周辺の郊外的な伸びやかさに対して、緊密な街の空間を構成する。

To delineate the boundary between the school premises and the community, a gently curving 150meters-long wall with the radius of 220meters extends opposite the municipal housing development, creating a pleasant tension in the pavement. The mall between the special classroom wing and the administrative wing is linked in concept with the wall and acts as the approach leading from the outside. The mall is a street simulated within the school building as well as the core of the space contained inside, creating a tightly interlinking urban space that contrasts with the relaxed and open atmosphere of the surrounding rural landscape.

所在地　　東京都稲城市
設計　　　船越徹＋アルコム
施工　　　西松建設・大石建設JV.
竣工　　　1992年7月
敷地面積　22,352.87m²
建築面積　4,170.20m²
延床面積　5,677.67m²
階数　　　地上3階
構造　　　鉄筋コンクリート造、一部鉄骨造
撮影　　　ナガミネスタジオ／35,38-39,41　新建築社／36上
　　　　　小林研二／36下,37,40

Location:　Inagi-city, Tokyo
Architect:　Tohru Funakoshi + ARCOM R&D, Architects
General contractor:　Joint venture of Nishimatsu Construction and Ohishi
Completion date:　July 1992
Site area:　240,604.05sq.ft.
Building area:　44,887.62sq.ft.
Total floor area:　61,113.87sq.ft.
Number of floors:　3 floors above ground
Structure:　Reinforced concrete structure and steel structure
Photographer:　Nagamine Studio / 35, 38-39, 41
Shinkenchiku-sha・Co.,Ltd. / 36: top
Kenji Kobayashi / 36: bottom, 37, 40

小国町立西里小学校
NISHIZATO PRIMARY SCHOOL, OGUNI

木島安史＋ＹＡＳ都市研究所
YASUFUMI KIJIMA + YAS & URBANISTS

南側全景　Overall view of the south side

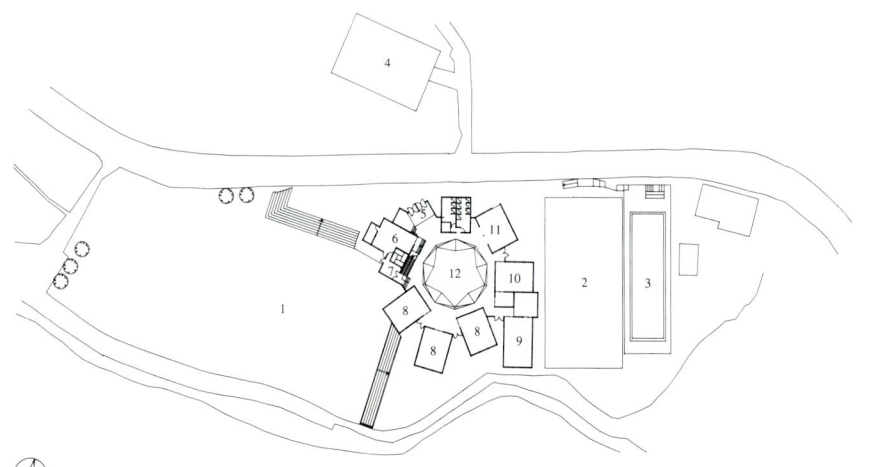

Site plan + 1st floor plan　1:1500

1　グラウンド　Playground
2　体育館（予定）　Gymnasium (plan)
3　既存プール　Existing swimming pool
4　既存体育館　Existing gymnasium
5　エントランス　Entrance
6　職員室　Faculty office
7　保健室　Infirmary
8　教室　Classroom
9　理科・図工室　Science lab. and art/craft room
10　音楽室　Music room
11　家庭科室　Home economics room
12　多目的ホール　Multi-purpose hall

南西側外観　Southwest facade

北西側外観　左、妻部分に校章が取り付けられている棟がエントランス　Northwest facade; the wing on the left with the school emblem at the gable is the entrance

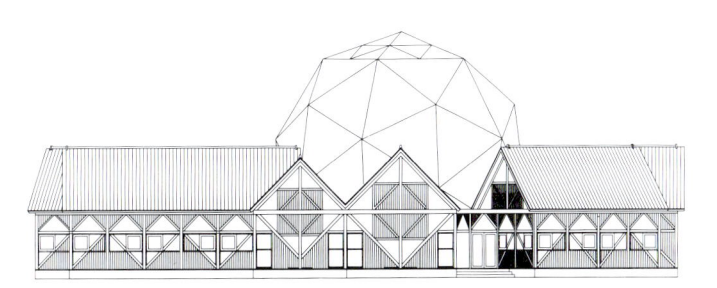

East elevation 1:400

ドーム内部の多目的ホール　Multi-purpose hall inside the dome

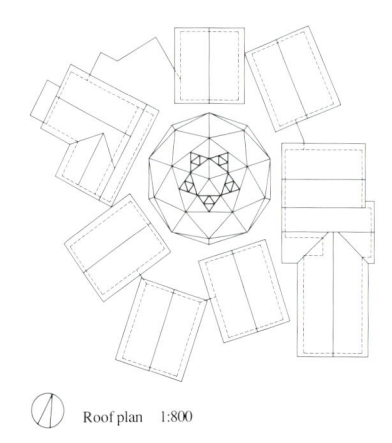

Roof plan　1:800

回廊から教室方向を見る　Looking at the classroom from the corridor

ドームと回廊の境部分　Colonnade connecting with the dome

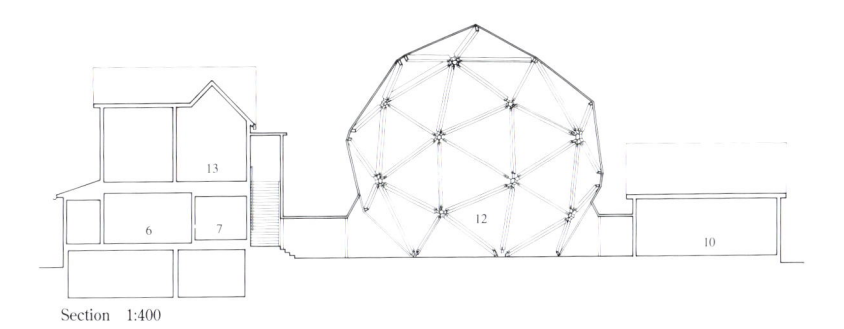

Section　1:400

6　職員室　Faculty office
7　保健室　Infirmary
10　音楽室　Music room
12　多目的ホール　Multi-purpose hall
13　校長室　Principal's office

多目的ホールより見上げ　Looking up in the multi-purpose hall

ドームジョイントのディテール　Joints of the dome, detail

教室　Classroom

熊本の山深い小さな町に建つこの小学校は、集落をイメージした切妻型の教室棟と、中央部の60面体のドームから構成されている。教室棟が持つ発散性とドームの持つ求心性の二面性を持たせながら、原風景としての建築を目指した群造型の試みである。中央ドームは多目的ホールと名付けられ、遊び場として、また集会室として多様な使われ方を想定しながら、この小学校のシンボルとして完結した小さな宇宙をイメージして造られた。

Situated in a small town in the deep mountains of Kumamoto Prefecture, the school buildings include a gable-roofed classroom wing that simulates a village and a dome in the center in the form of hexagesimal polyhedron. The diffusing nature of the classroom wing is contrasted with the centripetal form of the dome, a formative attempt at an archetypical landscape. The center dome forms a complete and compact cosmos, a symbol of the school, which is used as a multi-purpose hall acting as a playroom and a meeting room.

所在地　　熊本県小国町
設計　　　木島安史＋ＹＡＳ都市研究所
施工　　　橋本建設
竣工　　　1991年9月
敷地面積　7,245.00m²
建築面積　814.00m²
延床面積　949.00m²
階数　　　地上2階、地下1階
構造　　　木造、一部鉄筋コンクリート造
　　　　　ドーム：木造シングルレイヤードーム構造
撮影　　　山本伸生／42,46左上　　新建築社／43上,44,46右上,46下
　　　　　岡本公二／43下,45

Location: Oguni-town, Kumamoto
Architect: Yasufumi Kijima + YAS & Urbanists
General contractor: Hashimoto Construction Co.,Ltd.
Completion date: September 1991
Site area: 77,984.46sq.ft.
Building area: 8,761.81sq.ft.
Total floor area: 10,214.94sq.ft.
Number of floors: 2 floors above ground, 1 floor below ground
Structure: Timber construction and reinforced concrete structure
dome: single-layer timber dome structure
Photographer: Sinsey Yamamoto / 42, 46: top left
Shinkenchiku-sha・Co.,Ltd. / 43: top, 44, 46: top right, 46: bottom
Koji Okamoto / 43: bottom, 45

角館町立西長野小学校
NISHINAGANO PRIMARY SCHOOL

渡辺豊和建築工房
WATANABE TOYOKAZU KENCHIKU KOBO

南東側全景　Overall view of the southeast side

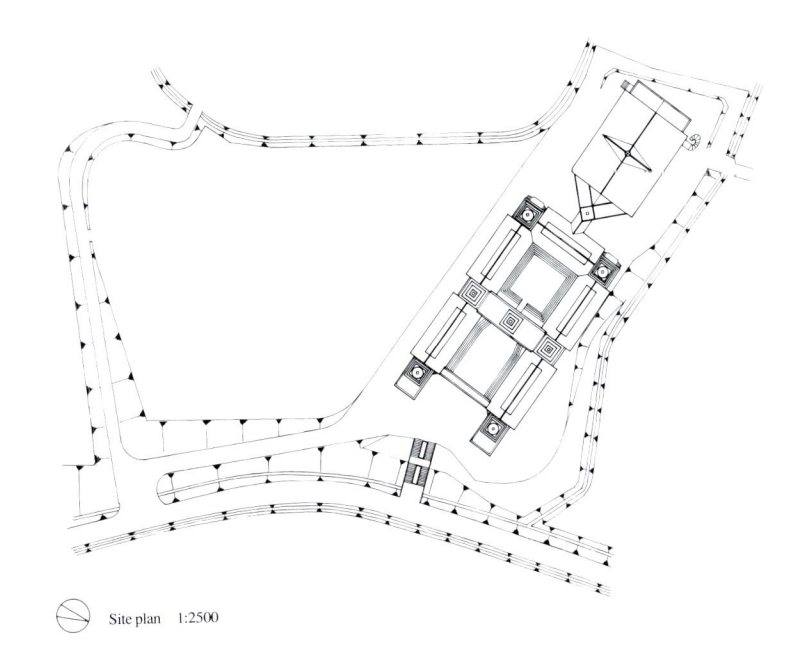

Site plan　1:2500

南側外観　South facade

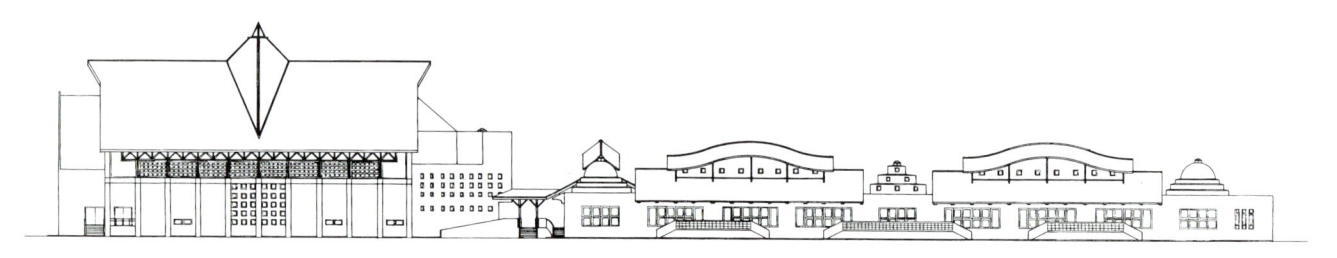

South elevation　1:800

ゲートより中庭奥のエントランスを見る　Looking from the gate at the entrance at the back of the courtyard

西側中庭　West courtyard

中庭を囲む廊下　Corridor surrounding the courtyard

エントランス　Entrance

1　中庭　Courtyard
2　職員エントランス　Entrance for faculty/staff
3　児童エントランス　Entrance for children
4　教室　Classroom
5　特殊学級教育相談室　Counselling room for the mentally and physically handicapped children
6　プレイルーム　Playroom
7　多目的ホール　Multi-purpose hall
8　家庭科室　Home economics room
9　図工室　Art/craft room
10　理科室　Science lab.
11　図書室　Library
12　保健室　Infirmary
13　職員室　Faculty office
14　校長室　Principal's office
15　音楽・視聴覚室　Music/audio-visual room
16　用務員室　Janitor's room
17　購買部　School shop
18　体育館　Gymnasium
19　ミーティングルーム　Meeting room

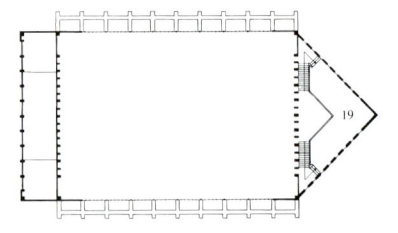

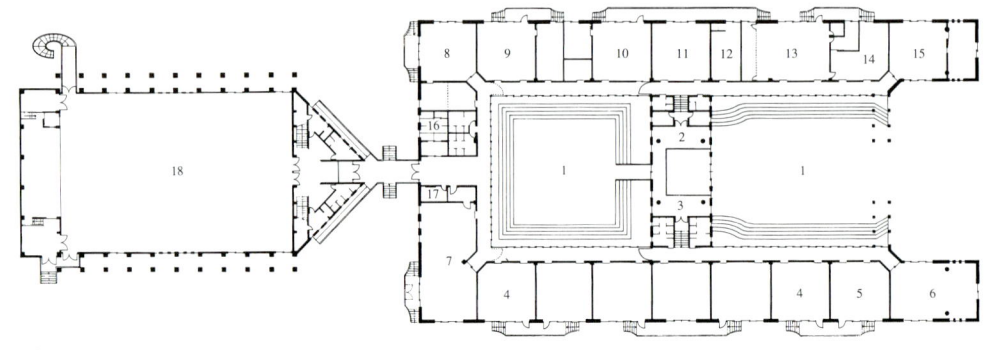

2nd floor plan

1st floor plan 1:1000

体育館 南側外観　South facade of the gymnasium

体育館　Gymnasium

校舎棟 南側外観　South facade of the school building

教室　Classroom

図書室 Library

購買部前廊下　Corridor in front of the school shop

城下町角館は小京都としての風情を今に伝える町並み保存地区として全国に有名であるが、西長野はその周辺農村地域である。そこで、武家屋敷の京風情緒に対し、西アジアの建築形態を構想した。広大なユーラシアのイメージを呼び醒まし、新たなる風景の拡張を企図してのことである。小学校は殊に農村地域では地区の集会場としても重要である。口型平面構成による中庭を階段状客席で囲み、地域の伝統芸能器楽の練習発表の場として計画した。

Kakunodate is well known as a well preserved historic castle town full of reminiscences of ancient cities like Kyoto. Nishinagano is situated in its outskirts in the rural area. To create an atmosphere contrasting to that of dignity and elegance of Kakunodate's mansions of warlords, the architectural forms of the western Asian region were pursued by creating a space that reminds us of a vast expanse of the Eurasian continent. Rural schools play an important role as a gathering place of the community. The courtyard formed as a square in plan view is surrounded by stepped seats for use as a stage for the traditional art and music of the region.

所在地	秋田県角館町
設計	渡辺豊和建築工房
施工	大木建設
竣工	1992年6月
敷地面積	23,000.00m²
建築面積	3,099.25m²
延床面積	2,868.20m²
階数	校舎棟：地上1階　体育館棟：地上2階
構造	鉄筋コンクリート造、一部木造
撮影	川元斉

Location: Kakunodate-town, Akita
Architect: Watanabe Toyokazu Kenchiku Kobo
General contractor: Ohki Corp.
Completion date: June 1992
Site area: 247,569.70sq.ft.
Building area: 33,360.02sq.ft.
Total floor area: 30,873.02sq.ft.
Number of floors: School building: 1 floor above ground
gymnasium: 2 floors above ground
Structure: Reinforced concrete structure and timber construction
Photographer: Hitoshi Kawamoto

つくば市立竹園西小学校
TAKEZONO-NISHI PRIMARY SCHOOL TSUKUBA

原広司＋アトリエ・ファイ建築研究所
HIROSHI HARA + ATELIER Φ

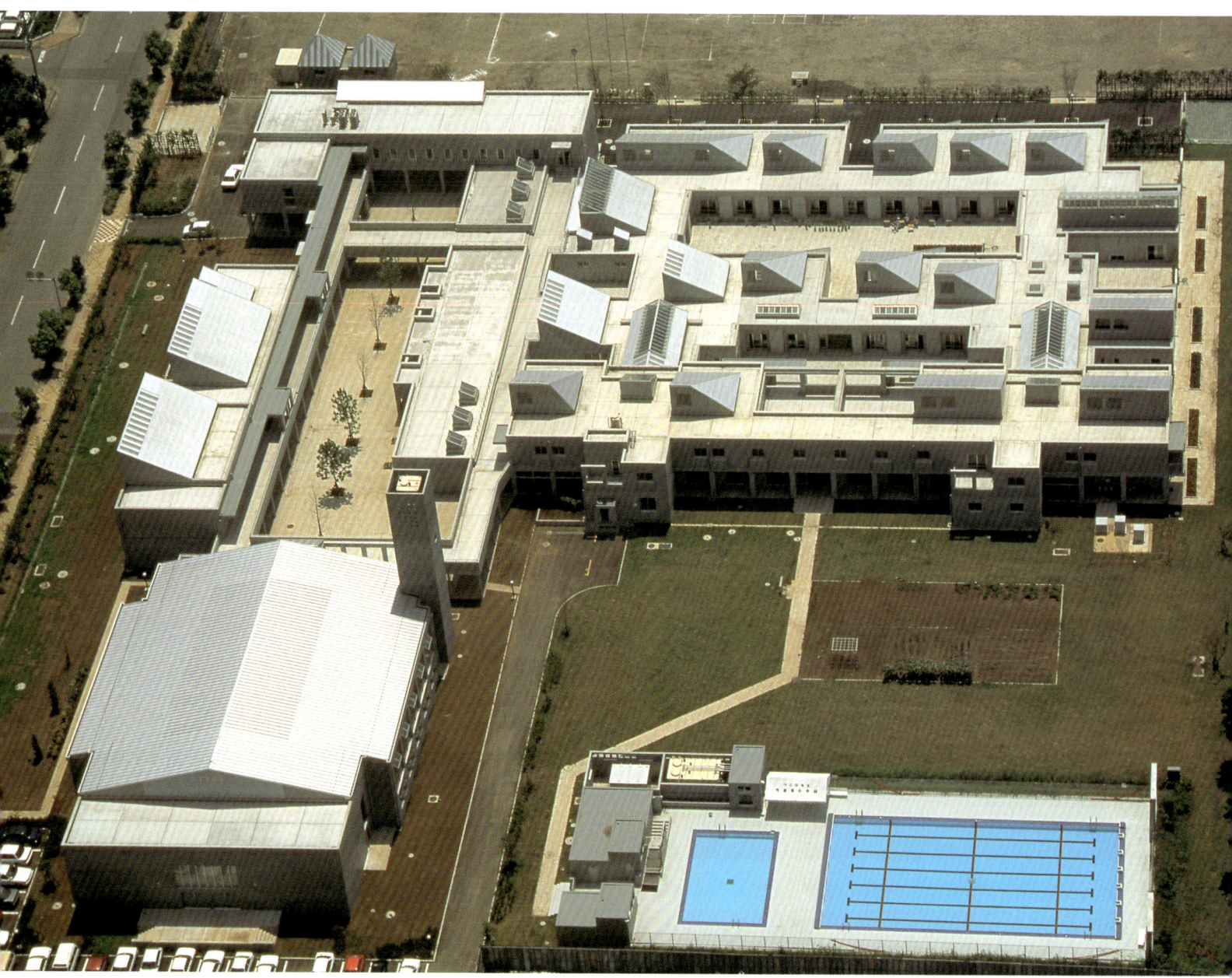

鳥瞰　Bird's eye view

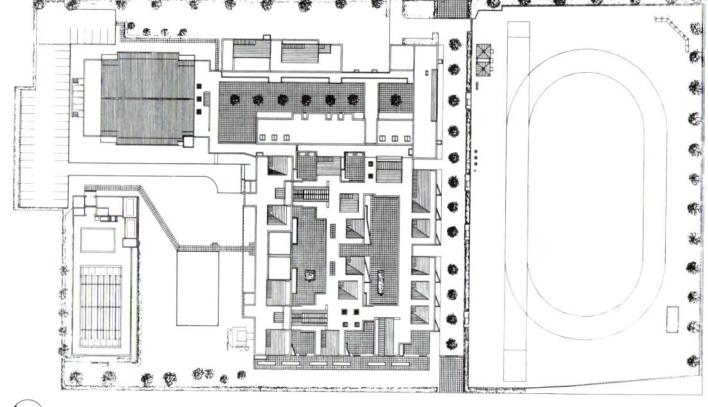

Site plan　1:2400

グラウンド側教室外観　Classroom facing playground

South elevation　1:700

East elevation　1:700

職員室屋上より回廊状の中庭と体育館を見る　Looking from the rooftop of the faculty office at the courtyard and the gymnasium

１階ピロティより回廊状の中庭を見る　正面奥に体育館　Looking in the polotis, the gymnasium at the back in the center

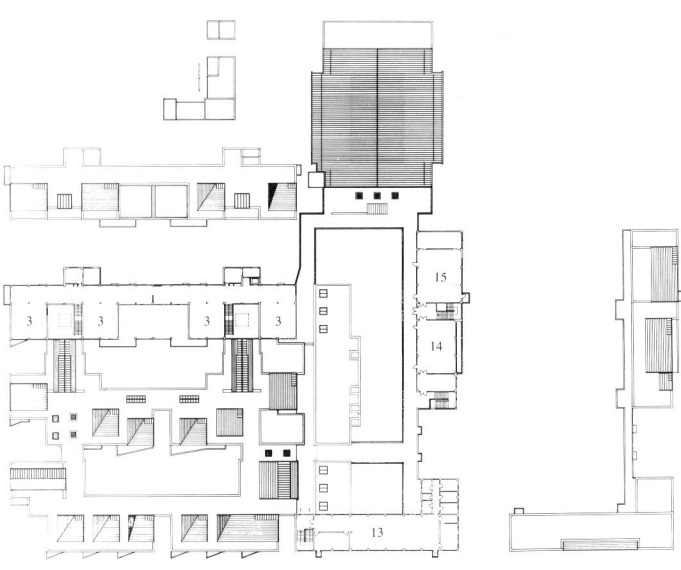

2nd floor plan

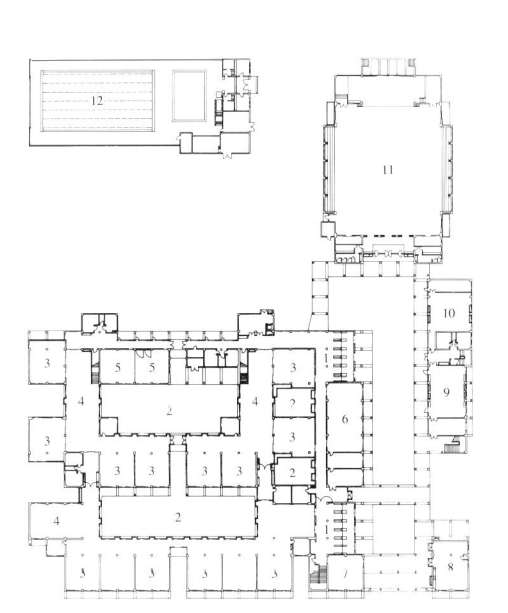

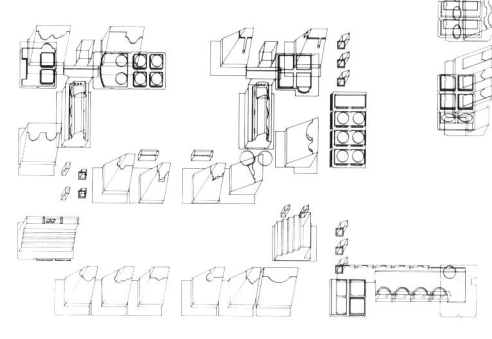

Axonometric drawing; roof

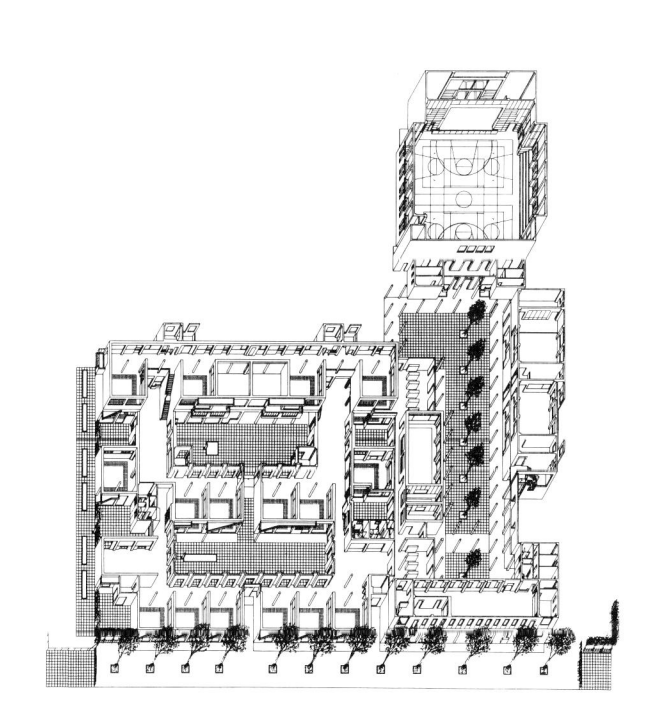

1st floor plan 1:1700

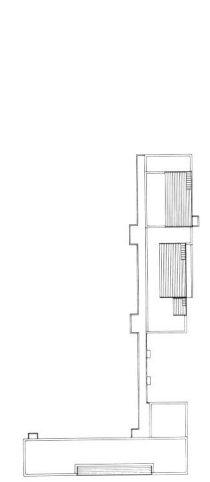

Axonometric drawing

1 エントランス Entrance
2 中庭 Courtyard
3 教室 Classroom
4 多目的教室 Multi-purpose classroom
5 図書室 Library
6 視聴覚室 Audio-visual room
7 児童会室 Student Council room
8 保健室 Infirmary
9 理科室 Science lab.
10 図工室 Art/craft room
11 体育館 Gymnasium
12 プール Swimming pool
13 職員室 Faculty office
14 家庭科室 Home economics room
15 音楽室 Music room

廊下兼オープンスペース　右は教室　Corridor/open space, classrooms on the right

多目的教室　Multi-purpose classroom

教室のハイサイドライトと天井の模様　High side-light and the pattern on the ceiling in the classroom

教室　Classroom

筑波研究学園都市の中心を南北に通る公園通り沿いに位置するこの建物は、敷地全体が公園の延長となるように計画されている。そのために建築の高さは低く抑えられているが、教室の屋根の相互に類似しつつも差異のある形態は、小刻みな地形をつくり出し、平坦な敷地に空間的変化を生み出している。内部空間においても、すべての教室の天井のデザインを変えるなどの工夫がされている。各教室には独自性を与えつつ多目的ホールや中庭など教室の延長空間を持ったオープンプランのシステムを採用し、一体感のある平面計画としている。

The school faces the Koen-dori or the Park Avenue that runs north and south in the center of Tsukuba City and is planned as an extension of the park. The low-rise buildings merge with the surrounding, but the classroom roofs with slightly differing shapes create visually and spatially subtle variations in the otherwise flat landscape. Inside, all the classrooms arranged as an open system have different ceiling designs and connect with the multi-purpose hall and the courtyard, creating an integral space as a whole.

所在地　　茨城県つくば市
設計　　　原広司＋アトリエ・ファイ建築研究所
施工　　　西松建設
竣工　　　1990年3月
敷地面積　27,546.57m²
建築面積　5,699.76m²
延床面積　6,030.78m²
階数　　　地上2階
構造　　　鉄筋コンクリート造、一部鉄骨造
撮影　　　大橋富夫／54-55,56下,58下　　新建築社／56上,58上,59

Location:　Tsukuba-city, Ibaraki
Architect:　Hiroshi Hara + Atelier Φ
General contractor:　Nishimatsu Construction Co.,Ltd.
Completion date:　March 1990
Site area:　296,508.52sq.ft.
Building area:　61,351.65sq.ft.
Total floor area:　64,914.71sq.ft.
Number of floors:　2 floors above ground
Structure:　Reinforced concrete structure and steel structure
Photographer:　Tomio Ohashi / 54-55, 56: bottom, 58: bottom
Shinkenchiku-sha・Co.,Ltd. / 56: top, 58: top, 59

中之口村立中之口西小学校
NAKANOKUCHI-NISHI PRIMARY SCHOOL

石本建築事務所
ISHIMOTO ARCHITECTURAL & ENGINEERING FIRM, INC.

校舎棟 南側外観　South facade of the school building

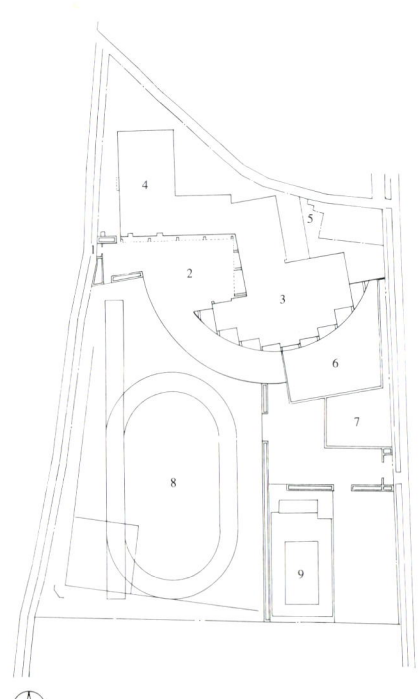

1　校門　School gate
2　前庭　Front yard
3　校舎棟　School building
4　体育館棟　Gymnasium
5　屋外ワークスペース　Outdoor work space
6　屋外学習スペース　Outdoor study area
7　庭園　Garden
8　グラウンド　Playground
9　プール　Swimming pool
10　テラス　Terrace

Site plan 1:3000

南東側外観　Southeast facade

西側全景　Overall view of the west side

南側より校舎外観を見る　Looking at the facade from south

校舎棟 北東側外観　Northeast facade of the school building

1階 多目的スペース　1st floor, multi-purpose space ▶

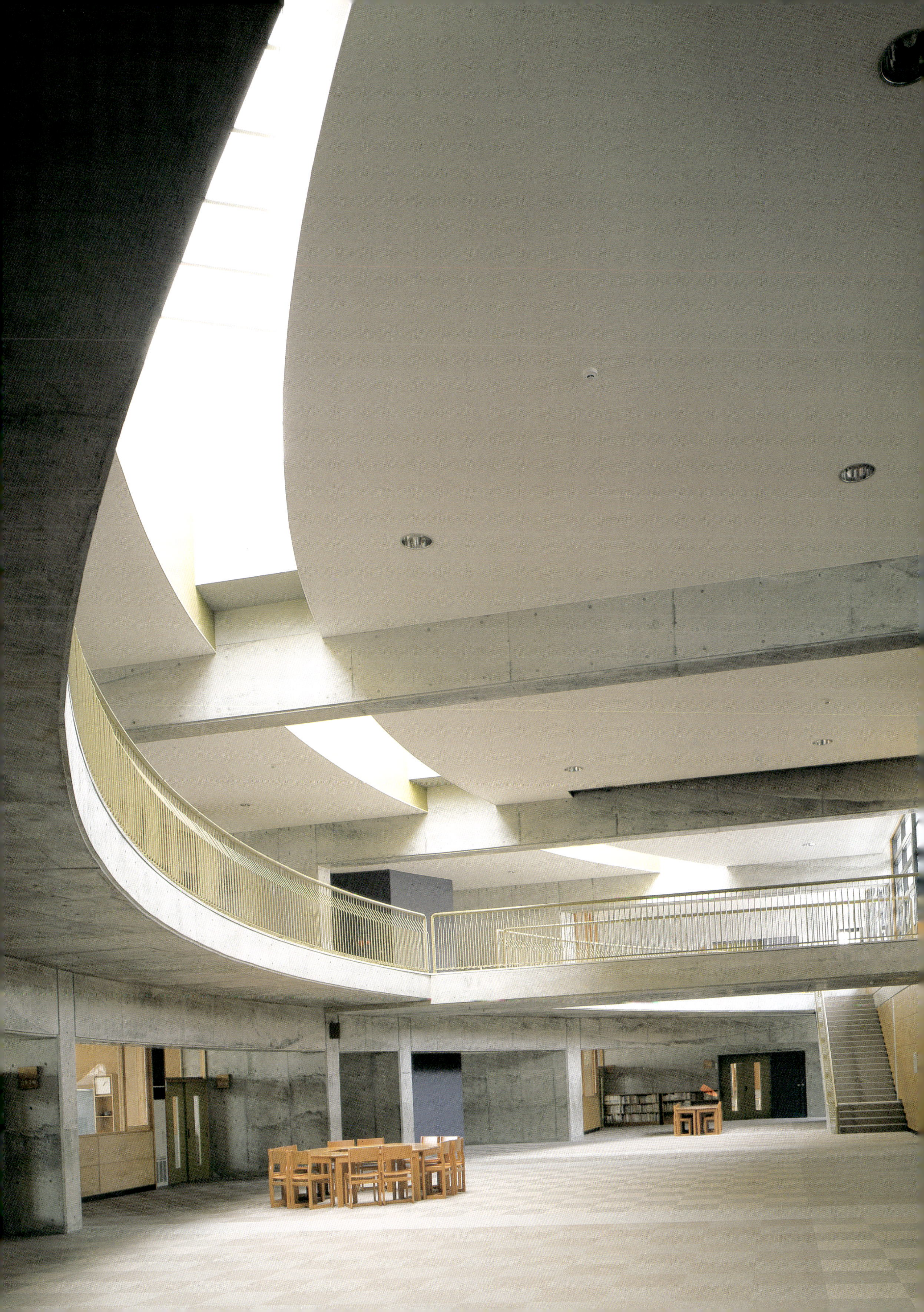

2階より多目的スペースを見下ろす　Looking down from the 2nd floor at the multi-purpose space

2階廊下　2nd floor, corridor

教室　Classroom

階段ホール　Stairway hall

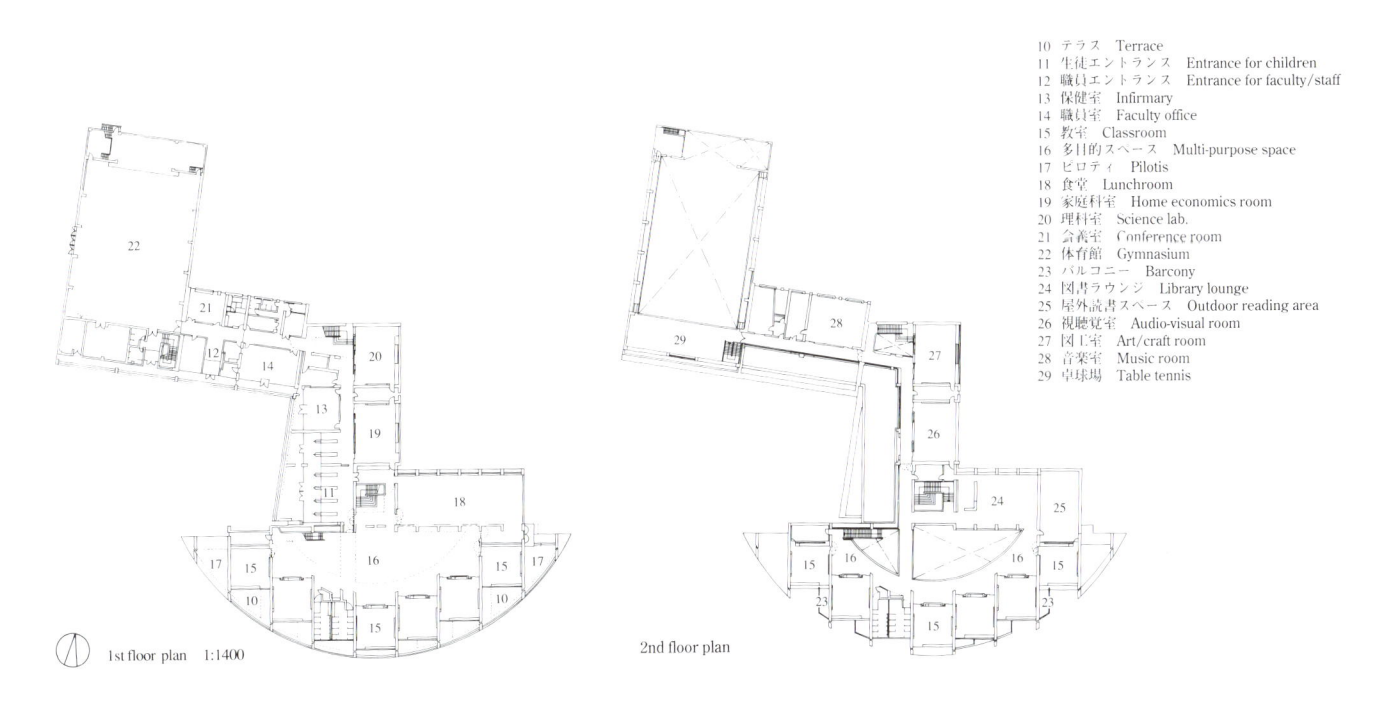

10 テラス	Terrace
11 生徒エントランス	Entrance for children
12 職員エントランス	Entrance for faculty/staff
13 保健室	Infirmary
14 職員室	Faculty office
15 教室	Classroom
16 多目的スペース	Multi-purpose space
17 ピロティ	Pilotis
18 食堂	Lunchroom
19 家庭科室	Home economics room
20 理科室	Science lab.
21 会議室	Conference room
22 体育館	Gymnasium
23 バルコニー	Barcony
24 図書ラウンジ	Library lounge
25 屋外読書スペース	Outdoor reading area
26 視聴覚室	Audio-visual room
27 図工室	Art/craft room
28 音楽室	Music room
29 卓球場	Table tennis

1st floor plan　1:1400

2nd floor plan

図書館　Library

食堂　Lunchroom

15 教室　Classroom
16 多目的スペース　Multi-purpose space
19 家庭科室　Home economics room
20 理科室　Science lab.
26 視聴覚室　Audio-visual room
27 図工室　Art/craft room
30 階段ホール　Stairway hall

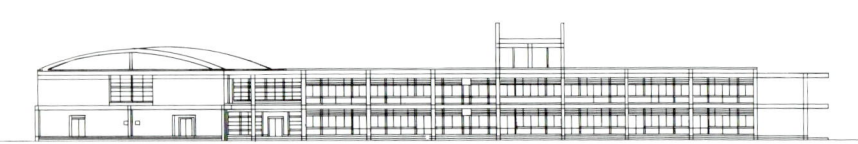

Section 1:900

South elevation 1:900

本校は越後平野のほぼ中央に位置し、緩やかな円弧を描く外観とともに、内部に豊かな多目的スペースを持った学校である。豊かな感性を育む空間づくりは、四季折々変化する田園の風景とともに子供たちにとって大切な原風景となる。2層吹抜の多目的スペースは1、2階の教室群と一体化され、彼らの生活空間の一部となり、学年を超えた触れ合いを誘発する。子供たちの体験の中から記憶に残る楽しい建築であって欲しいと願ったものである。

Situated substantially in the center of the Echigo Plain, the school building has a gently curving facade and contains a spacious multi-purpose hall inside. The design aims at offering a space that fosters supple sensitivity in children. Children will long cherish the memories of the school and the days spent there surrounded by nature that shifts from season to season. The multi-purpose hall that extends the height of two stories is integrally connected with the classrooms on the first and the second floors and invites children to mix with each other irrespective of the age.

所在地　　新潟県中之口村
設計　　　石本建築事務所
施工　　　加賀田組
竣工　　　1991年9月
敷地面積　20,929.00m²
建築面積　3,371.40m²
延床面積　4,994.00m²
階数　　　地上2階
構造　　　鉄筋コンクリート造（ボイドラーメン構造）、一部鉄骨造
撮影　　　加藤嘉六／60,61上,63,64上,64右下,65
　　　　　小林研二／61下,62下,64左下,66　久代正人／62上

Location: Nakanokuchi-village, Niigata
Architect: Ishimoto Architectural & Engineering Firm, Inc.
General contractor: Kagata-gumi
Completion date: September 1991
Site area: 225,277.66sq.ft.
Building area: 36,289.41sq.ft.
Total floor area: 53,754.92sq.ft.
Number of floors: 2 floors above ground
Structure: Reinforced concrete structure (rigid frame structure in the void) and steel structure
Photographer: Karoku Kato / 60, 61: top, 63, 64: bottom right, 65
Kenji Kobayashi / 61: bottom, 62: bottom, 64: bottom left, 66
Masato Kushiro / 62: top

中学校／高等学校　Junior and Senior High Schools

淡路町立岩屋中学校
IWAYA JUNIOR HIGH SCHOOL

Team Zoo いるか設計集団
TEAM ZOO ATELIER IRUKA CO.,LTD.

3階 教室より体育館と広場を見下ろす　Looking down at the gymnasium and the plaza from the 3rd floor classroom

南西側外観　Southwest facade

屋上テラスより中庭方向を見る　Looking toward courtyard from rooftop terrace

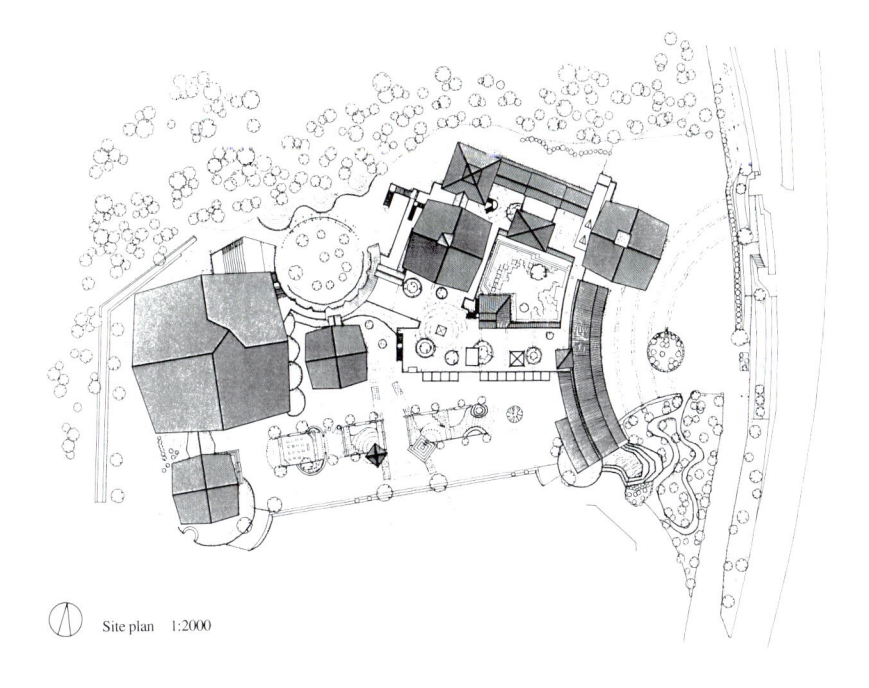

Site plan 1:2000

校舎南側 "思い出の小道"　"Memory Lane" on the south of the school building

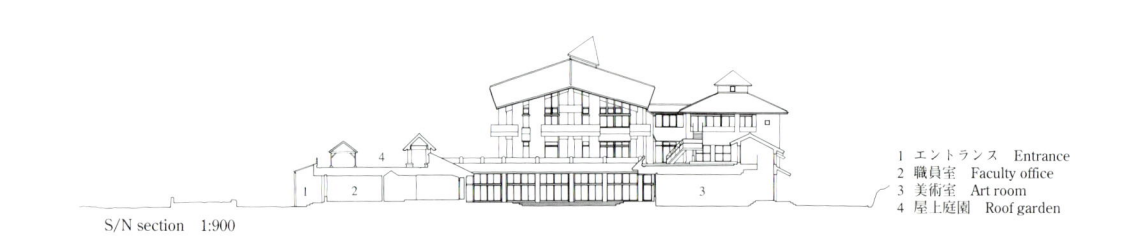

S/N section 1:900

1 エントランス　Entrance
2 職員室　Faculty office
3 美術室　Art room
4 屋上庭園　Roof garden

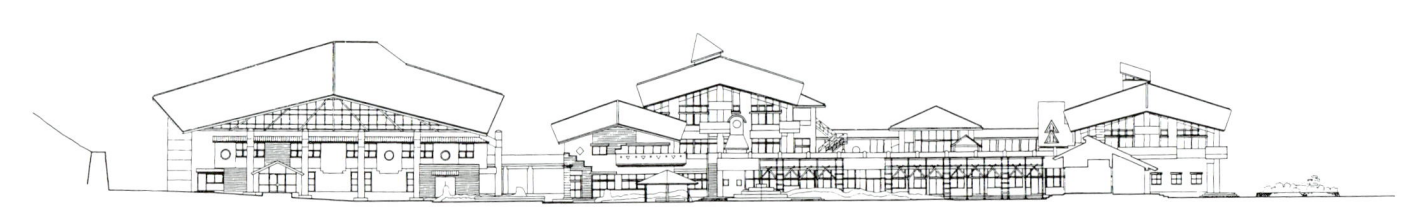

South elevation 1:900

ワークスペースから教室を見る　Looking at the classroom from the work space

廊下から美術室を見る　Looking into the art room from the corridor

2階へ通じる段状の生徒会コーナー　Student Council quarters with steps leading to 2nd floor

東側教室棟と西側教室棟をつなぐ2階廊下　2nd floor corridor connecting east and west classroom wings

体育館　Gymnasium

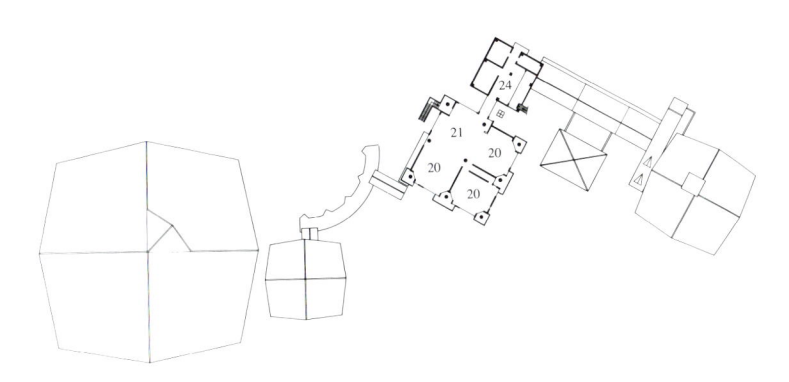

3rd floor plan

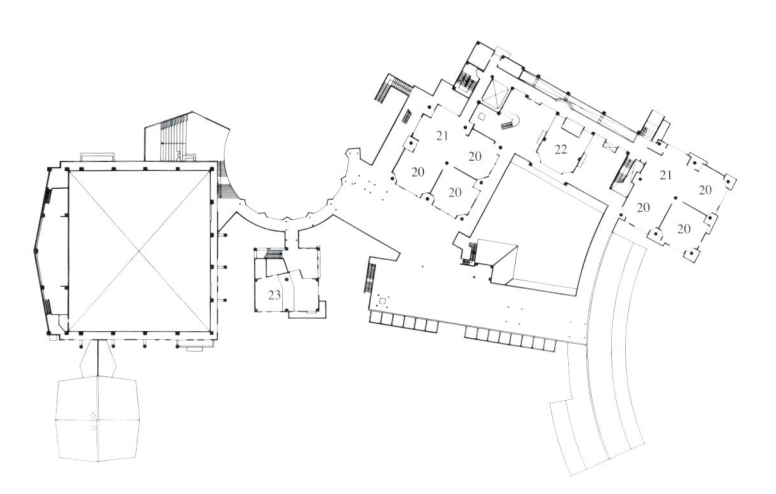

2nd floor plan

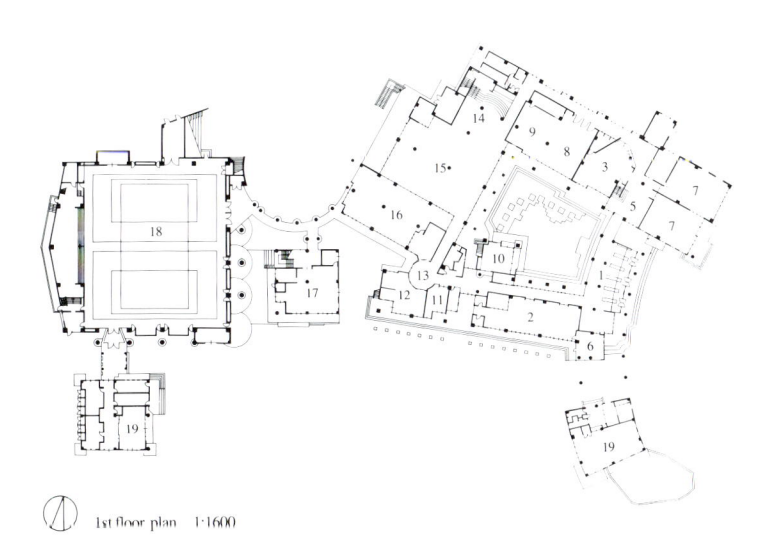

1st floor plan 1:1600

1. エントランス　Entrance
2. 職員室　Faculty office
3. 美術室　Art room
5. 学生ラウンジ　Students' lounge
6. 校長室　Principal's office
7. 理科室　Science lab.
8. 被服室　Sewing class
9. 調理室　Cooking class
10. 作法室・生徒相談室　Etiquette training/guidance room
11. 特殊学級室　Classroom for the mentally and physically handicapped
12. 保健室　Infirmary
13. 円形ホール　Circular hall
14. 生徒会コーナー　Student Council quarters
15. メディアセンター　Media Center
16. コンピューター室　Computer room
17. 技術室　Craft workshop
18. 体育館　Gymnasium
19. ミーティングルーム　Meeting room
20. 教室　Classroom
21. ワークスペース　Work space
22. 視聴覚室　Audio-visual room
23. 音楽室　Music room
24. ラウンジ　Lounge

3階教室より屋上テラスを見下ろす
Looking down at the rooftop terrace from the 3rd floor classroom

この学校は海辺にある。1階に管理部門と特別教室群、学校全体のオープンスペースであるメディアセンターを配置し、2階以上はワークスペースと海がよく見えるテラスを持つ教室群を計画した。建て替えであるため旧校舎の躯体を部分的に残し、地場の色瓦を使ってモザイク貼りを、職人さんの指導を受けながら生徒参加で行った。校舎の内・外に作った小さなベンチやアルコーヴは生徒の語らいの楽しいスペースになっている。

The school building stands at the seaside. Administration offices, special classrooms, and a Media Center which also functions as an open space, are laid out on the 1st floor. Classrooms, work spaces and terraces overlooking the sea are on the 2nd floor and above. The former school building was renovated, preserving some of its structural elements and incorporating them in the new design. Students helped the craftsman in decorating the walls with mosaic work using colored tiles produced in the region. Small benches and alcoves scattered around the premises provide comfortable spaces for conversation.

所在地　　兵庫県淡路町
設計　　　Team Zoo いるか設計集団
施工　　　青木建設・森長建設・マトザキ建設JV.
竣工　　　1993年3月
敷地面積　34,333.00m²
建築面積　4,996.82m²
延床面積　5,676.35m²
階数　　　地上3階
構造　　　鉄筋コンクリート造、一部鉄骨造
撮影　　　新建築社

Location: Awaji-town, Hyogo
Architect: Team Zoo Atelier Iruka Co.,Ltd.
General contractor: Joint venture of Aoki, Moricho and Matozaki
Completion date: March 1993
Site area: 369,556.97sq.ft.
Building area: 53,785.27sq.ft.
Total floor area: 61,099.66sq.ft.
Number of floors: 3 floors above ground
Structure: Reinforced concrete structure and steel structure
Photographer: Shinkenchiku-sha・Co.,Ltd.

内子町立大瀬中学校
OSE MIDDLE SCHOOL

原広司＋アトリエ・ファイ建築研究所
HIROSHI HARA + ATELIER Φ

鳥瞰　Bird's eye view

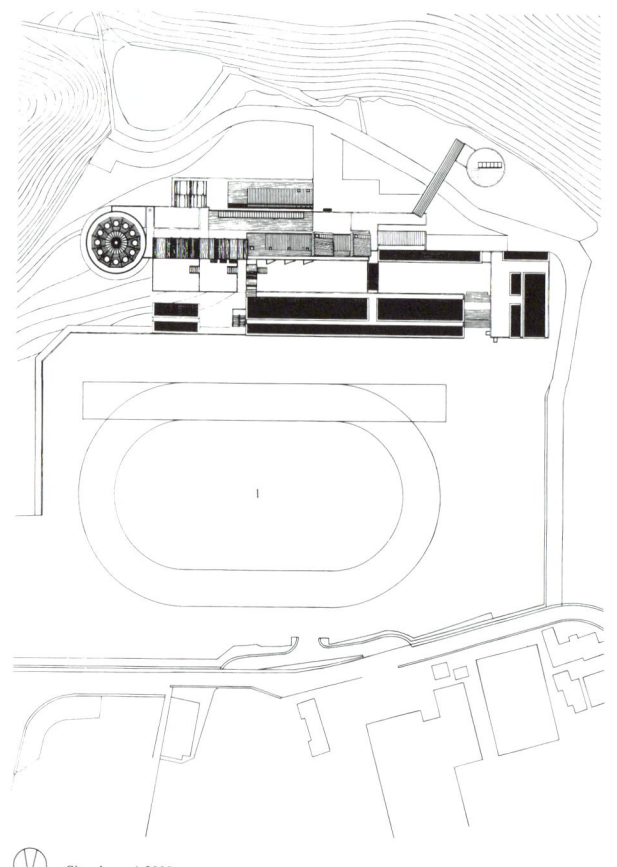

グラウンドより北側全景を見る　Looking at the north facade from the playground

Site plan 1:2000
1 グラウンド　Playground

左手前に普通教室棟、奥に特別教室棟を見る
Classroom wing in the foreground on the left, special classroom wing at the back

美術教室北側より北東を望む　Looking northeast from the north of art room

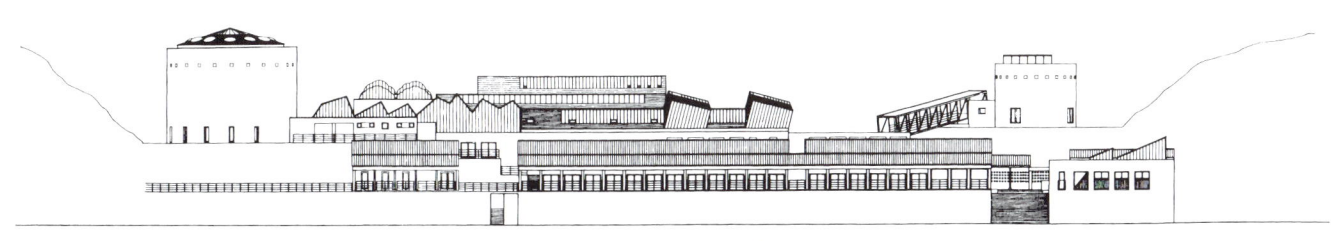

North elevation　1:900

中庭西側から見る　Looking from the west side of courtyard

中庭　奥はエントランス　Courtyard, entrance at the back

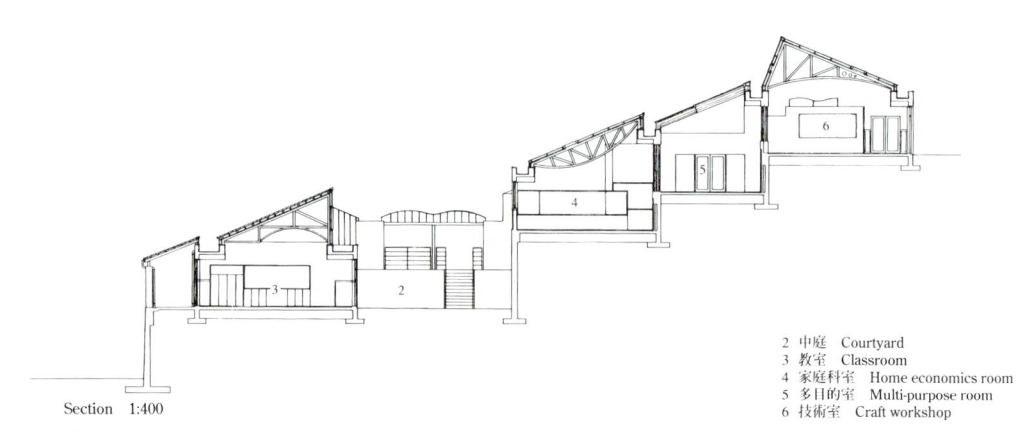

Section　1:400

2　中庭　　Courtyard
3　教室　　Classroom
4　家庭科室　Home economics room
5　多目的室　Multi-purpose room
6　技術室　Craft workshop

図書室と家庭科室の間の階段　Stairway between library and home economics room

理科室 天井見上げ　Looking up at the ceiling in the science lab.

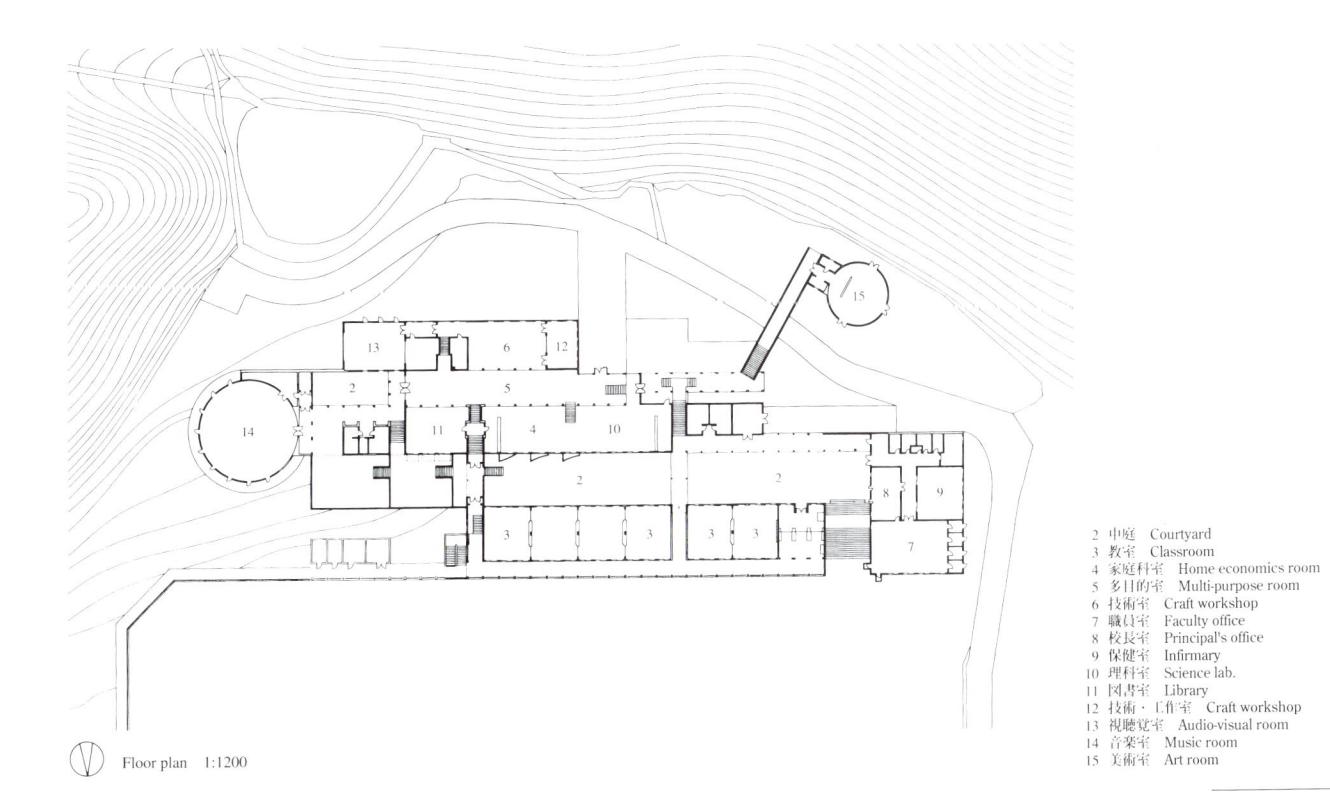

Floor plan 1:1200

2 中庭　Courtyard
3 教室　Classroom
4 家庭科室　Home economics room
5 多目的室　Multi-purpose room
6 技術室　Craft workshop
7 職員室　Faculty office
8 校長室　Principal's office
9 保健室　Infirmary
10 理科室　Science lab.
11 図書室　Library
12 技術・工作室　Craft workshop
13 視聴覚室　Audio-visual room
14 音楽室　Music room
15 美術室　Art room

多目的室越しに右奥の家庭科室を見る　Looking at the home economics room at the far right across multi-purpose room

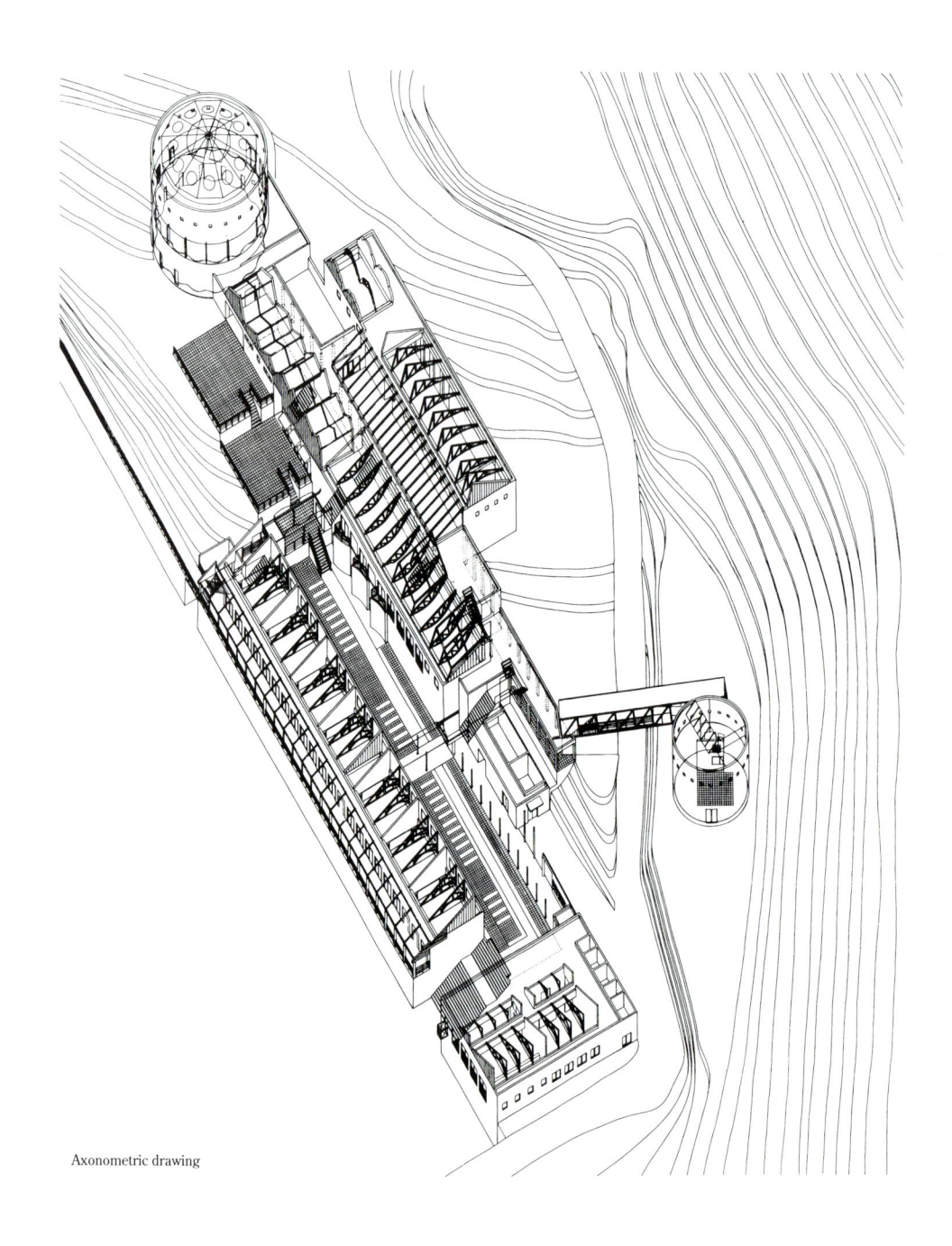

Axonometric drawing

教室 天井見上げ　Looking up at the ceiling in the classroom

教室　Classroom

美術室 天井見上げ　Looking up at the ceiling in the art room

音楽室 天井見上げ
Looking up at the ceiling in the music room

教室南側トップサイドライト　Top side light on the south of classroom

理科室 天井見上げ　Looking up at the ceiling in the science lab.

視聴覚室 天井見上げ　Looking up at the ceiling in the audio-visual room

文学者大江健三郎の生地である大瀬は、鬱蒼とした森に囲まれた小さな谷間に位置する。深い森を背後に持つ南側緩斜面に、既存の地形や自然ができるだけそのままの状態で残される形で建物は計画されている。森を背景に手前に木造小屋組の和風屋根、後方には多様なエレメントを持つ金属屋根が配され、重層化されたファサードが形成されている。平面的には普通教室と特別教室が明確に分けられている。これはこの建物が中学校であると同時に、地域のコミュニティセンターとして機能することが意図されているためである。

Ose, the birthplace of novelist Kenzaburo Ohe, is situated in a small valley surrounded by thick forests, and the site stretches on a gentle slope facing south. The school buildings are designed to keep the surrounding natural environment and the terrain intact. The Japanese style roofs with wooden trusses in the foreground and the metallic roofs comprising different elements in the back add diversity to the multi-layered facade. A clear distinction is made between the regular and the special classrooms in the floor plan, indicating that the school building is opened to the local community as well.

所在地　　愛媛県内子町
設計　　　原広司＋アトリエ・ファイ建築研究所
施工　　　清水建設
竣工　　　1992年7月
敷地面積　21,964.76m²
建築面積　2,685.73m²
延床面積　2,206.02m²
階数　　　地上1階
構造　　　鉄筋コンクリート造　屋根：鉄骨造、木造
撮影　　　大橋富夫

Location:　Uchiko-town, Ehime
Architect:　Hiroshi Hara + Atelier Φ
General contractor:　Shimizu Corp.
Completion date:　July 1992
Site area:　236,426.42sq.ft.
Building area:　28,908.93sq.ft.
Total floor area:　23,745.38sq.ft.
Number of floor:　1 floor above ground
Structure:　Reinforced concrete structure　roof: steel structure and timber construction
Photographer:　Tomio Ohashi

金山町立金山中学校
KANEYAMA JUNIOR HIGH SCHOOL

木曽三岳奥村設計所・東京芸術大学益子研究室　奥村昭雄　益子義弘
Akio Okumura　Yoshihiro Masko　KISO MITAKE OKUMURA DESIGN ACTIVITIES,
TOKYO NATIONAL UNIVERSITY OF FINE ARTS AND MUSIC / MASKO LABORATORY

南側全景の各季節　教室棟の屋根は全面が太陽熱集熱面　South facade in four seasons: solar collectors on the classroom roofs

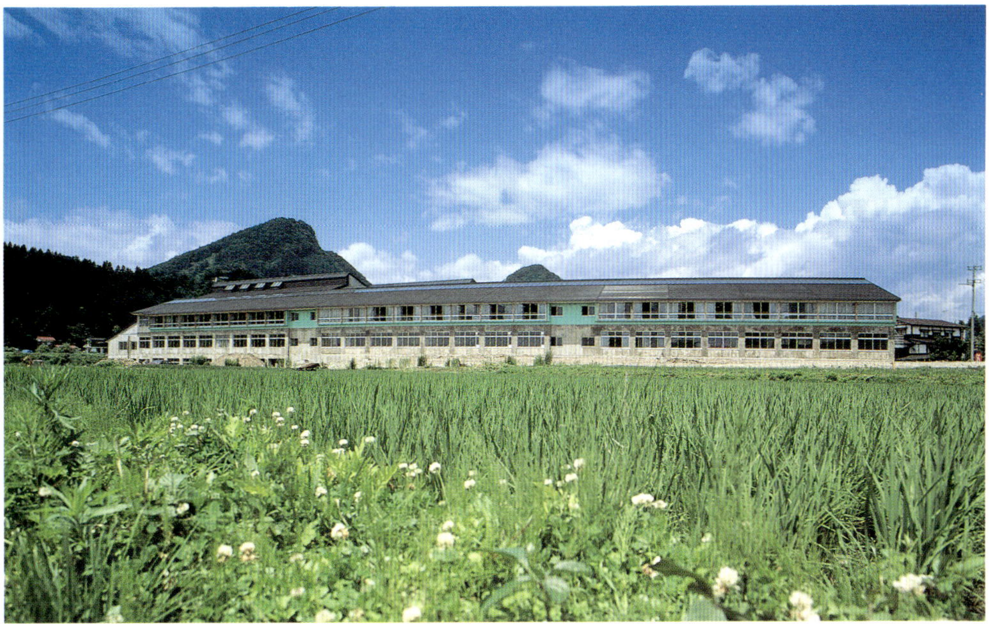

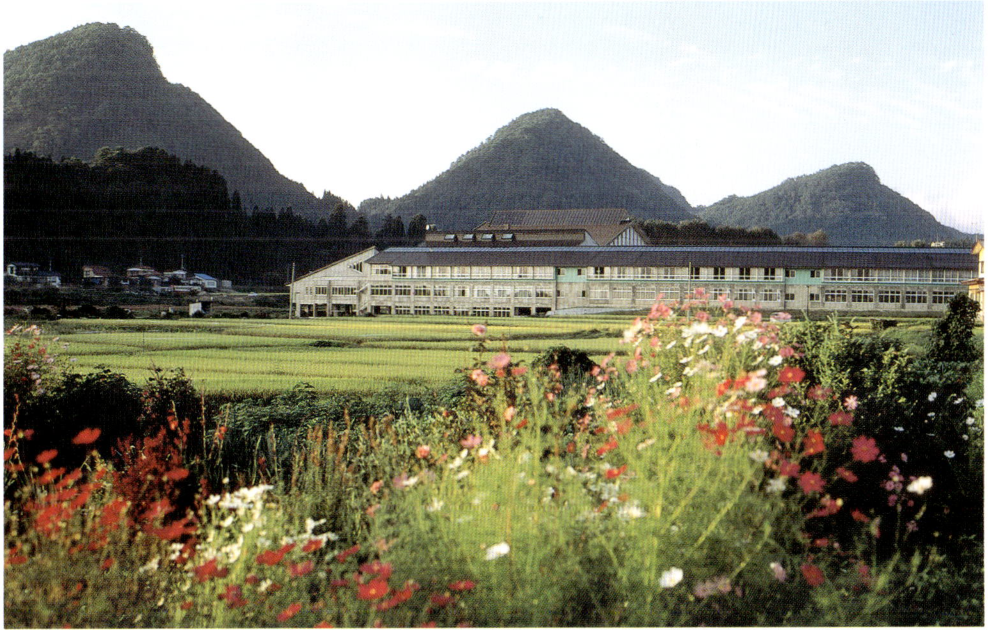

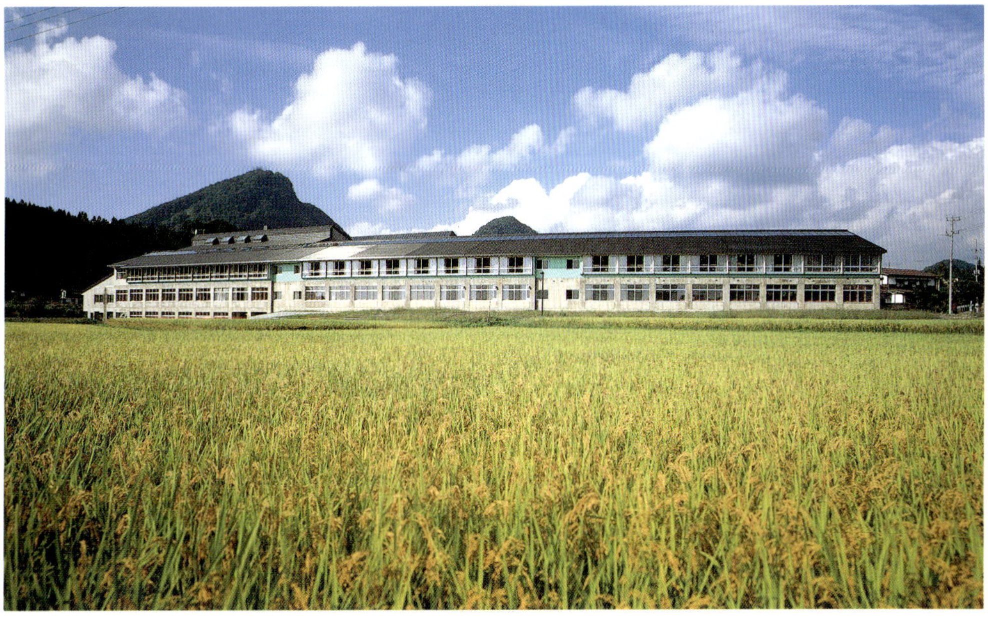

エントランスと多目的スペース外観　Exterior of the entrance and the multi-purpose space

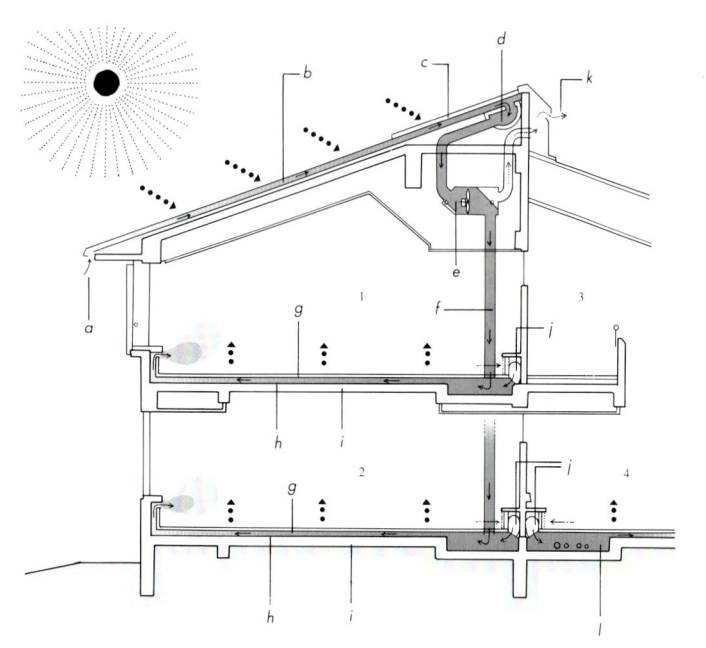

教室棟のシステム図　Solar power system in the classroom wing

1 教室　Classroom
2 特別教室　Special classroom
3 廊下　Corridor
4 多目的スペース　Multi-purpose space

a 外気取入口　Air inlet port
b 普通屋根集熱面　Solar collector
c ガラス付き集熱面　Solar collector with glass covering
d 棟ダクト　Duct
e ハンドリングボックス　Fan and damper
f 竪ダクト　Descending duct
g 木質仕上床　Wood flooring
h 空気層　Air
i 蓄熱コンクリートスラブ　Heat storage concrete slab
j 補助暖房器　Auxiliary heater
k 夏排気　Exhaust air in summer
l 配管スペース　Piping space

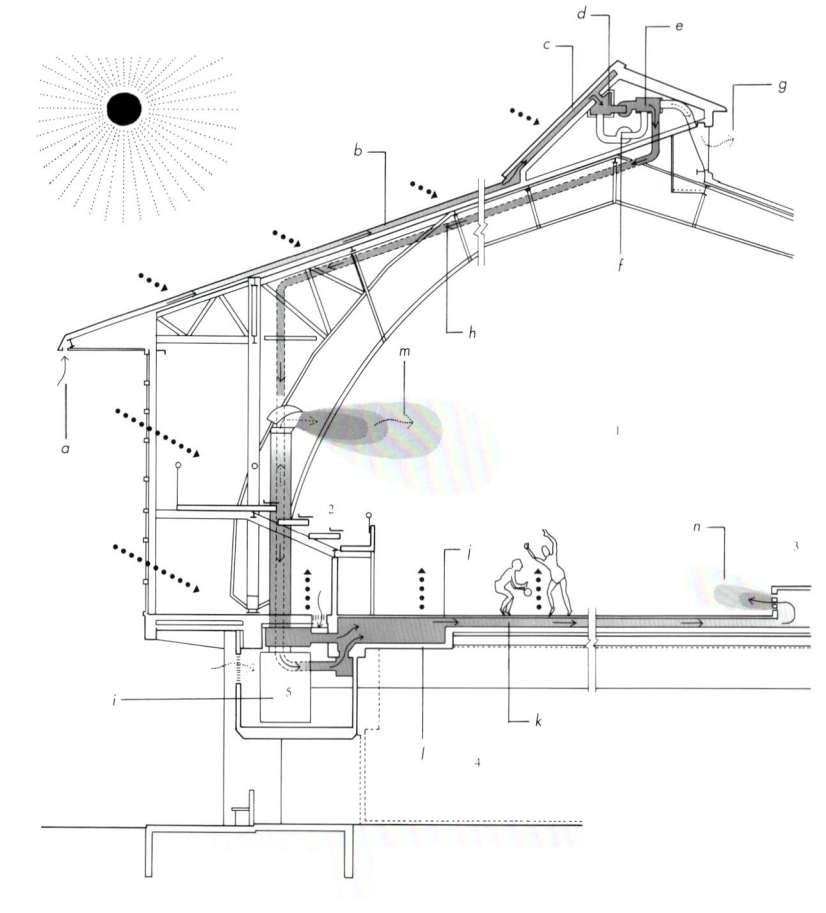

体育館のシステム図　Solar power system in the gymnasium

1 アリーナ　Arena
2 観覧席　Seats
3 ステージ　Stage
4 ピロティ　Pilotis
5 機械室　Machine room

a 外気取入口　Air inlet port
b 普通屋根集熱面　Solar collector
c ガラス付き集熱面　Solar collector with glass covering
d 棟ダクト　Duct
e 床下への送風ファン　Fan for supplying air into the underfloor space
f 融・落雪用ファン　Fan for melting the snow on the roof
g 夏排気　Exhaust air in summer
h 立下りダクト　Descending duct
i 空調機　Air conditioning system
j 木質仕上床　Wood flooring
k 空気層　Air
l 蓄熱コンクリートスラブ　Heat storage concrete slab
m 空調吹出口：空調空気風量の1/2は直接室内へ、残り1/2は床下を通る
　Outlet for air from the air conditioning system: one half of the air volume goes directly into the room, and the other half is sent underfloor.
n 床下からの吹出口　Outlet for the air in the underfloor space

比較的雪の少ない山形平野と違って、鳥海山の東側に当たる秋田との県境の地帯は、積雪2m位にもなる豪雪地である。金山町も11月から1月までは太陽を拝むことはめったになく、雪の中に埋もれてしまう。暖房の必要期間は長く、月平均気温が15℃以下の月は8ヵ月間にもおよぶ。一方で、盆地気候の夏の暑さもまた格別で、しばしば最高気温のニュースに登場する。雪と暑さは"米どころ"の条件である。外的条件を利用して室内環境を適正化する各種の手法を、パッシブソーラーシステムは用意している。金山中学では、そのひとつである"OMソーラー"システム…空気式屋根面集熱と床下躯体蓄熱による床暖房を中心にして、断熱、冬の日射取得、夏の日射遮蔽と屋根面排熱などのパッシブ手法を組み合わせている。完成後丸2年が経過したが、教室、体育館ともに、ほとんど朝の立ち上がり時だけの補助暖房だけで、均一で温度変化の少ない室内環境が得られている。夏も、室内は25℃を超えることはなかった。

Unlike the less snowy Yamagata Plain, Kaneyama on the east of Mt. Chokai bordering Akita Prefecture is buried deep in the 2-meters snow with the sun rarely shining between November and January. Heating is indispensable during the long winter, and the monthly mean temperature drops below +15℃ for almost eight months. On the other hand, because of the basin climate, it becomes exceptionally hot during the summer, often scoring the highest temperature in the country. Snow and summer heat are essential qualifications for good rice crop. The passive solar power system offers various measures to control the indoor spaces under comfortable conditions by taking advantage of the external conditions. The "OM solar system" adopted in Kaneyama Junior High School mainly consists of rooftop solar collectors and underfloor heat storage concrete slabs. Other passive measures such as heat insulation, maximum utilization of winter sunshine, shielding of summer sunshine and heat radiation through roof surfaces are also employed. The indoor environment is kept at constant and comfortable temperature conditions after two years since its completion with the auxiliary heaters turned on briefly in winter mornings. The room temperature has not risen above 25℃ in summer.

金山川越しに西側外観を見る　Looking at the west facade from across the Kaneyama River

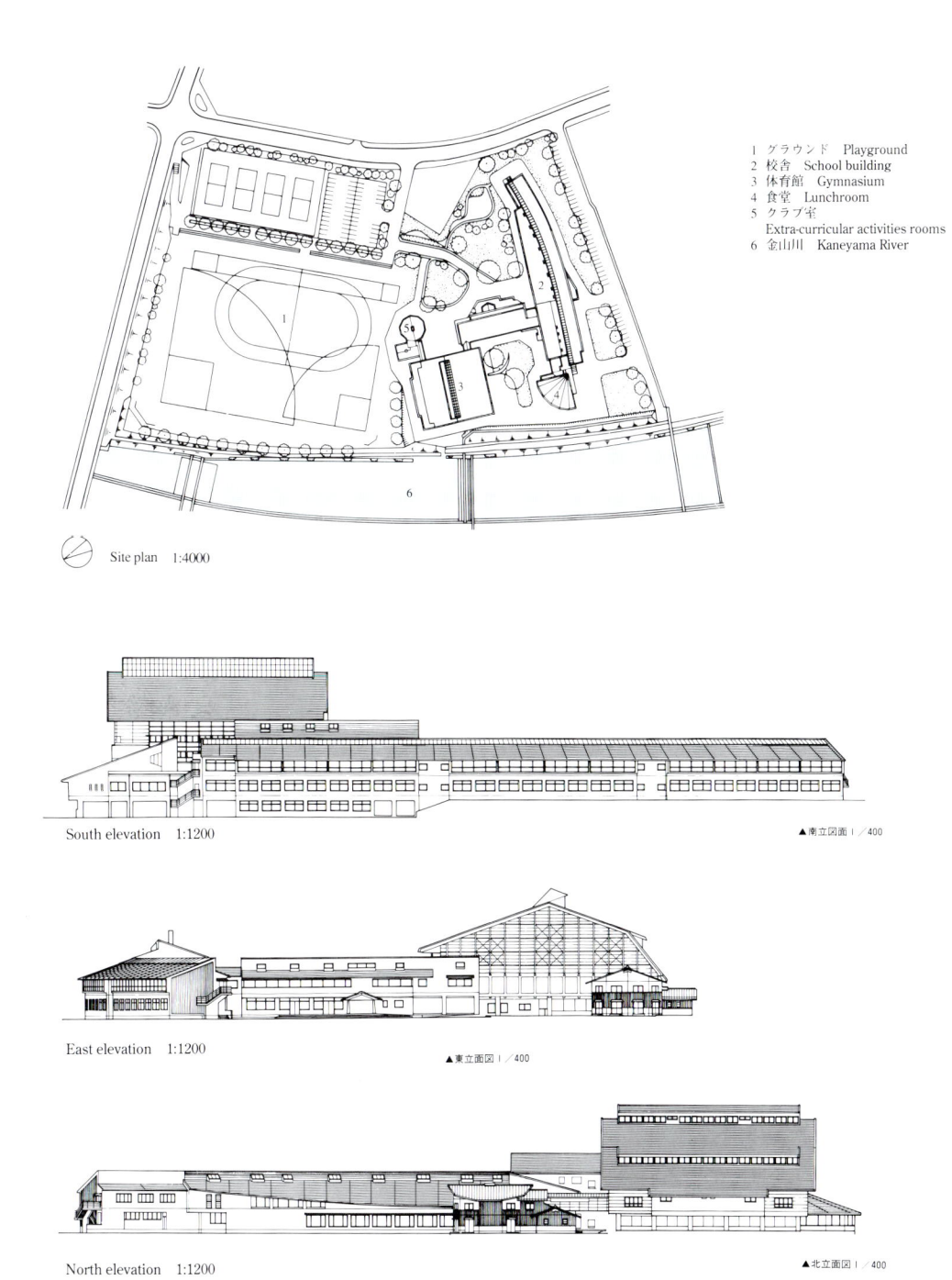

1　グラウンド　Playground
2　校舎　School building
3　体育館　Gymnasium
4　食堂　Lunchroom
5　クラブ室　Extra-curricular activities rooms
6　金山川　Kaneyama River

Site plan　1:4000

South elevation　1:1200　▲南立面図 1／400

East elevation　1:1200　▲東立面図 1／400

North elevation　1:1200　▲北立面図 1／400

東階段から多目的スペースを見る　Looking at the multi-purpose space from the east stairway

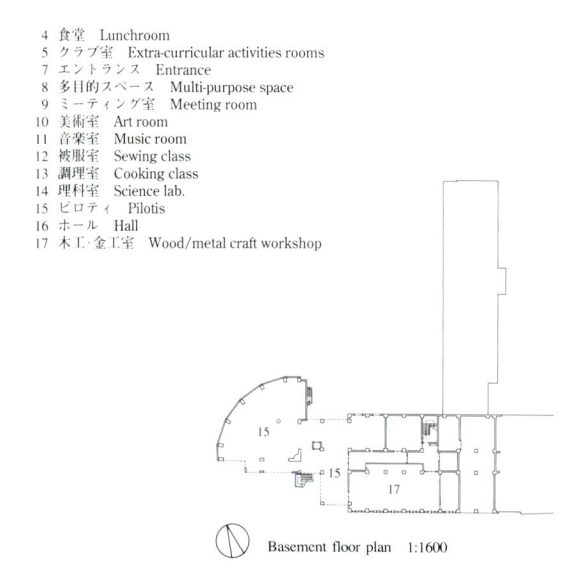

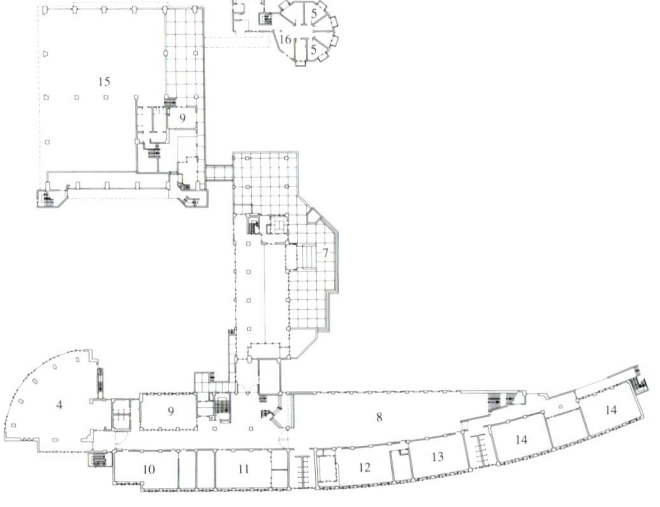

```
4  食堂        Lunchroom
5  クラブ室     Extra-curricular activities rooms
7  エントランス  Entrance
8  多目的スペース Multi-purpose space
9  ミーティング室 Meeting room
10 美術室       Art room
11 音楽室       Music room
12 被服室       Sewing class
13 調理室       Cooking class
14 理科室       Science lab.
15 ピロティ     Pilotis
16 ホール       Hall
17 木工・金工室  Wood/metal craft workshop
```

Basement floor plan　1:1600

1st floor plan

多目的スペース　Multi-purpose space

教室　Classroom

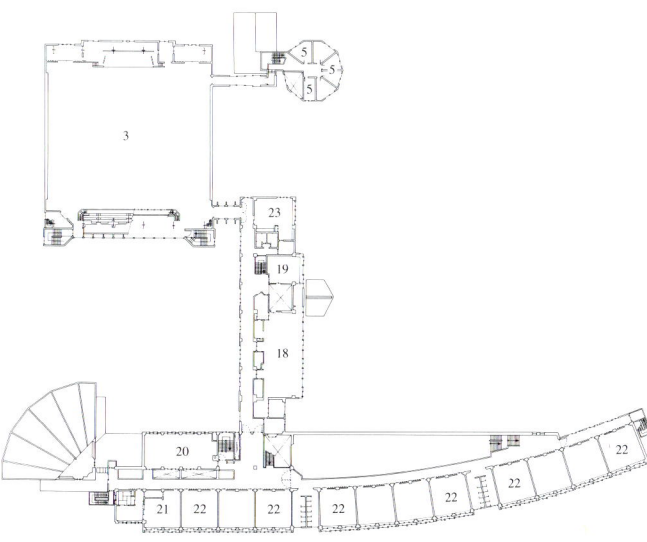

3	体育館　Gymnasium
5	クラブ室　Extra-curricular activities rooms
16	ホール　Hall
18	職員室　Faculty office
19	校長室　Principal's office
20	コンピューター教室　Computer room
21	特殊学級室　Classroom for the mentally and physically handicapped
22	教室　Classroom
23	保健室　Infirmary
24	図書室　Library
25	視聴覚室　Audio-visual room

2nd floor plan

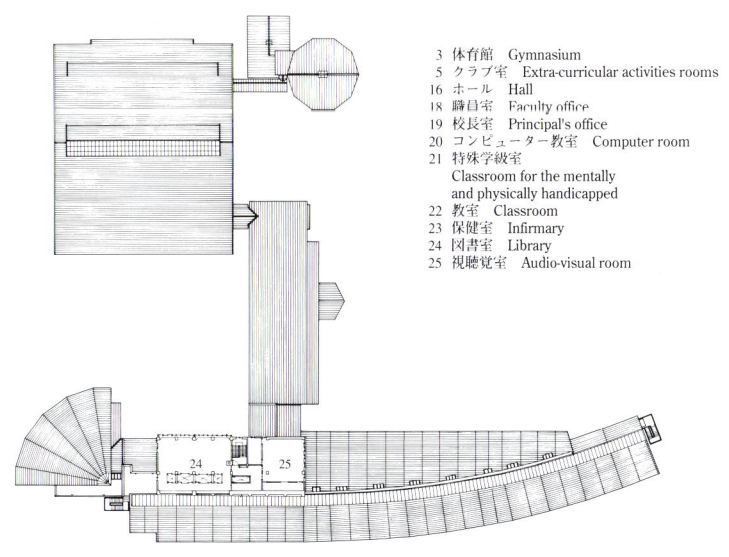

3rd floor plan

食堂　Lunchroom

体育館　Gymnasium

山形県の北端、豪雪地に建つパッシブソーラーシステムを採り入れた中学校である。冬は−15℃を割り、夏は35℃を超え、年間の気温較差は50℃以上になる地域ではあるが、自然室温で＋5℃から25℃の範囲に保つことができた。冬の朝の内だけわずかの補助暖房を加えるだけで、むらのない変化の緩やかな室内環境が得られた。寒冷で特に多雪な地方では、永い冬期間、生徒たちの基礎体力の維持が難しい。温度環境の整った広い屋内空間、体育館だけでなく多目的なホールや廊下の役割が大切である。

Located in the snowbelt at the northern end of Yamagata Prefecture, the school adopted the passive solar power system because of the seasonal temperature fluctuation that ranges from -15℃ in winter to +35℃ in summer. The temperature difference of 50℃ is mitigated as the system maintains the room temperature at +5℃ in winter and +25℃ in summer. In winter, auxiliary heaters are turned on only in the morning to warm the rooms to a comfortable temperature. Well-heated indoor spaces such as multi-purpose halls and corridors play an equally important role as the gymnasium in enhancing the basal physical strength of the students during the long winter time of cold and snowy weather.

所在地　山形県金山町
設計　木曽三岳奥村設計所・東京芸術大学益子研究室
　　　奥村昭雄　益子義弘
施工　清水建設・沼田建設JV.
竣工　1992年7月
敷地面積　46,206.03m²
建築面積　5,018.09m²
延床面積　7,973.02m²
階数　地上3階、地下1階
構造　校舎：鉄筋コンクリート造、一部鉄骨造
　　　体育館：鉄筋コンクリート造、一部鉄骨造
撮影　上田明／84-85,89-90　新建築社／86-88

Location:　Kaneyama-town, Yamagata
Architect:　Akio Okumura　Yoshihiro Masuko
Kiso Mitake Okumura Design Activities, Tokyo National University of Fine Arts And Music / Masko Laboratory
General contractor:　Joint venture of Shimizu and Numata
Completion date:　July 1992
Site area:　497,357.08sq.ft.
Building area:　54,014.22sq.ft.
Total floor area:　85,820.79sq.ft.
Number of floors:　3 floors above ground, 1 floor below ground
Structure:　School building: reinforced concrete structure and steel structure　gymnasium: reinforced concrete structure and steel structure
Photographer:　Akira Ueda / 84-85, 89-90
Shinkenchiku-sha・Co.,Ltd. / 86-88

新宿区立落合中学校
OCHIAI JUNIOR HIGH SCHOOL

船越徹＋アルコム
TOHRU FUNAKOSHI + ARCOM R&D, ARCHITECTS

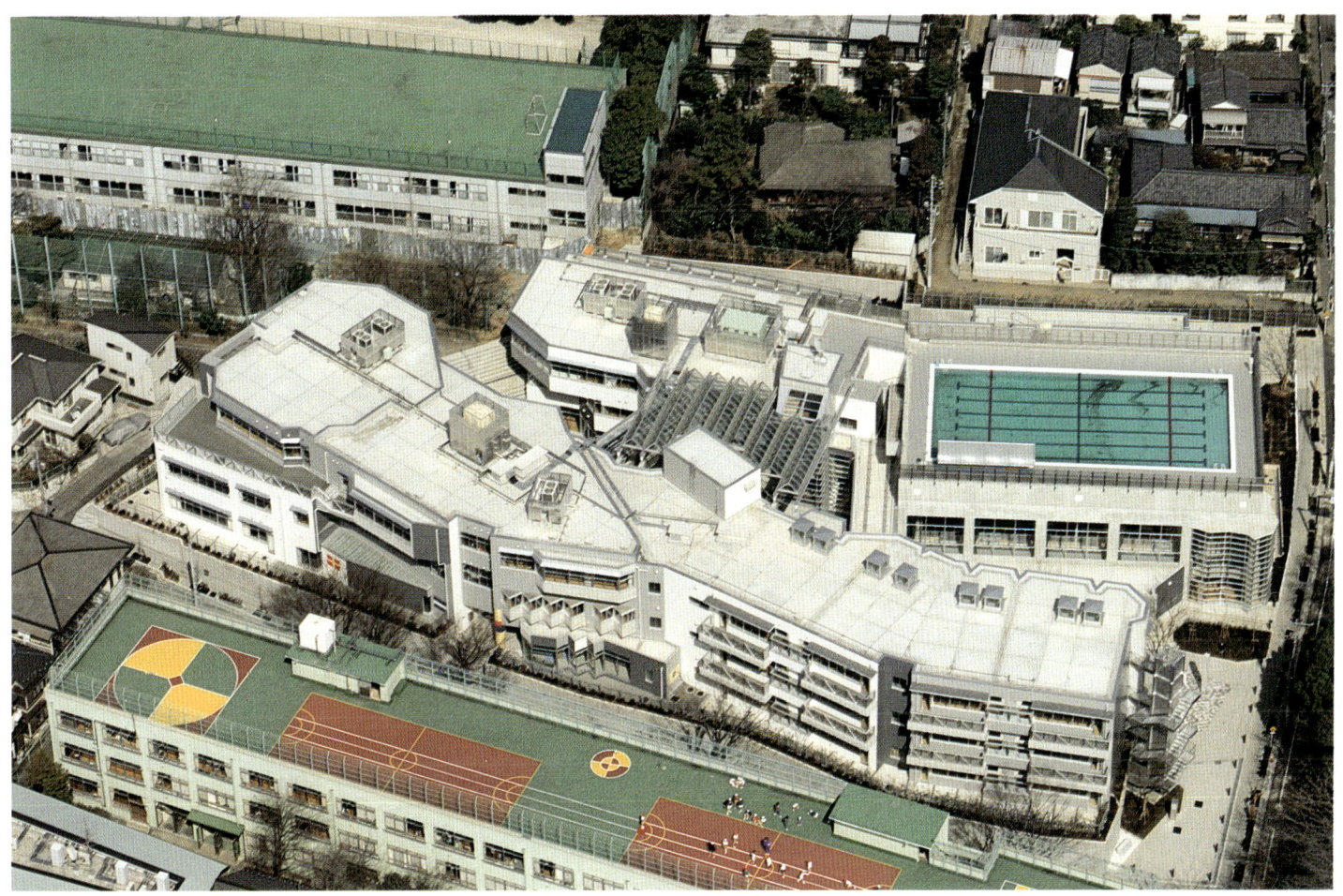

鳥瞰　Bird's eye view

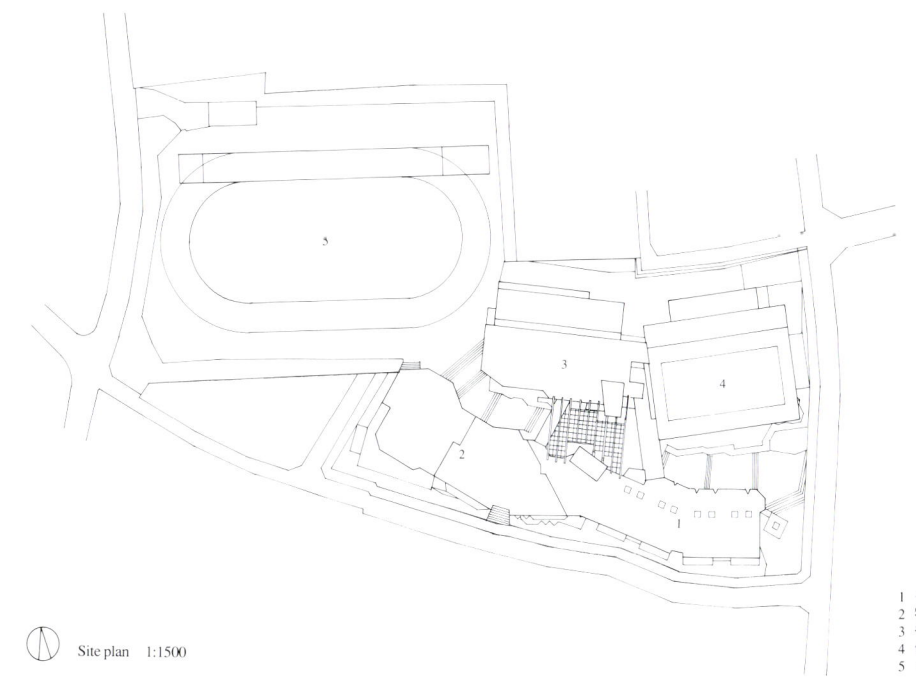

Site plan　1:1500

1　普通教室棟　Classroom wing
2　特別教室棟　Special classroom wing
3　管理棟　Administration wing
4　体育館　Gymnasium
5　グラウンド　Playground

特別教室棟 南側外観　South facade of the special classroom wing

普通教室棟 南東側外観　Southeast facade of the classroom wing

正面入口　左に普通教室棟、右に体育館棟　Front entrance, classrooms on the left and gymnasium on the right

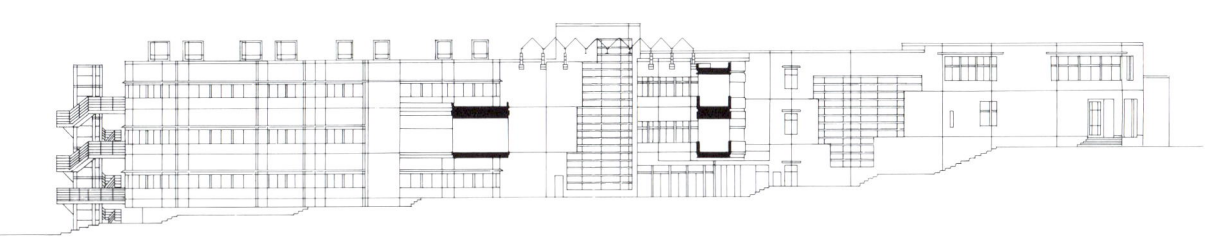

North elevation　1:600

中庭、連絡ブリッジ　左に管理棟、右に特別教室棟　Courtyard; administration wing on the left is connected by a bridge with special classroom wing on the right

ガラス屋根下中庭　左に普通教室棟、右に管理棟　Courtyard under glass roof; classroom wing on the left, administration wing on the right ▶

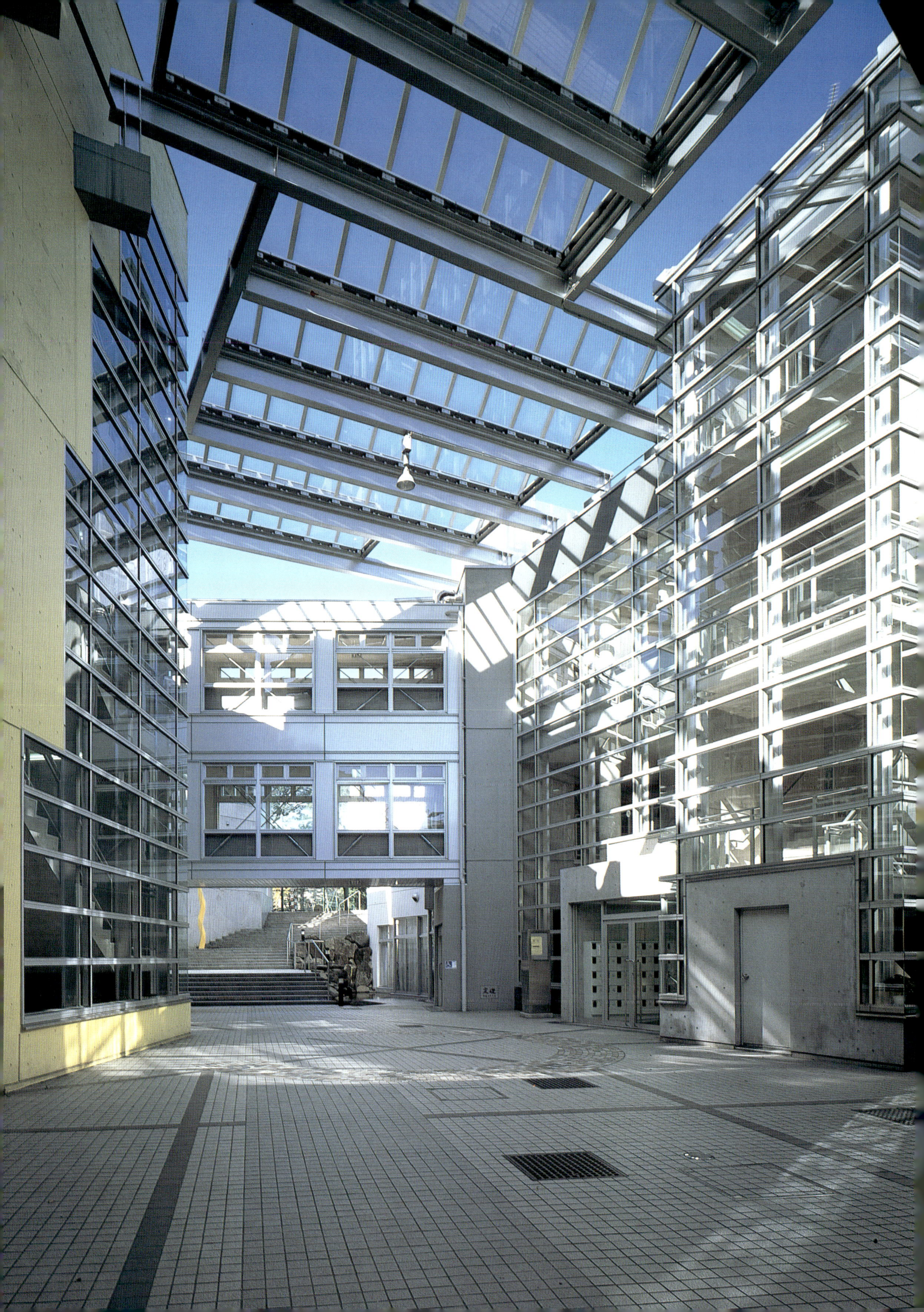

コリドール　Corridor

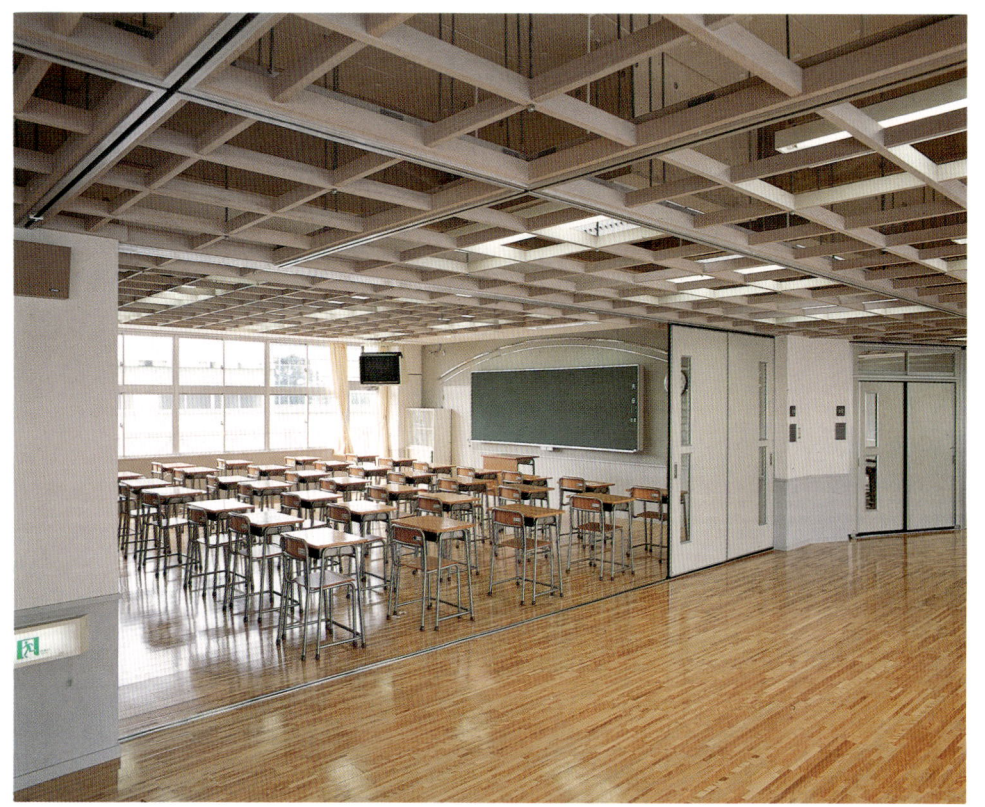

教室　Classroom

多目的スペース　Multi-purpose space

敷地は閑静な住宅地にあり、瓢箪型で8mの高低差を持つ。ここに建築基準法55条2項の12m認定を受け、12クラスの普通教室（将来の教科教室型に対して人文系、数学系、語学系に当てるように計画）、12の特別教室、体育館、屋上プール等を2棟に配置した。その間に一部ガラス屋根のある、アプローチからグラウンドまでの通り抜け空間を設け、両側の不規則に続く外壁をコンクリート打ち放しと3種類のグレーで塗分け、あたかも渓谷のアナロジーとしてデザインした。

Located in the quiet residential area, the gourd-shaped site has an 8-meters difference in the ground level. Pursuant to Article 55-2 of the Building Standards Act stipulating the height restriction to 12-meters, two wings containing 12 regular classrooms that can be converted in future into classrooms specially adapted to respective courses of curriculum such as humanities, science and language studies, 12 special classrooms, a gymnasium, a rooftop swimming pool, etc. are built. The two wings oppose each other across an open space partially covered with a glass roof. The open space acts as a passage leading from the approach to the playground. The buildings' outer walls of exposed concrete on both sides of the passage have irregular surfaces and are painted with three shades of gray to give an image of a mountain gorge.

1階 食堂兼多目的室　Lunchroom/multi-purpose room on the 1st floor

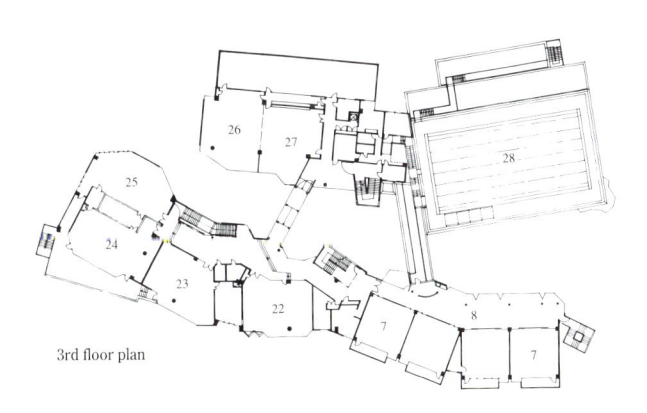

3rd floor plan

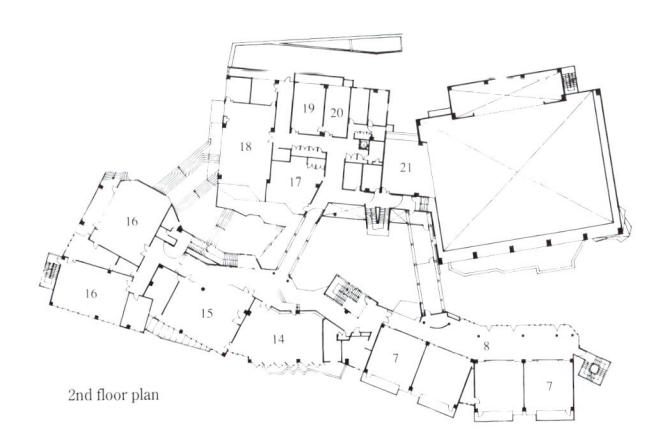

2nd floor plan

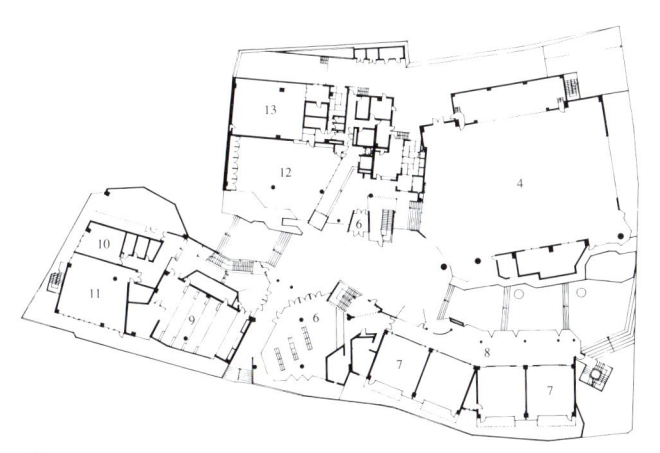

1st floor plan　1:1200

所在地	東京都新宿区
設計	船越徹＋アルコム
施工	淺沼組・生研建設JV.
竣工	1993年3月
敷地面積	9,577.41m²
建築面積	3,075.25m²
延床面積	6,600.16m²
階数	地上3階
構造	校舎：鉄筋コンクリート造
	体育館、プール：鉄骨鉄筋コンクリート造
撮影	中田眞澄／'91,93-94,96-97　岡田泰治／'92,95

Location: Shinjuku-ward, Tokyo
Architect: Tohru Funakoshi + ARCOM R&D, Architects
General contractor: Joint venture of Asanuma-gumi and Seiken-kensetsu
Completion date: March 1993
Site area: 103,090.28sq.ft.
Building area: 33,101.68sq.ft.
Total floor area: 71,043.46sq.ft.
Number of floors: 3 floors above ground
Structure: School building: reinforced concrete structure
gymnasium and swimming pool: steel framed reinforced concrete structure
Photographer: Masumi Nakada / 91, 93 94, 96-97
Taiji Okada / 92, 95

4　体育館　Gymnasium
6　エントランス　Entrance
7　教室　Classroom
8　多目的スペース　Multi-purpose space
9　音楽室　Music room
10　生徒会室　Student Council room
11　視聴覚室　Audio-visual room
12　食堂兼多目的室　Lunchroom/multi-purpose room
13　厨房　Kitchen
14　図書室　Library
15　コンピューター室　Computer room
16　理科室　Science lab.
17　保健室　Infirmary
18　職員室　Faculty office
19　校長室　Principal's office
20　事務室　Office
21　会議室　Conference room
22　特別活動室　Special activities room
23　美術室　Art room
24　金工室　Metal craft workshop
25　木工室　Wood craft workshop
26　調理室　Cooking class
27　被服室　Sewing class
28　プール　Swimming pool

三春町立桜中学校
SAKURA JUNIOR HIGH SCHOOL

香山アトリエ／環境造形研究所
KŌYAMA ATELIER

中庭越しに校舎を見る　Looking at the school building across the courtyard

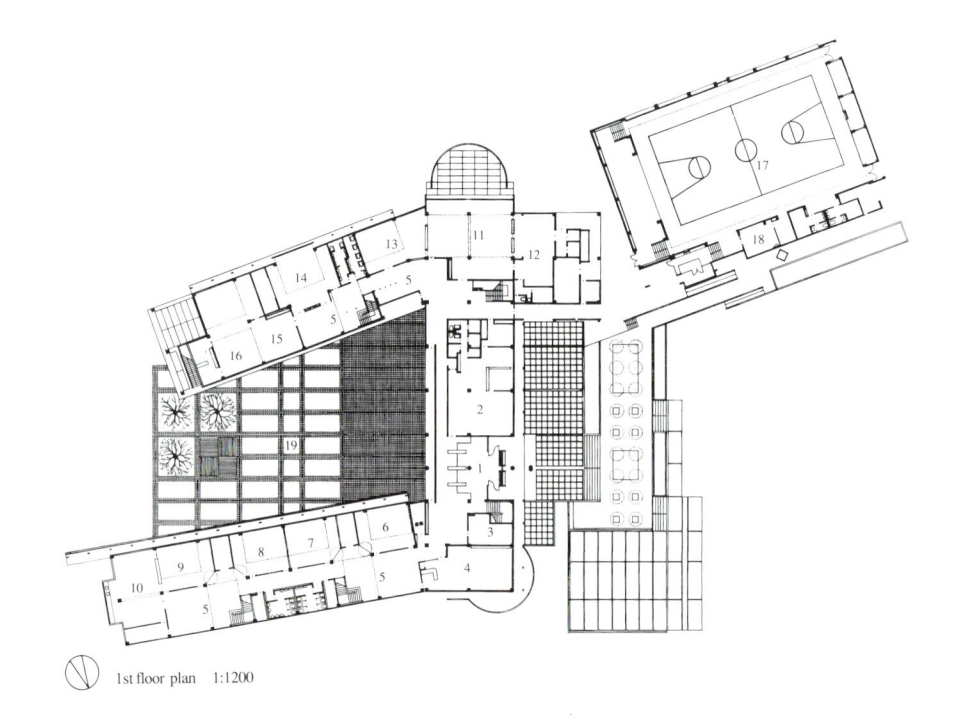

1st floor plan　1:1200

柱廊より中庭を見る　Looking at the courtyard from the colonnade

正面エントランスと前庭　Entrance and front garden

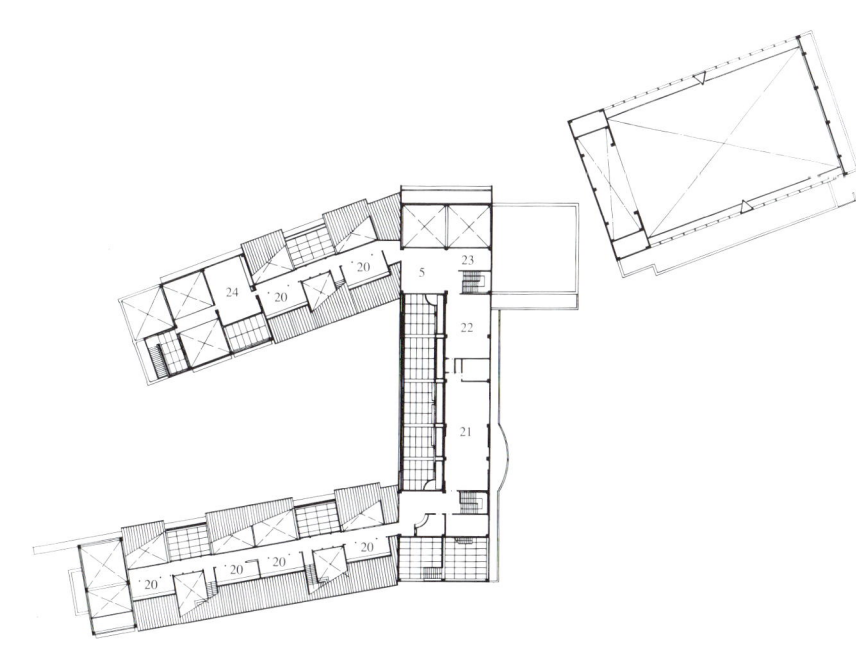

1 エントランス　Entrance
2 校務センター　Administration center
3 保健室　Infirmary
4 図書館　Library
5 オープンスペース　Open space
6 社会教室　Social studies class
7 国語教室　Japanese language class
8 数学教室　Mathematics class
9 講義室　Lecture room
10 理科室　Science lab.
11 食堂　Lunchroom
12 厨房　Kitchen
13 調理室　Cooking class
14 音楽室　Music room
15 技術室　Craft workshop
16 美術室　Art room
17 体育館　Gymnasium
18 ミーティングルーム　Meeting room
19 中庭　Courtyard
20 ホームベース　Homebase
21 コンピューター室　Computer room
22 英語教室　English language class
23 生徒会コーナー　Quarters for Student Council activities
24 被服室・講義室　Sewing class/lecture room

2nd floor plan

オープンスペース　Open space

2階ホームベース　2nd floor, homebase

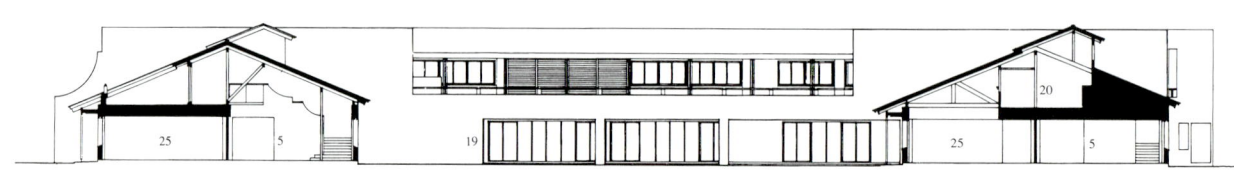

Section 1:400

5　オープンスペース　Open space
19　中庭　Courtyard
20　ホームベース　Homebase
25　教室　Classroom

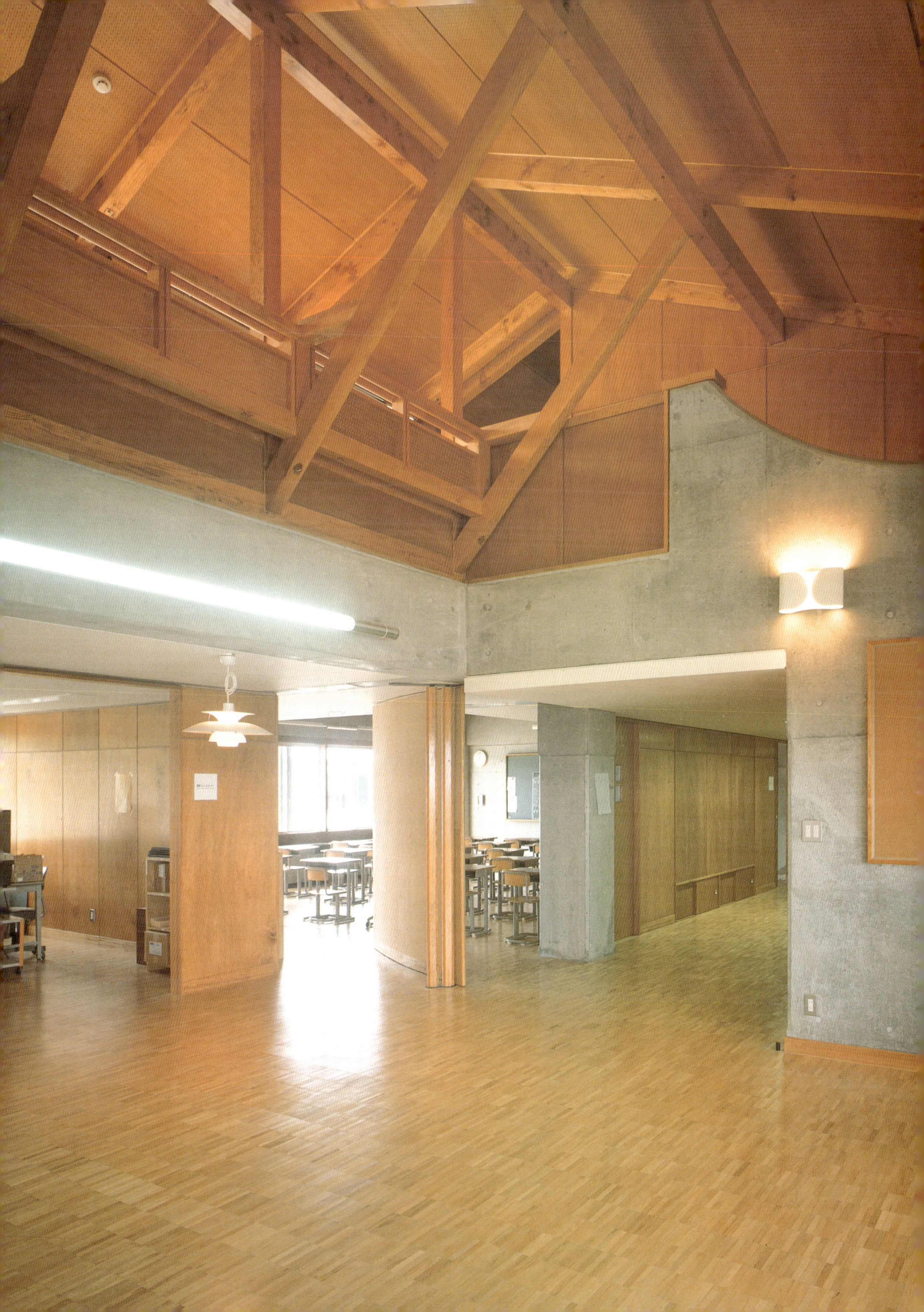

教室　Classroom

教室より中庭を見る　Looking at the courtyard from the classroom

1階 食堂　1st floor, lunchroom

体育館 北側外観　North facade of the gymnasium

体育館　Gymnasium

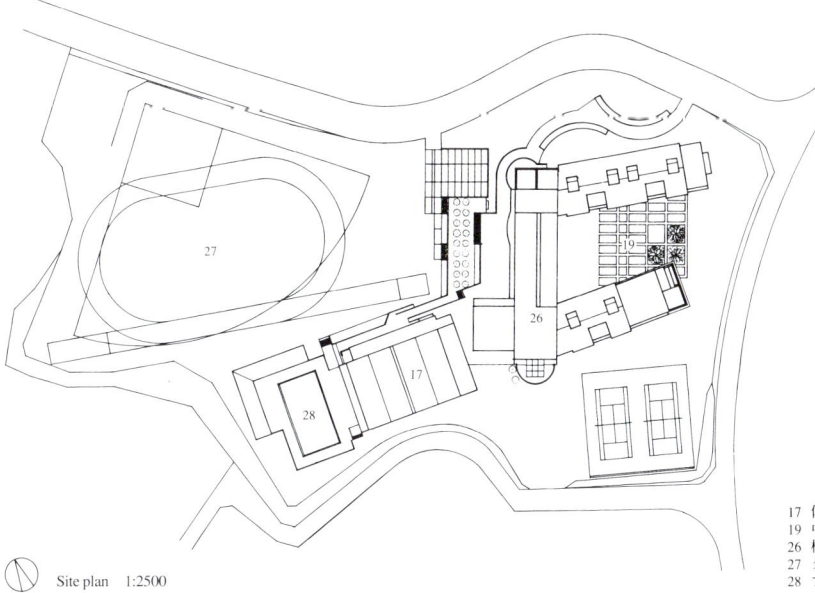

東北の小さな町の、小規模な中学校である。敷地は緩い丘の上にある。その上に射す日の光、そこから見える遠い山並み、そして強い北風を考えて配置が決められている。構造は、鉄筋コンクリートの柱、梁、壁の上に木造の小屋組をかぶせた複合構造である。それが風景に溶け込む形態を生み、内部に変化ある親しみやすい空間を作り出す。教科教室型という新しい方式で運営される学校にとってふさわしい多様な空間が、この複合構造から生み出された。

This is a small school in a small town standing on a gently sloping hill in the Tohoku District. The layout of the buildings was planned with due consideration of the sunshine, the command of the distant mountain view and the strong north wind that blows on the hill. A composite structure of RC columns, beams and walls combined with wooden trusses creates a form that fuses with the surrounding landscape and that contains cozy and diversified indoor spaces. The composite structure was a successful choice for a school which adopts the new system of allotting classrooms to particular courses, not to homerooms.

所在地	福島県三春町
設計	香山アトリエ／環境造形研究所
施工	大林組
竣工	1991年10月
敷地面積	27,474.11m²
建築面積	3,954.94m²
延床面積	4,432.91m²
階数	地上2階
構造	校舎：鉄筋コンクリート造、一部木造
	体育館：鉄筋コンクリート造、鉄骨造
撮影	香山壽夫／98　新建築社／99上,100上,102-103
	渡邊和俊／100下,101

Location:　Miharu-town, Fukushima
Architect:　Kōyama Atelier
General contractor:　Obayashi Corp.
Completion date:　October 1991
Site area:　295,728.57sq.ft.
Building area:　42,570.58sq.ft.
Total floor area:　47,715.40sq.ft.
Number of floors:　2 floors above ground
Structure:　School building: reinforced concrete structure and timber construction　gymnasium: reinforced concrete structure and steel structure
Photographer:　Hisao Kohyama / 98
Shinkenchiku-sha・Co.,Ltd. / 99: top, 100: top, 102-103
Kazutoshi Watanabe / 100: bottom, 101

17　体育館　Gymnasium
19　中庭　Courtyard
26　校舎　School building
27　グラウンド　Playground
28　プール　Swimming pool

Site plan 1:2500

睦学園 神戸国際中学校
KOBE INTERNATIONAL JUNIOR HIGH SCHOOL

竹中工務店
TAKENAKA CORP.

1号館大階段 "メモリアルステップ" 右上部は図書室　"Memorial Steps" of grand stairway in the Building No. 1, library on the upper right

広場より西側全景　West facade from the open field

東側アプローチより校舎棟全景　左は体育館　Entire view of school building seen from approach; gymnasium on the left

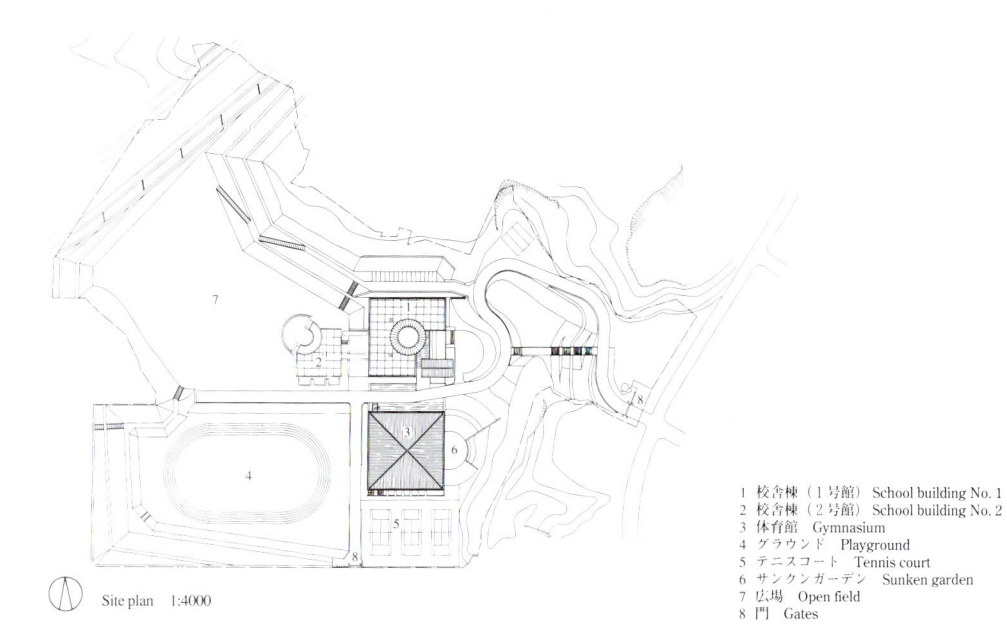

Site plan　1:4000

1 校舎棟（1号館）　School building No. 1
2 校舎棟（2号館）　School building No. 2
3 体育館　Gymnasium
4 グラウンド　Playground
5 テニスコート　Tennis court
6 サンクンガーデン　Sunken garden
7 広場　Open field
8 門　Gates

睦ホール外周階段見上げ　Looking up at the stairway along the outer perimeter of the Mutsumi Hall

睦ホール2階　Mutsumi Hall, 2nd floor

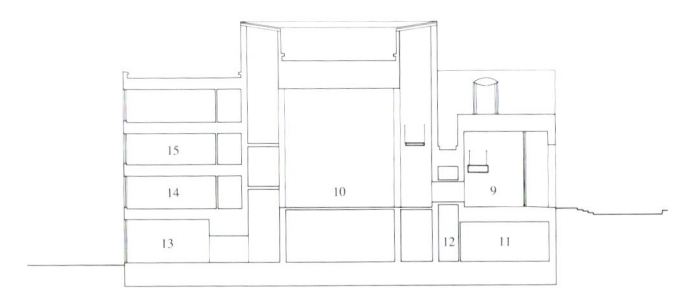

Section　1:700

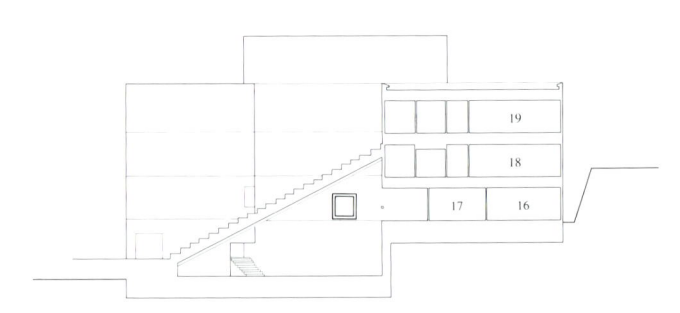

Section　1:700

9　エントランスホール　Entrance hall
10　睦ホール　Mutsumi Hall
11　多目的室　Multi-purpose room
12　ホール　Hall
13　食堂　Lunchroom
14　進路指導室　Guidance room
15　保健室　Infirmary
16　OAルーム　OA Lab.
17　事務室　Office
18　研究室　Faculty office
19　ニューメディア学習室　New media studies

体育館地下1階プール　Swimming pool in basement 1 of the gymnasium

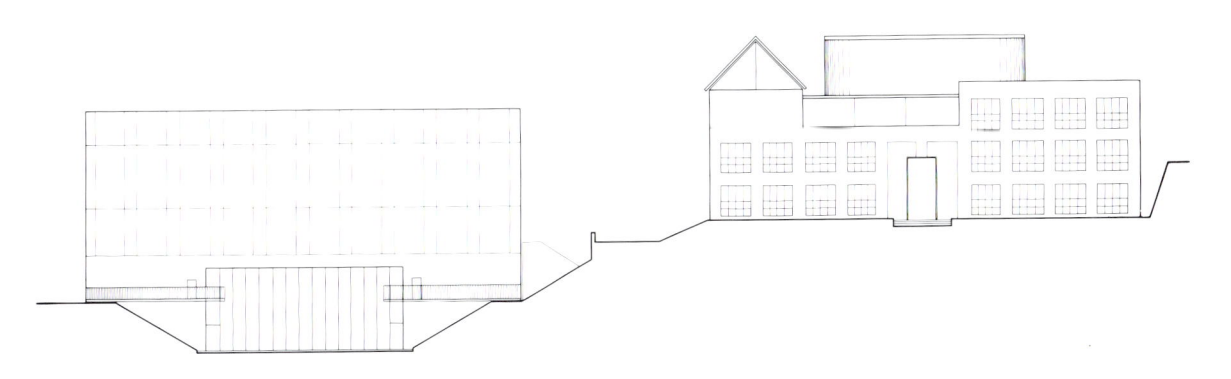

East elevation　1:700

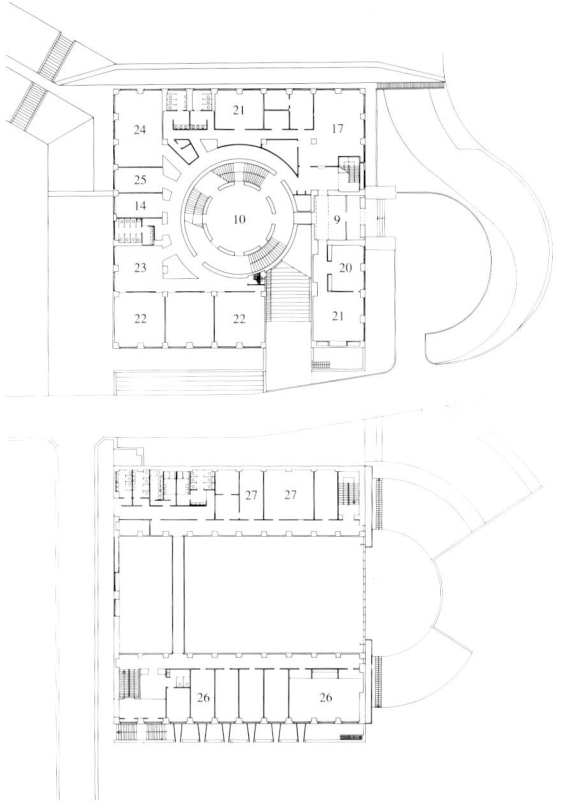

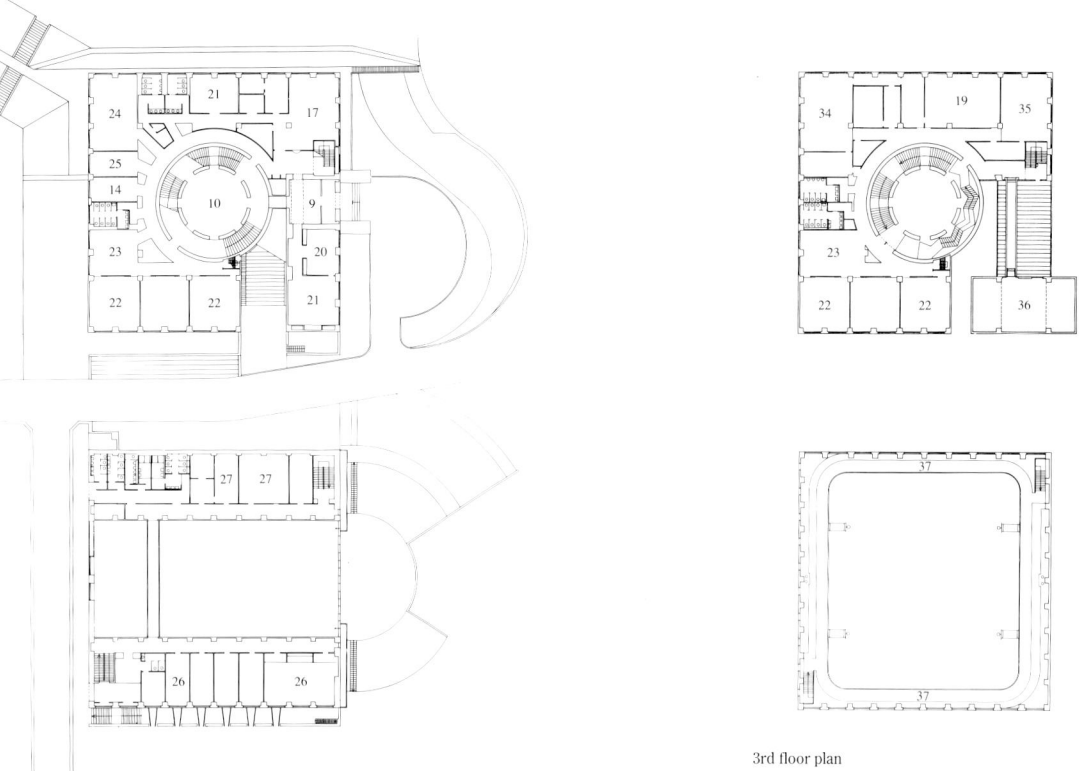

1st floor plan

3rd floor plan

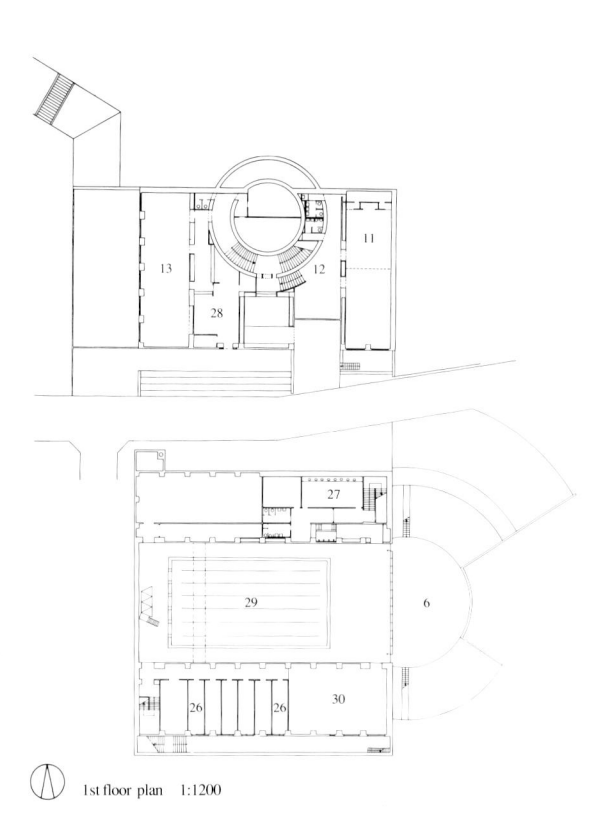

1st floor plan 1:1200

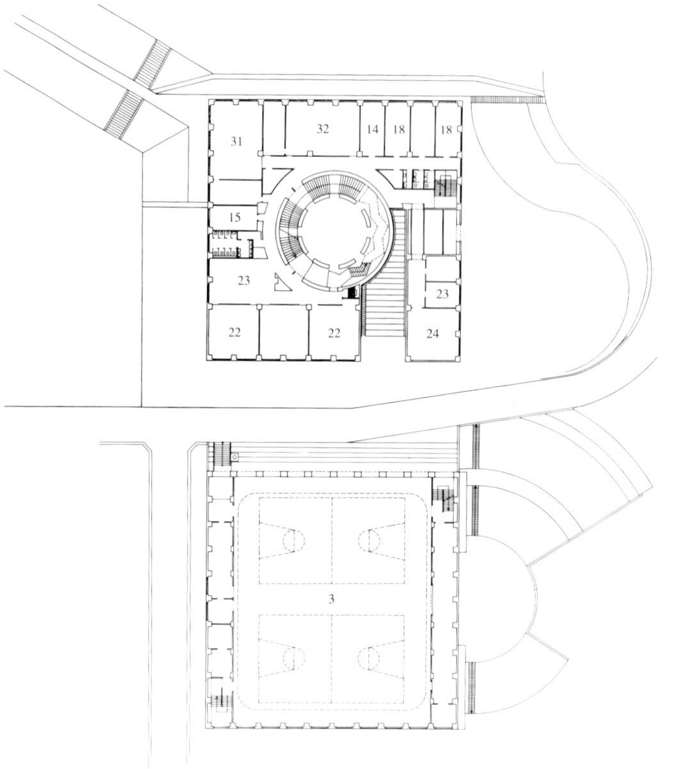

2nd floor plan

3 体育館 Gymnasium	23 コモンスペース Common space
6 サンクンガーデン Sunken garden	24 会議室 Conference room
9 エントランスホール Entrance hall	25 役員室 Chief staff room
10 睦ホール Mutsumi Hall	26 クラブ室 Extra-curricular activities room
11 多目的室 Multi-purpose room	27 ロッカールーム Locker room
12 ホール Hall	28 厨房 Kitchen
13 食堂 Lunchroom	29 プール Swimming pool
14 進路指導室 Guidance room	30 トレーニングルーム Training gym
15 保健室 Infirmary	31 理科室 Science lab.
17 事務室 Office	32 調理室 Cooking class
18 研究室 Faculty office	33 副校長室 Vice Principal's office
19 ニューメディア学習室 New media studies	34 ＬＬ教室 Language Lab.
20 理事長室 Director's room	35 美術室 Art room
21 応接室 Reception room	36 図書室 Library
22 教室 Classroom	37 ランニングトラック Track

3階図書室へのガラス張り廊下　Glass paneled corridor leading to the 3rd floor library

図書室　Library

生徒たちの"記憶の場の創出"を目指したキャンパスである。一般に級友や教師の思い出はともかく、生活の背景となった学舎の記憶は時とともに極めておぼろ気になる。この学舎が、学校施設として、生徒たちの思い出がつなぎとめられ、そして幾重にも重なる"場"（大階段、家形の図書館、円形階段ホール等）が点在するものであって欲しかったのである。それらが、感受性豊かな年頃の甘酸っぱい思い出のシーンとして、彼らの心に刻まれてゆくことを願っている。

We aimed at creating a campus that "remains in the memories" of students. Memories of the school itself are often cast into oblivion with lapse of time, if not those of classmates and teachers. Our design concept is focused on creating an architecture that remains in the memory of students and that contains layers of "spaces" (the wide stairway, the library shaped like a free standing house, the circular stairway hall, etc.). We hope that these elements will be engraved in their mind to remind them of their sweet-sour days of their youth.

所在地　　兵庫県神戸市
設計・施工　竹中工務店
竣工　　1992年8月
敷地面積　47,659.65m²
建築面積　3,401.24m²
延床面積　10,001.63m²
階数　　地上3階　地下1階
構造　　鉄筋コンクリート造
撮影　　村井修／104,106,109　新建築社／105
　　　　竹中工務店　吉村行雄／107

Location: Kobe-city, Hyogo
Architect / General contractor: Takenaka Corp.
Completion date: August 1992
Site area: 513,003.70sq.ft.
Building area: 36,610.61sq.ft.
Total floor area: 107,656.54sq.ft.
Number of floors: 3 floors above ground, 1 floor below ground
Structure: Reinforced concrete structure
Photographer: Osamu Murai / 104, 106, 109
Shinkenchiku-sha・Co.,Ltd. / 105
Yukio Yoshimura　Takenaka Corp./ 107

熊本県立東稜高等学校
TORYO HIGH SCHOOL, KUMAMOTO

木島安史＋ＹＡＳ都市研究所
YASUFUMI KIJIMA + YAS & URBANISTS

鳥瞰　Bird's eye view

北側外観　左から理科棟、体育館、クラブ室　North facade: from left, science studies wing, gymnasium, extra-curricular activities rooms

校門より前庭越しに管理棟を見る　Looking at the administration wing from the school gate across the front garden

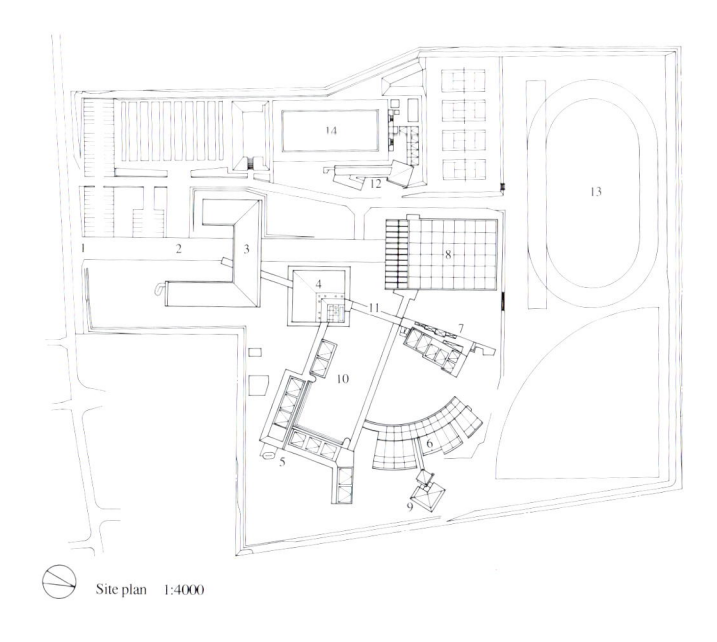

Site plan　1:4000

1　校門　School gate
2　前庭　Front yard
3　管理棟　Administration wing
4　昇降口棟　Entrance
5　普通教室棟　Classroom wing
6　芸術棟　Art/music studies wing
7　理科棟　Science studies wing
8　体育館　Gymnasium
9　礼法室　Etiquette training room
10　中庭　Courtyard
11　渡り廊下　Corridor
12　クラブ室　Extra-curricular activities room
13　グラウンド　Playground
14　プール　Swimming pool

中庭より普通教室棟、右に昇降口棟を見る　Looking at the classroom wing from the courtyard, entrance on the right

普通教室棟より中庭越し奥に体育館を見る　Looking from the classroom wing at the gymnasium at the back across courtyard

渡り廊下と奥に中庭を見る　Looking at the connecting corridor and courtyard at the back

理科棟　Science studies wing

昇降口棟1階　Entrance, 1st floor

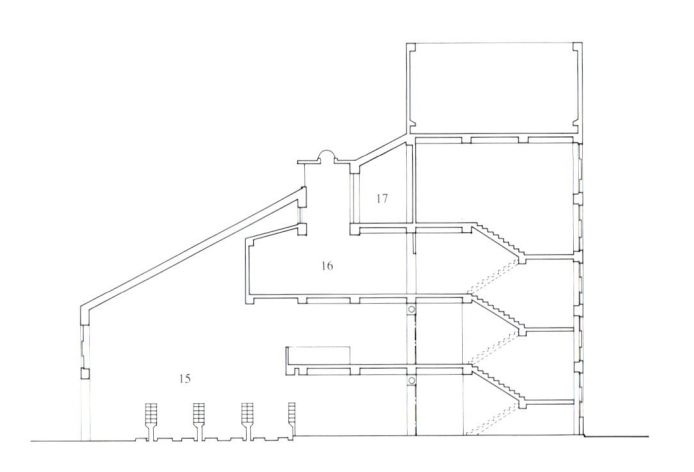

Section 1:400

8 体育館	Gymnasium
9 礼法室	Etiquette training room
11 渡り廊下	Corridor
15 エントランス	Entrance
16 学習室	Study room
17 生活指導室	Guidance room
18 生徒会室	Student Council room
19 オープンギャラリー	Open gallery
20 教室	Classroom
21 被服室	Sewing class
22 調理室	Cooking class
23 書道室	Calligraphy room
24 美術室	Art room
25 音楽室	Music room
26 理科室	Science lab.
27 保健室	Infirmary
28 図書室	Library
29 校長室	Principal's office
30 会議室	Conference room
31 事務室	Office

1st floor plan 1:1800

芸術棟 教室　Art/music studies wing

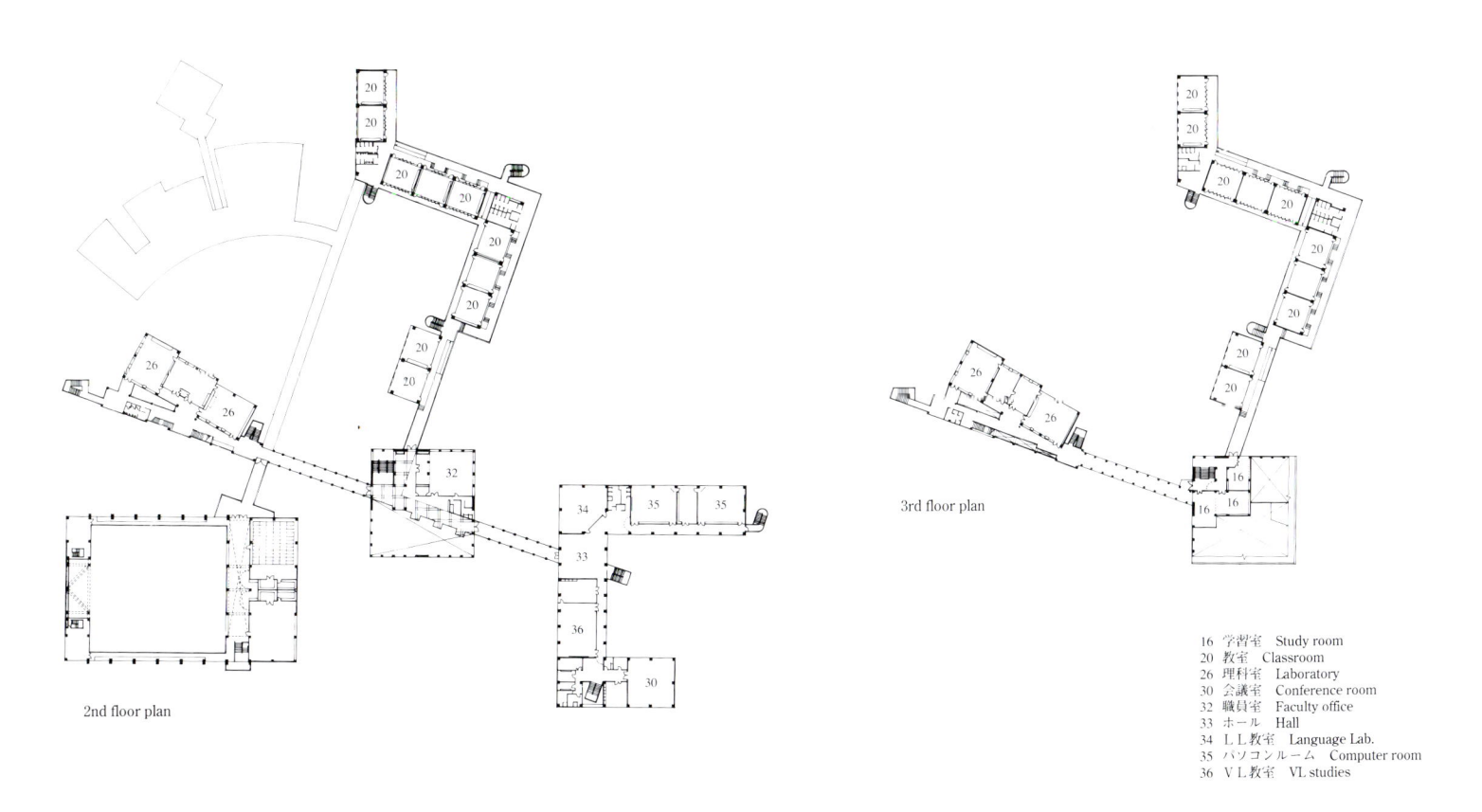

2nd floor plan

3rd floor plan

16　学習室　Study room
20　教室　Classroom
26　理科室　Laboratory
30　会議室　Conference room
32　職員室　Faculty office
33　ホール　Hall
34　L L 教室　Language Lab.
35　パソコンルーム　Computer room
36　V L 教室　VL studies

体育館　Gymnasium

本校は、分散型の自由な配置計画ができた。原則として、南側の明るく広い半屋外の廊下で各棟を結びながら、外部と内部が一体化したオープンで自由度に豊んだ学園を目指した。全体配置は角度の異なる軸線によって決定された。管理棟、昇降口棟、理科棟は前面道路に平行な軸、そしてそれら3棟を貫く2階建ての廊下は南北軸である。そして管理棟と体育館が中心角を揃え、配置計画の骨格が形成されている。

The site allowed a scattered layout of buildings. Basically, the spacious semi-outdoor corridors on the south connect the wings to create a campus in which the indoor spaces are integrally linked with the outdoor spaces. The layout is planned along different axis lines. The axes of the administration wing, the wing containing the stairways and the science building run parallel to the road in front of the site, and the two-storied corridor runs north and south penetrating these three wings. The gymnasium and the administration wing are aligned at the central angle, forming the skeleton of the layout.

所在地　　熊本市
設計　　　木島安史＋ＹＡＳ都市研究所
施工　　　サンエー建設　水上建設　日動工務店　坂口建設
　　　　　豊工務店　光進建設　川上建設
竣工　　　1990年3月
敷地面積　65,000.00m²
建築面積　8,256.00m²
延床面積　13,152.97m²
階数　　　昇降口棟：地上4階　管理棟：地上2階
　　　　　普通教室棟、理科棟：地上3階　芸術棟：地上1階
　　　　　体育館、クラブ室：地上2階
構造　　　昇降口棟、管理棟、普通教室棟、理科棟：鉄筋コンクリート造　芸術棟：木造、一部鉄筋コンクリート造
　　　　　体育館：鉄筋コンクリート造、一部木造
　　　　　クラブ室：鉄筋コンクリート造
撮影　　　荒井政夫

Location:　Kumamoto-city, Kumamoto
Architect:　Yasufumi Kijima + YAS & Urbanists
General contractor:　Sanei Construction Co.,Ltd.　Mizukami Construction Co.,Ltd.　Nichido Construction Co.,Ltd.　Sakaguchi Construction Co.,Ltd.　Yutaka Construction Co.,Ltd.　Koshin Construction Co.,Ltd.　Kawakami Construction Co.,Ltd.
Completion date:　March 1990
Site area:　699,653.50sq.ft.
Building area:　88,866.76sq.ft.
Total floor area:　141,577.25sq.ft.
Number of floors:　Entrance: 4 floors above ground
administration wing: 2 floors above ground
classroom wing and science studies wing: 3 floors above ground
art/music studies wing: 1 floor above ground　gymnasium and extra-curricular activities rooms: 2 floors above ground
Structure:　Entrance, administration wing, classroom wing and science studies wing: reinforced concrete structure
art/music studies wing: timber construction and reinforced concrete structure　gymnasium: reinforced concrete structure and timber construction　extra-curricular activities rooms: reinforced concrete structure
Photographer:　Masao Arai

複合施設　Combined Facilities

育英学院サレジオ小・中学校
SALESIANS OF DON BOSCO SALESIO PRIMARY AND JUNIOR HIGH SCHOOL

藤木隆男建築研究所
FUJIKI TAKAO ATELIER, INC.

西側外観　手前は小学校教室群　West facade: primary school classrooms in the front

Site plan 1:2200

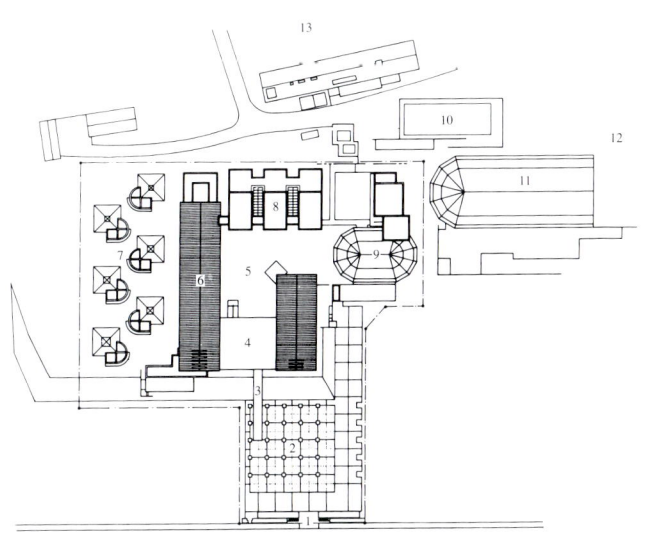

1 正門 Front gate
2 広場 Plaza
3 ブリッジ Bridge
4 ポーチ Porch
5 中庭 Courtyard
6 特別教室棟 Special classroom wing
7 小学校棟 Primary school wing
8 中学校棟 Junior high school wing
9 講堂 Auditorium
10 プール Swimming pool
11 体育館 Gymnasium
12 グラウンド Playground
13 東京サレジオ学園 Tokyo Salesian Boys' Home

特別教室棟より講堂を見る　Looking at the auditorium from the special classroom wing

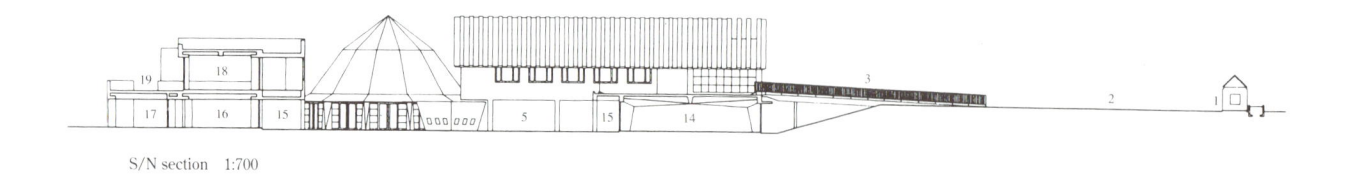

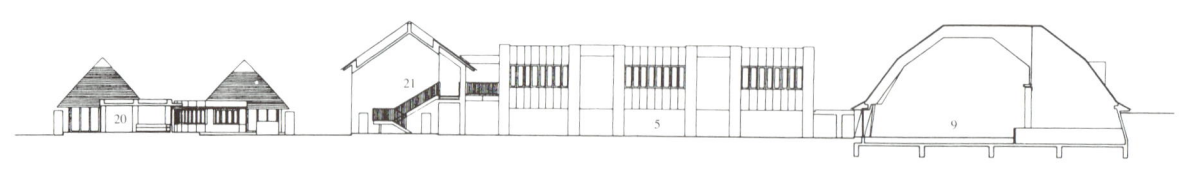

S/N section　1:700

E/W section　1:700

1　正門　Front gate
2　広場　Plaza
3　ブリッジ　Bridge
5　中庭　Courtyard
9　講堂　Auditrium
14　食堂　Lunchroom
15　回廊　Corridor
16　中学生ホール　Hall for junior high school students
17　生徒会室　Student Council room
18　中学教室　Junior high school classroom
19　ルーフテラス　Roof terrace
20　小学教室　Primary school classroom
21　ピロティ　Pilotis

講堂より特別教室棟を見る　Looking at the special classroom wing from the auditorium

中庭　Courtyard

エントランスよりパソコン室を見る　Looking at the computer room from the entrance

中学生ホール　2階は教室　Hall for junior high school students; classrooms on the 2nd floor

小学教室の天井見上げ　Looking up at the ceiling in primary school classroom

小学教室　Primary school classroom

中学教室　Junior high school classroom

講堂 Auditorium

食堂 Lunchroom

鳥瞰 Bird's eye view

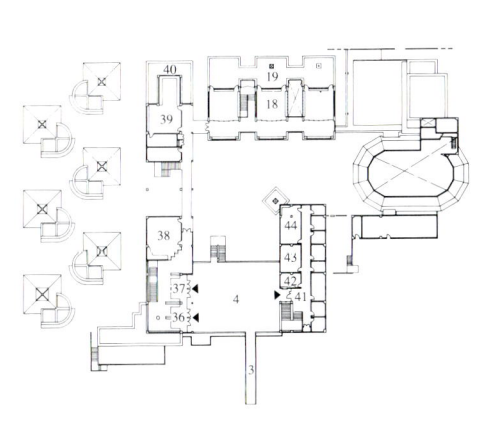

2nd floor plan

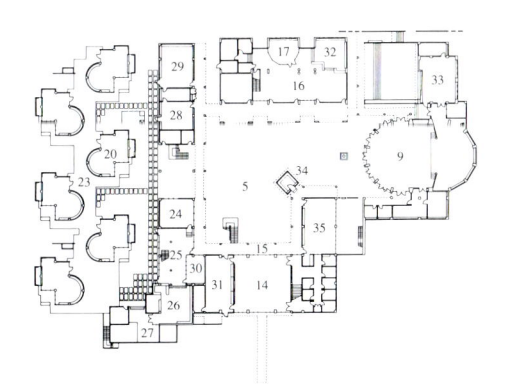

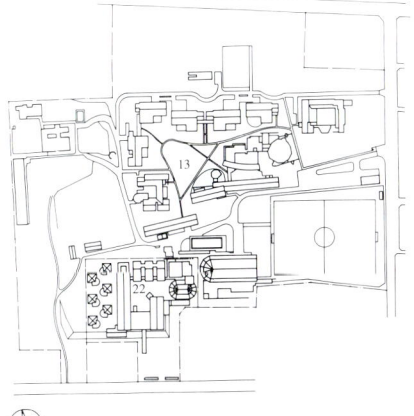

Total site plan 1:6500

1st floor plan 1:1600

- 3 ブリッジ　Bridge
- 4 ポーチ　Porch
- 5 中庭　Courtyard
- 9 講堂　Auditrium
- 13 東京サレジオ学園　Tokyo Salesian Boys' Home
- 14 食堂　Lunchroom
- 15 回廊　Corridor
- 16 中学生ホール　Hall for junior high school students
- 17 生徒会室　Student Council room
- 18 中学教室　Junior high school classroom
- 19 ルーフテラス　Roof terrace
- 20 小学教室　Primary school classroom
- 22 育英学院サレジオ小・中学校　Salesians of Don Bosco Salesio Primary and Junior High School
- 23 デッキ　Deck
- 24 スタジオ　Studio
- 25 小学生ホール　Hall for primary school students
- 26 小・図書館　Library, primary school
- 27 テラス　Terrace
- 28 小・理科室　Science lab., primary school
- 29 中・理科室　Science lab., junior high school
- 30 児童会室　Assembly room
- 31 家庭科室　Home economics room
- 32 中・図書館　Library, junior high school
- 33 音楽室　Music room
- 34 宗教司牧室　Rectory
- 35 職員室　Faculty office
- 36 小学エントランス　Entrance, primary school
- 37 中学エントランス　Entrance, junior high school
- 38 パソコン室　Computer room
- 39 技術・美術室　Art/craft workshop
- 40 ルーフガーデン　Roof garden
- 41 エントランス　Entrance
- 42 事務室　Office
- 43 会議室　Conference room
- 44 校長・応接室　Principal's office/reception room

住宅や大学、研究所に囲まれた武蔵野の風景の中に、勾配屋根、低層、分散配置の"小さな"学校建築をはめ込むこと。ホームルームを拠点とする、屋外空間と一体となった学校生活の展開を目指し、オープンスクール形式を採らず、むしろ教室の独立完結性を志向している。また、併設の小・中学校に自立性と変化を持たせるため、それぞれに"村"と"街"としての建築の構造や空間の質を与え、9年間の学校生活にメリハリや豊かさを持たせることを求めている。

Low-rises with pitched roof are scattered in the premises as a "small-scale school" amid the verdure of Musashino surrounded by private houses, universities and research centers. Home-room based system instead of open school system is employed, and each home-room constitutes an independent space which is closely linked with the outdoor areas. To respect the independence and autonomy of the primary and secondary schools as well as to give diversity to the architecture as a whole, the buildings are designed to simulate a "village" and a "town" respectively in their structure and quality of the space. The nine years of school life here will give children rich and colorful experiences.

所在地　東京都小平市
設計　藤木隆男建築研究所
施工　日本国土開発
竣工　1993年3月
敷地面積　8,136.00m²
建築面積　2,764.27m²
延床面積　3,125.24m²
階数　地上2階
構造　鉄筋コンクリート造、一部木造（小学校棟小屋組）、鉄骨造（講堂棟小屋組）
撮影　高瀬良夫

Location: Kodaira-city, Tokyo
Architect: Fujiki Takao Atelier, Inc.
General contractor: JDC Corp.
Completion date: March 1993
Site area: 87,575.09sq.ft.
Building area: 29,754.33sq.ft.
Total floor area: 33,639.77sq.ft.
Number of floors: 2 floors above ground
Structure: Reinforced concrete structure, timber construction (roof truss in primary school building) and steel structure (roof truss in auditorium)
Photographer: Yoshio Takase

慶應義塾湘南藤沢中等部・高等部
KEIO SHONAN-FUJISAWA JUNIOR & SENIOR HIGH SCHOOL

谷口建築設計研究所　谷口吉生
Yoshio Taniguchi　TANIGUCHI AND ASSOCIATES

エントランスより左に高層棟、右に体育館を見る　Looking at the high-rise building on the left, and gymnasium on the right from the entrance

正面低層部 体育館西側外観　Low-rise building in the center, gymnasium west facade

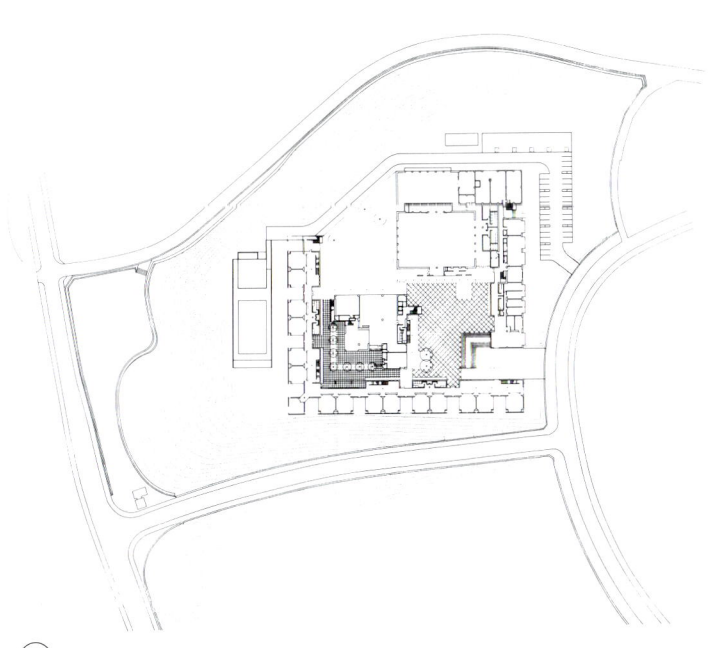

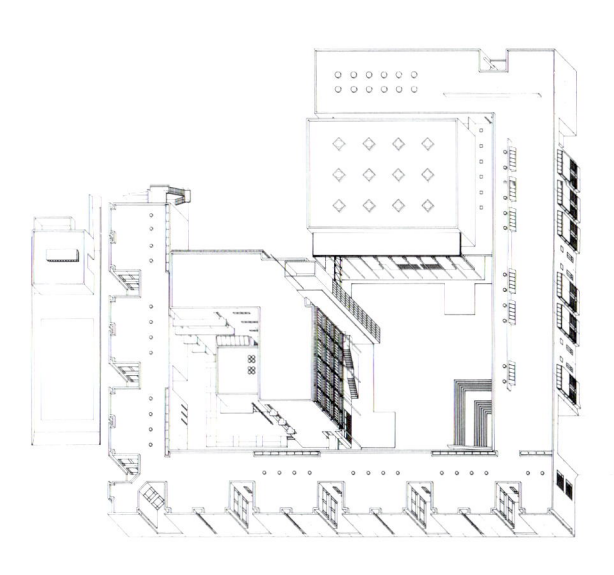

Site plan　1:3500

Axonometric drawing

前面道路に接する低層部のエントランス　Entrance in the low-rise building facing front road

北側外観　North facade

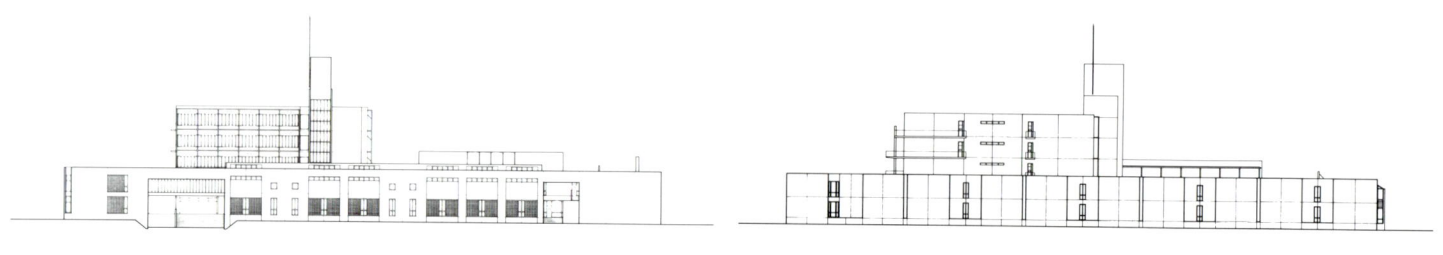

North elevation　1:1400

East elevation　1:1400

高層部吹抜　Light-well in the high-rise building ▶

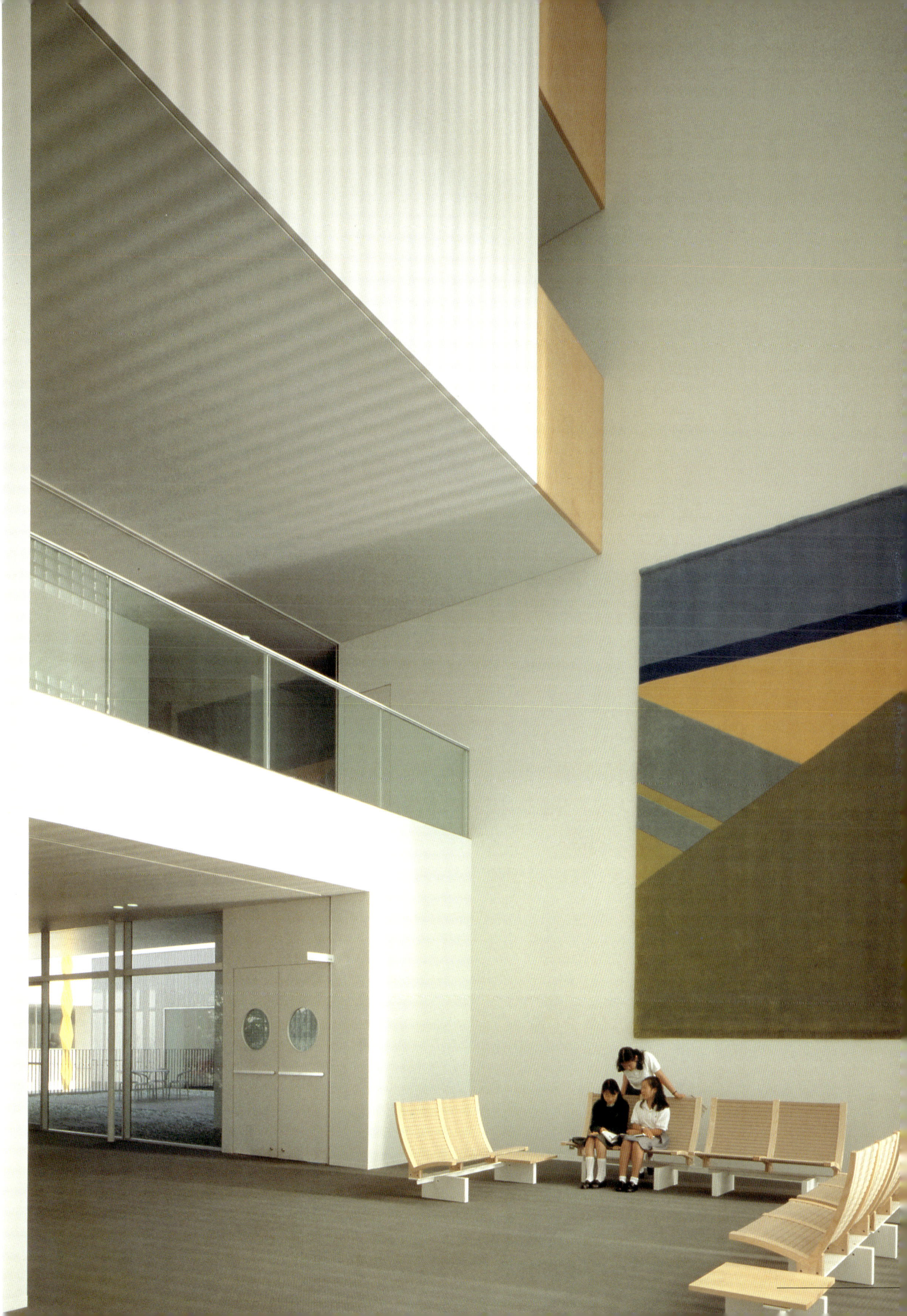

低層部吹抜見上げ　Looking up in the light-well of the low-rise building

普通教室　Classroom

教室入口とコリドール　Classroom door and corridor

教室棟2階コリドール　2nd floor corridor in the classroom wing

図書室 閲覧コーナー　Library reading room

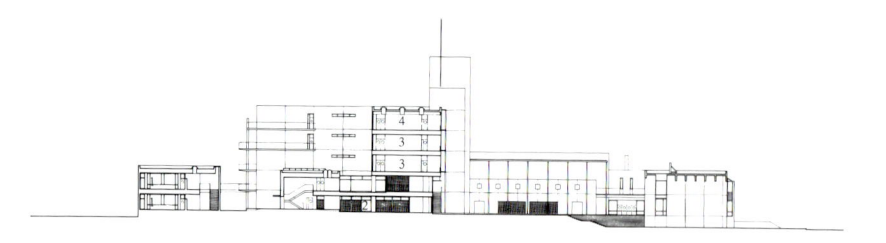

Section　1:1400

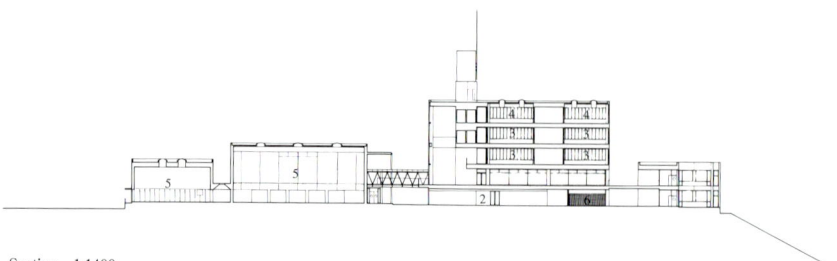

Section　1:1400

1　教室　Classroom
2　図書室　Library
3　理科室　Science lab.
4　美術室　Art room
5　体育館　Gymnasium
6　保健室　Infirmary

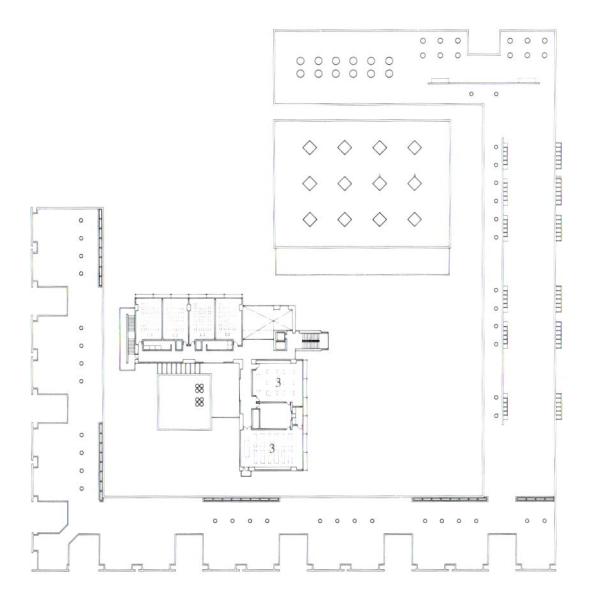

3rd floor plan

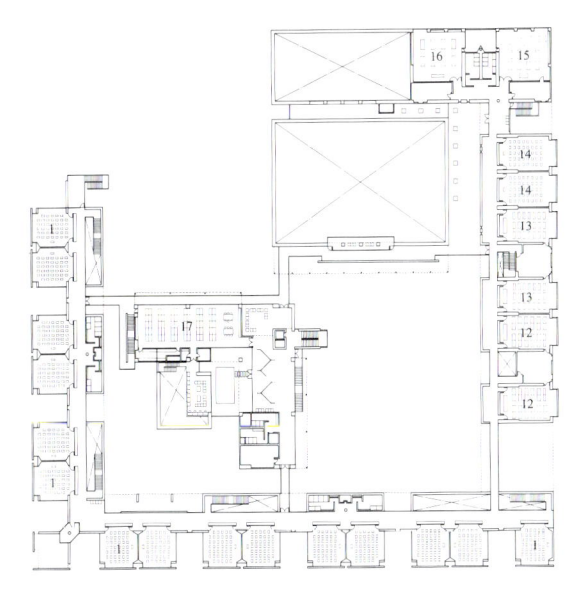

2nd floor plan

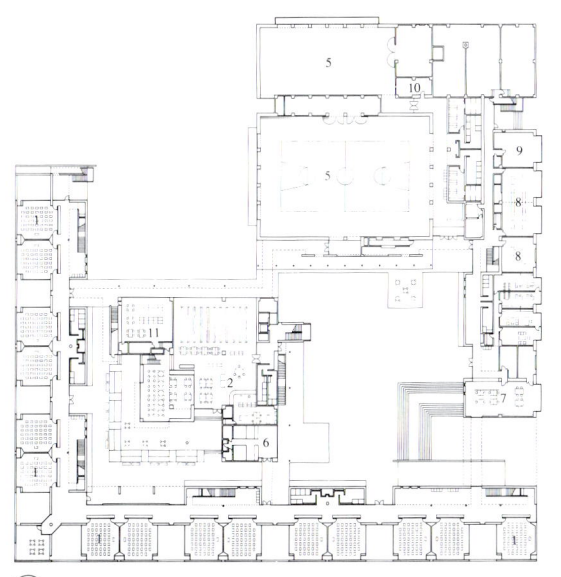

1st floor plan 1:1600

体育館 Gymnasium

1 教室   Classroom
2 図書室   Library
3 理科室   Science lab.
5 体育館   Gymnasium
6 保健室   Infirmary
7 事務室   Office
8 会議室   Conference room
9 管理室   Administration room
10 体育教員室 Office for gymnastic teachers
11 教材研究室
   Laboratory for developing teaching materials
12 ＡＶＣ教室 AVC
13 ＬＬ教室   Language Lab.
14 多目的室   Multi-purpose room
15 技術科室   Craft workshop
16 家庭科室   Home economics room
17 教員室   Faculty office

敷地は藤沢郊外の緑におおわれた高台の上に位置する。大学と共有するキャンパス内に独自の領域を設定するために、普通教室で構成される低層部によって外周を囲った。その内部に高層の特別教室棟と体育館を配することにより、両者の間に多様な外部空間が出現する。建築と周辺、家具、備品、サインにわたるまで意匠統一された環境と、多様な空間を持つ美しい街として、この学校を位置付けることを設計の基本方針とした。

The school is situated within the university campus on a verdurous hill in the suburbs of Fujisawa City. Low-rise buildings containing classrooms delineate the area allotted to the junior and senior high schools. A gymnasium and a high-rise containing special classrooms stand within the enclosure, creating diversified outdoor spaces between the buildings. The architecture, surroundings, furniture, fixtures and signs are all designed based on a unified concept to create attractive scenes of diversified characters.

所在地   神奈川県藤沢市
設計   谷口建築設計研究所　谷口吉生
施工   竹中工務店・安藤建設・戸田建設JV.
竣工   1992年3月
敷地面積   75,302.00m²
建築面積   7,630.00m²
延床面積   13,157.00m²
階数   地上5階、塔屋1階
構造   鉄筋コンクリート造、鉄骨鉄筋コンクリート造、
          一部鉄骨造
撮影   新建築社／126, 128-130, 132　北嶋俊治／127, 131, 133

Location: Fujisawa-city, Kanagawa
Architect: Yoshio Taniguchi Taniguchi and Associates
General contractor: Joint venture of Takenaka, Ando Construction and Toda
Completion date: March 1992
Site area: 810,543.19sq.ft.
Building area: 82,128.56sq.ft.
Total floor area: 141,620.63sq.ft.
Number of floors: 5 floors above ground, tower on the 1st floor
Structure: Reinforced concrete structure, steel framed reinforced concrete structure and steel structure
Photographer: Shinkenchiku-sha・Co.,Ltd. / 126, 128-130, 132
Toshiharu Kitajima / 127, 131, 133

千里国際学園
SENRI INTERNATIONAL SCHOOL

長島孝一＋ＡＵＲ
KOICHI NAGASHIMA + AUR ARCHITECTURE · URBAN DESIGN · RESEARCH · CONSULTANTS CO.,LTD.

鳥瞰　Bird's eye view

北側外観　North facade

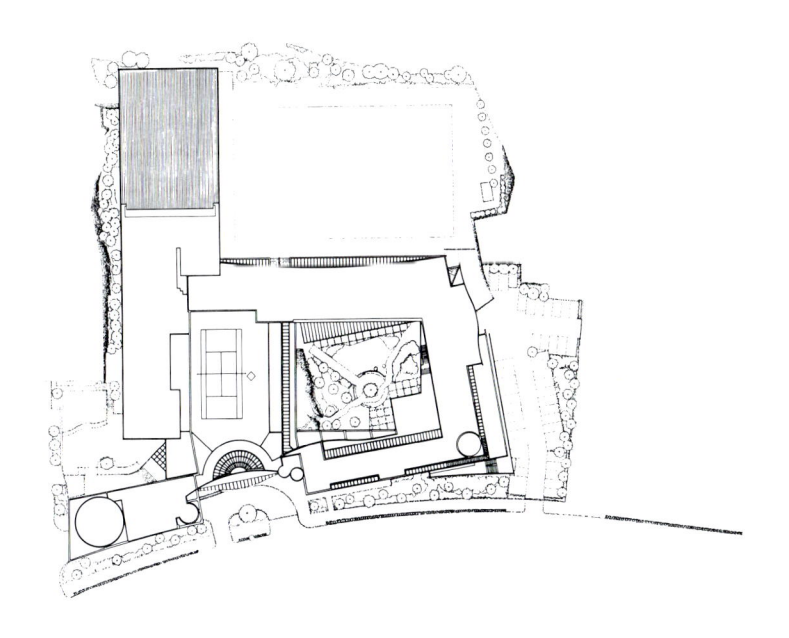

Site plan　1:2000

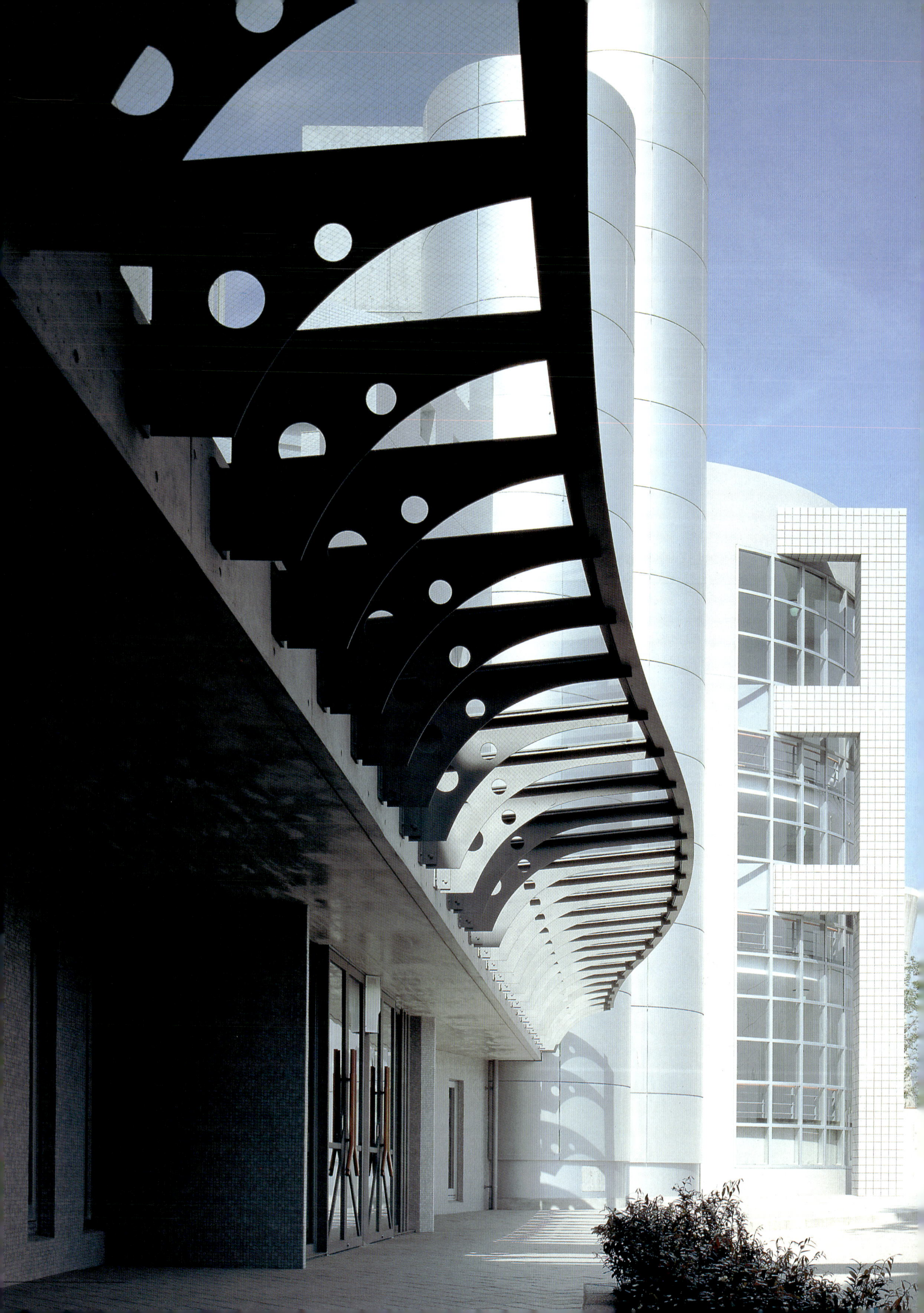

エントランスホール　Entrance hall

図書館2階より中庭を見る　Looking into the courtyard from the 2nd floor in the library

◀ エントランスのキャノピーとシリンダー見上げ
　Looking up at the entrance canopy and cylinders

中庭と食堂とをつなぐ生徒ラウンジ　Students' lounge connecting lunchroom and courtyard

中庭に突き出たラウンジ外観　Lounge projecting into the courtyard

中庭と図書館の間の擁壁　Retention wall between courtyard and library

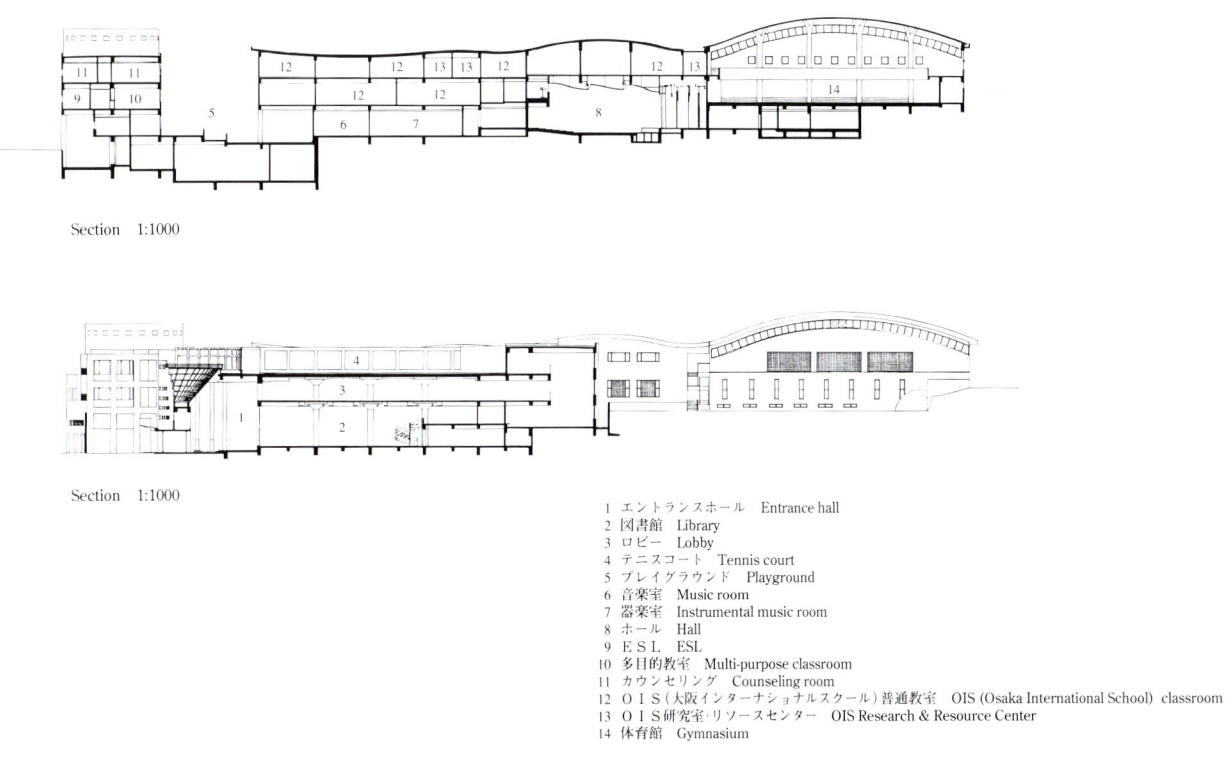

Section 1:1000

Section 1:1000

1 エントランスホール　Entrance hall
2 図書館　Library
3 ロビー　Lobby
4 テニスコート　Tennis court
5 プレイグラウンド　Playground
6 音楽室　Music room
7 器楽室　Instrumental music room
8 ホール　Hall
9 ＥＳＬ　ESL
10 多目的教室　Multi-purpose classroom
11 カウンセリング　Counseling room
12 ＯＩＳ（大阪インターナショナルスクール）普通教室　OIS (Osaka International School) classroom
13 ＯＩＳ研究室・リソースセンター　OIS Research & Resource Center
14 体育館　Gymnasium

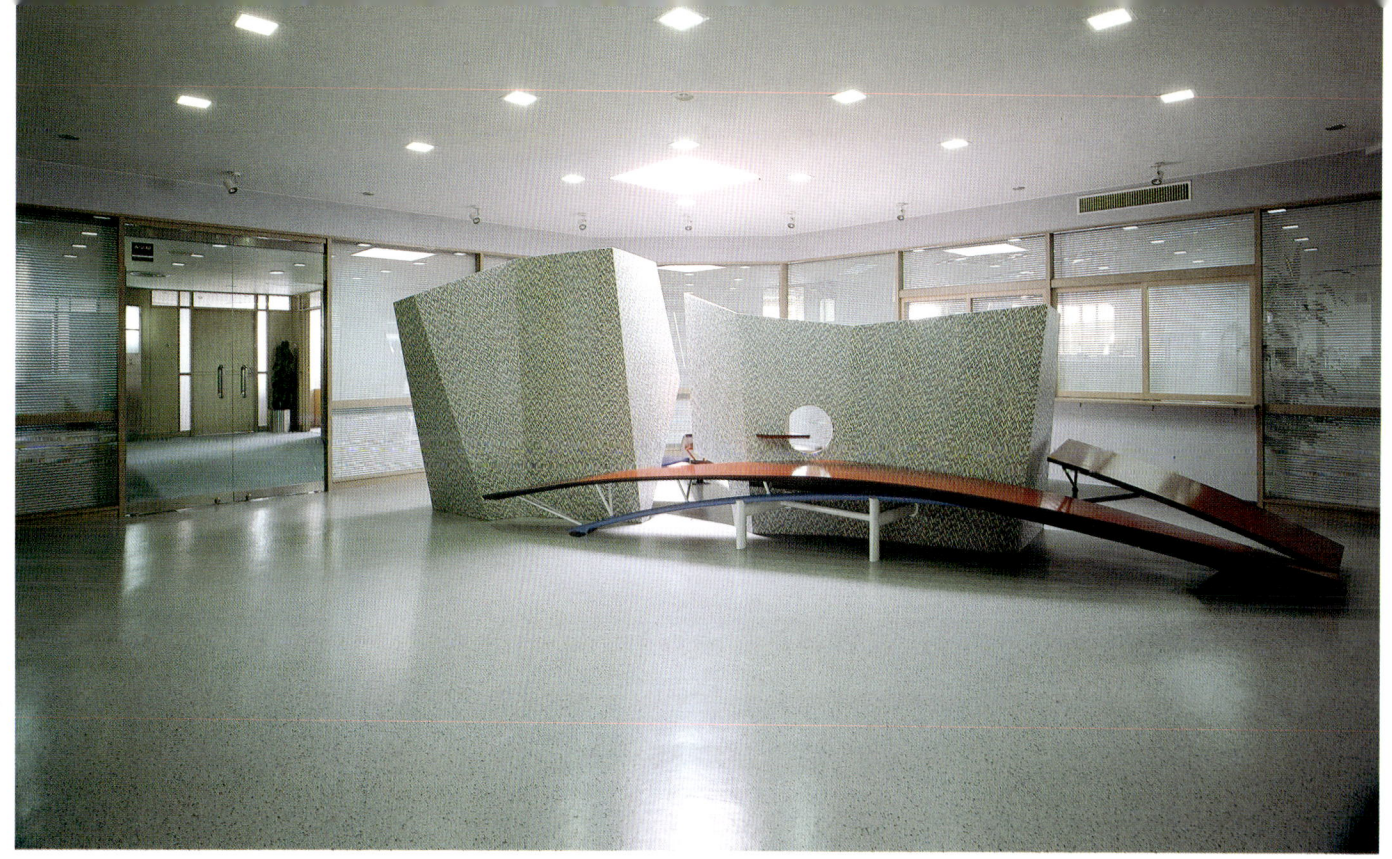

2階 教職員ラウンジ前のセンターロビー　Center lobby in front of the faculty lounge on the 2nd floor

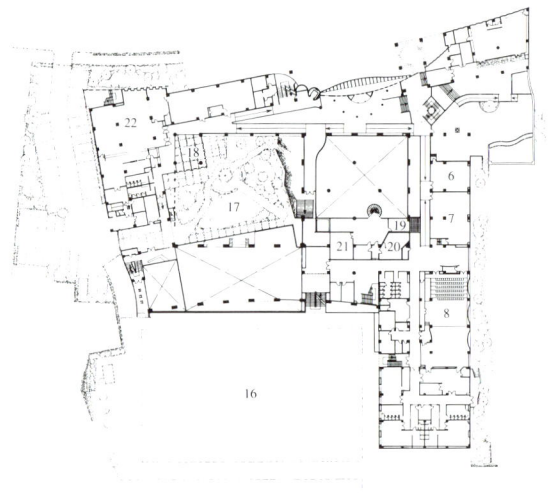

1st floor plan

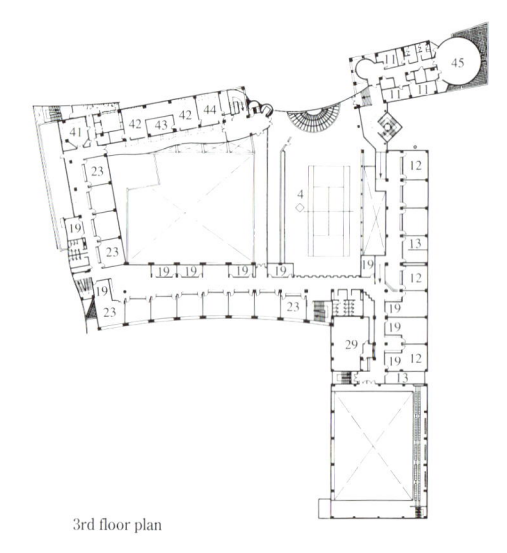

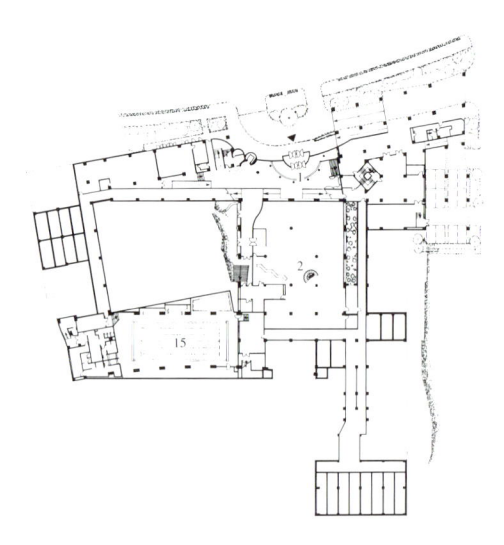

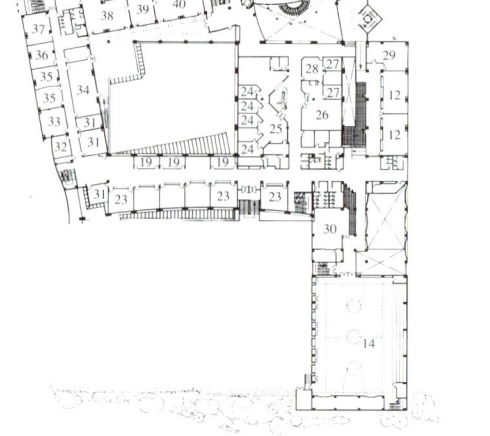

3rd floor plan

Basement floor plan　1:2000

2nd floor plan

光庭に沿ったスロープ　Slope along light court

千里丘陵の竹林を切り開き造成された住宅地に建つ、外国人子弟、帰国子女、一般生徒を対象としたインターナショナルスクールである。多様な文化的背景を持つ生徒、教師間の"交流"をキーコンセプトとして設計された。共用スペースを都市の広場と道に見立てて、その基本的システムであるノード（結節点）とコリドール（軸）のシステムを適用し、廊下同士の交点にたまりの場をつくり、廊下を家具や光の導入の仕方により個性化することで、魅力的な交流の場の形成を目指した。

The school is situated within a housing development cleared from a bamboo forest and enrolls non-Japanese, Japanese returnees from overseas as well as Japanese students. The key concept is the "cultural exchange" among students and teachers of diverse ethnicity and cultural backgrounds. Common spaces are likened to an urban plaza and streets, where the basic system of nodes and corridors is employed, and cozy and attractive gathering spaces are created at the junctions of corridors partitioned by furniture and utilizing the effects of light.

180人収容のホール　Hall with 180 seats

所在地　　大阪府箕面市
設計　　　長島孝一＋AUR
施工　　　鴻池組
竣工　　　1991年3月
敷地面積　15,061.90㎡
建築面積　7,090.07㎡
延床面積　16,669.96㎡
階数　　　地上4階、地下1階
構造　　　鉄筋コンクリート造、鉄骨造
撮影　　　古舘克明

Location:　Minoh-city, Osaka
Architect:　Koichi Nagashima + AUR Architecture・Urban Design・Research・Consultants Co.,Ltd.
General contractor:　Konoike Corp.
Completion date:　March 1991
Site area:　162,124.78sq.ft.
Building area:　76,316.80sq.ft.
Total floor area:　179,433.78sq.ft.
Number of floors:　4 floors above ground, 1 floor below ground
Structure:　Reinforced concrete structure and steel structure
Photographer:　Furudate Katsuaki

1　エントランスホール　Entrance hall
2　図書館　Library
4　テニスコート　Tennis court
6　音楽室　Music room
7　器楽室　Instrumental music room
8　ホール　Hall
9　ESL　ESL
10　多目的教室　Multi-purpose classroom
11　カウンセリング　Counseling room
12　OIS（大阪インターナショナルスクール）普通教室　OIS (Osaka International School) classroom
13　OIS研究室・リソースセンター　OIS Research & Resource Center
14　体育館　Gymnasium
15　プール　Swimming pool
16　グラウンド　Ground
17　中庭　Courtyard
18　ラウンジ　Lounge
19　セミナー室　Seminar room
20　スタジオ　Studio
21　AV室　Audio-visual room
22　食堂　Lunchroom
23　OIA（大阪国際文化中学校・高等学校）普通教室　OIA (Osaka Intercultural Academy) classroom
24　理事長室・OIA校長室　Director's office/OIA Principal's office
25　アドミニストレーションルーム　Administration room
26　教職員ラウンジ　Faculty lounge
27　OIS校長室・OIA教頭室　OIS Principal's offices/OIA Vice Principal's offices
28　インフォメーションセンター　Infomation center
29　コンピューター室　Computer room
30　小体育館　Small gymnasium
31　国語科研究室　Japanese Language Dept. office
32　数学科研究室　Mathematics Dept. office
33　語学科研究室　Foreign Language Dept. office
34　生物教室　Biology lab.
35　語学学習センター　Language study center
36　社会科研究室　Social Studies Dept. office
37　社会科教室　Social studies class
38　化学教室　Chemistry lab.
39　理科研究室　Science Dept. office
40　物理教室　Physics class
41　プラネタリウム　Planetarium
42　美術室・工芸室　Art/craft workshop
43　美術科研究室　Art Dept. office
44　造形教室　Formative art workshop
45　会議室　Conference room

三春町中郷学校
NAKASATO COMMUNITY SCHOOL, MIHARU

鈴木恂＋ＡＭＳ
MAKOTO SUZUKI + AMS ARCHITECTS

北側の丘からアプローチテラスを見る　Looking at the approach terrace from the hill on the north

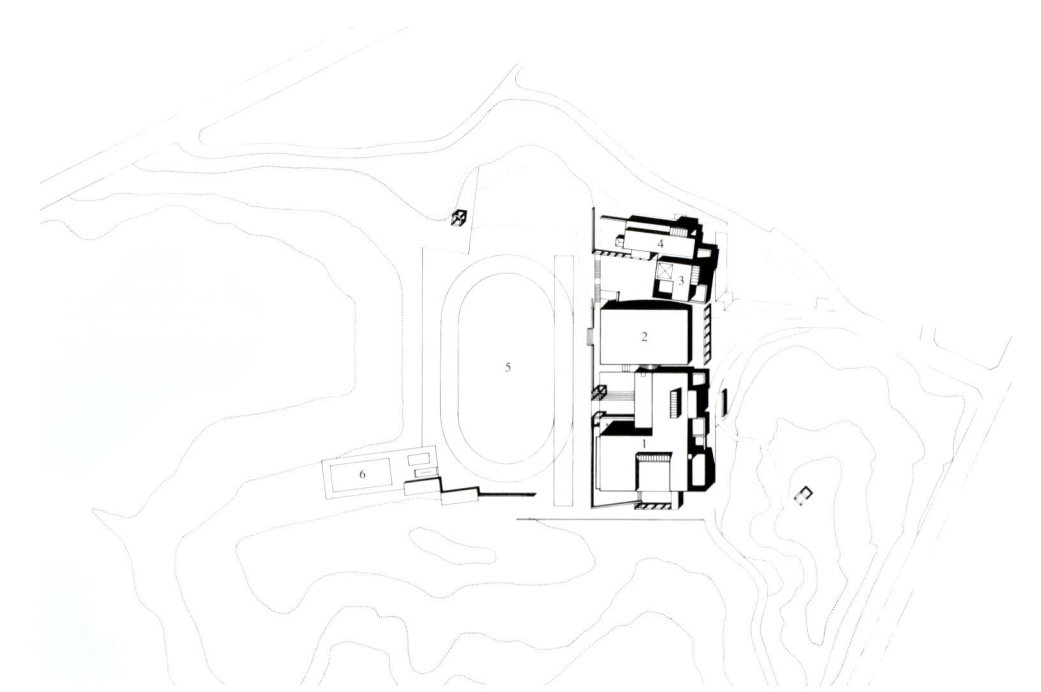

1 小学校　Elementary school
2 体育館　Gymnasium
3 公民館　Public hall
4 幼稚園　Kindergarten
5 グラウンド　Playground
6 プール　Swimming pool

Site plan 1:3000

北側アプローチテラス　Approach terrace on the north

南側中庭　Courtyard on the south

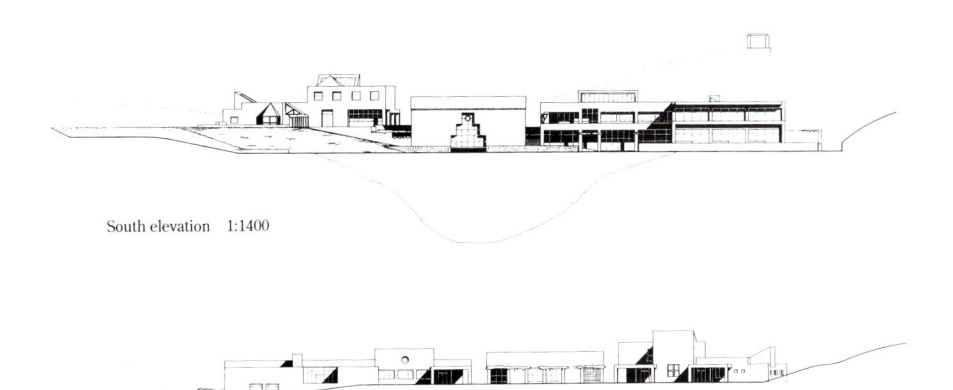

South elevation　1:1400

North elevation　1:1400

143

小学校南側　図工広場　Art/craft plaza on the south of the primary school

小学校と体育館の間より校庭を見る
Looking at the playground through
the primary school building and the gymnasium

地階 音楽室前廊下　Basement floor, corridor in front of the music room

多目的ホール　右は図書コーナー　Multi-purpose hall, reading area on the right

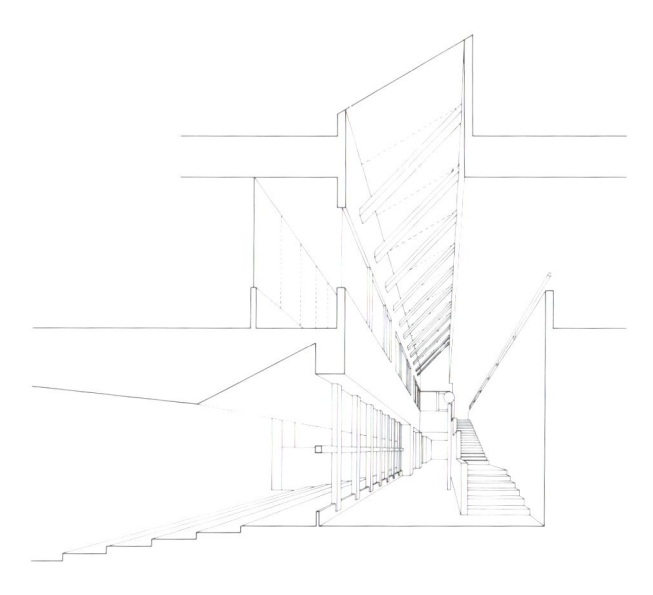

Perspective drawing

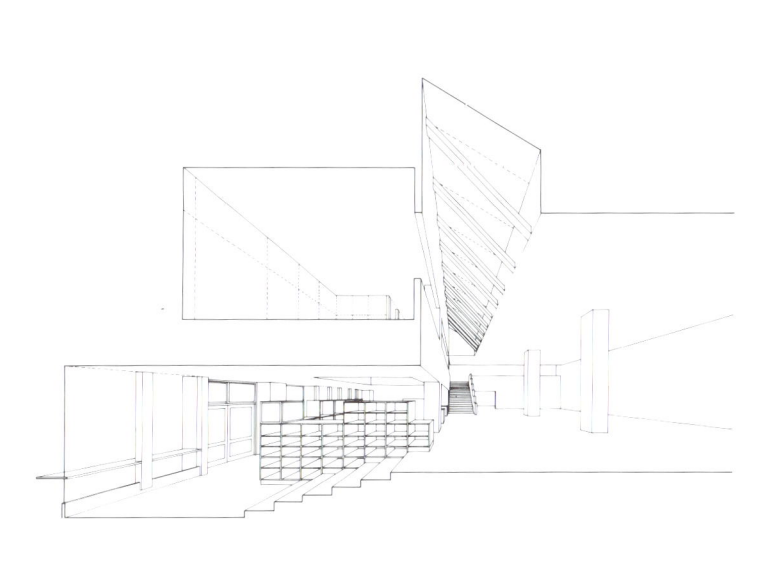

Perspective drawing

多目的ホールから図書コーナーを見る　Looking at the reading area from the multi-purpose hall

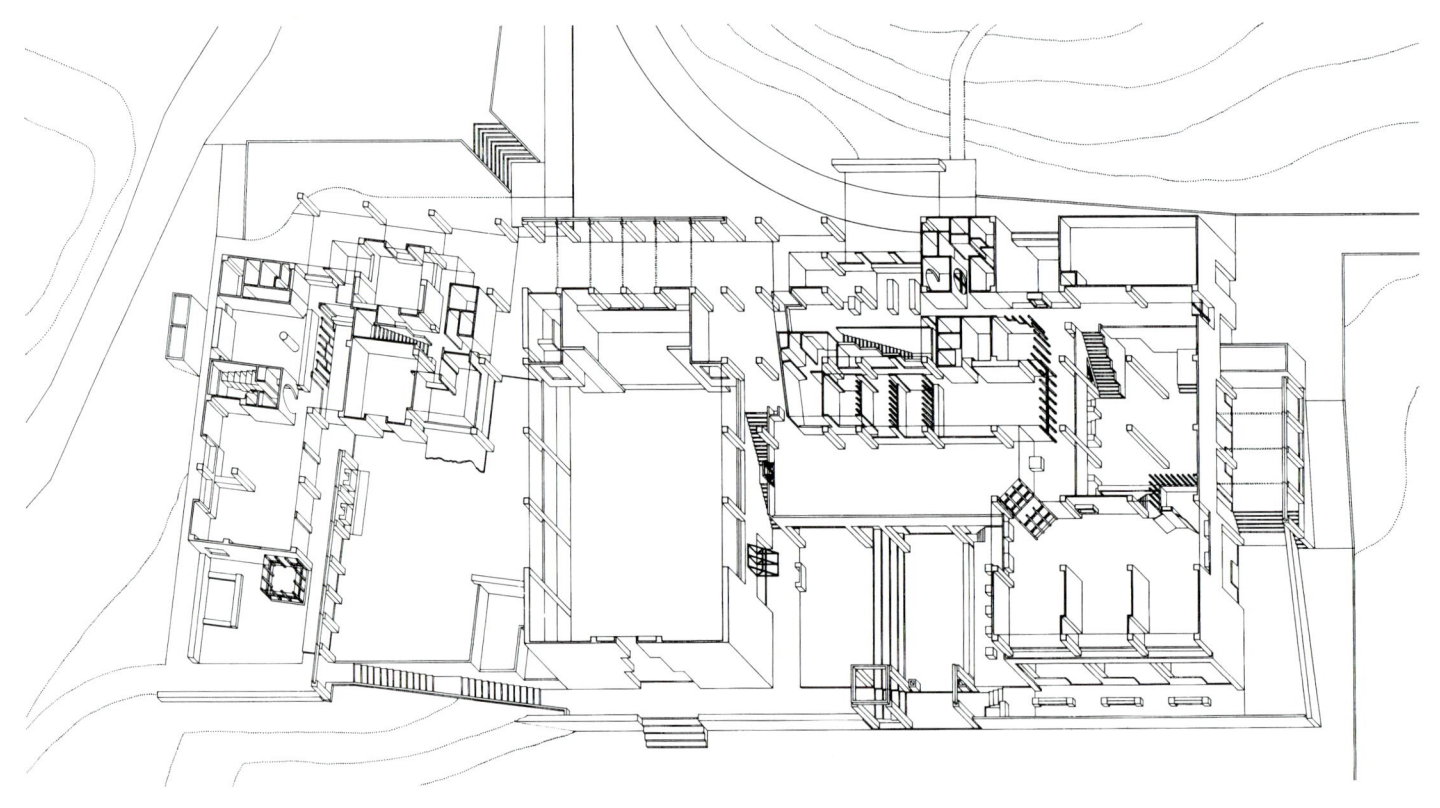

Axonometric drawing

体育館　Gymnasium

2	体育館　Gymnasium
7	幼稚園エントランス　Entrance, kindergarten
8	公民館エントランス　Entrance, public hall
9	小学校エントランス　Entrance, elementary school
10	職員室　Faculty office
11	遊戯室　Playroom
12	保育室　Nursery
13	園庭　Kindergarten playground
14	図書ラウンジ　Library lounge
15	調理室　Cooking class
16	アプローチテラス　Approach terrace
17	教務センター　Administration center
18	国際交流コーナー　Plaza for international exchange
19	テラス　Terrace
20	オープンスペース　Open space
21	教室　Classroom
22	多目的ホール　Multi-purpose hall
23	図書コーナー　Reading area
24	コンピューターコーナー　Computer lab.
25	厨房　Kitchen
26	図工室　Art/craft room
27	図工広場　Art/craft plaza
28	音楽室　Music room
29	音楽広場　Music plaza
30	理科室　Science lab.
31	体育広場　Exercise plaza

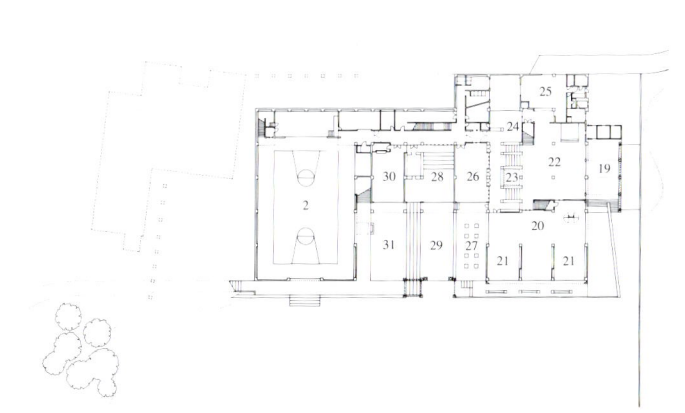

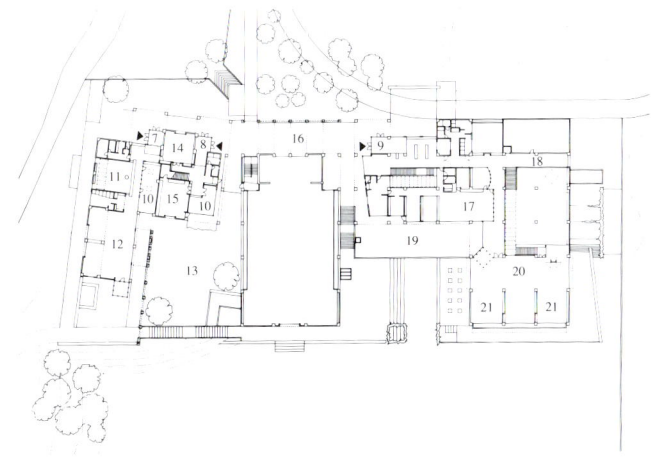

Basement floor plan　1:1600

1st floor plan

幼稚園　遊戯室　Kindergarten, playroom

幼稚園の園庭に面したテラス　Terrace facing the kindergarten playground

間もなく敷地はダム湖に突き出した小さな岬の一角となる。小学校、体育館、公民館、幼稚園の4施設から成る建築群は、丘陵を水平に広がっていき、あたかもその風景を捉えようとしている。各施設は自立性を確保しつつ空間の連続性をつくり出している。施設の中心に立つそれぞれの光のゾーンは、各施設のアイデンティティを表象する最も象徴的空間であり、地域の人々の活動を受け止め、子供たちの個性を引き出していく魅力的な場所の情景をつくり出している。

The site is situated on a small headland projecting into an artificial lake. A primary school, a gymnasium, a community center and a kindergarten stand on a hill as if to take command of the landscape. Each group of buildings is independent of the others, and yet they are within a continuum of space. Each facility is centered around a zone of light which is the symbol of its identity. The concept is to provide an attractive and educational environment for the children and the community.

所在地　福島県三春町
設計　鈴木恂＋AMS
施工　小学校：大林組　幼稚園・公民館：渡伝組
竣工　1990年3月
敷地面積　57,177.00m²
建築面積　3,248.00m²
延床面積　4,247.00m²
階数　地上2階、地下1階
構造　鉄筋コンクリート造、一部鉄骨造
撮影　鈴木悠

Location: Miharu-town, Fukushima
Architect: Makoto Suzuki + AMS Architects
General contractor: Primary school: Obayashi Corp.
kindergarten and public hall: Wataden-gumi Co.,Ltd.
Completion date: March 1990
Site area: 615,447.51sq.ft.
Building area: 34,961.15sq.ft.
Total floor area: 45,714.28sq.ft.
Number of floors: 2 floors above ground, 1 floor below ground
Structure: Reinforced concrete structure and steel structure
Photographer: Yutaka Suzuki

大学　Universities / Colleges

金沢工業高等専門学校
KANAZAWA TECHNICAL COLLEGE

水野一郎・田中光＋金沢計画研究所
ICHIRO MIZUNO, HIKARU TANAKA + KANAZAWA PLANNING RESEARCH

広場　Plaza

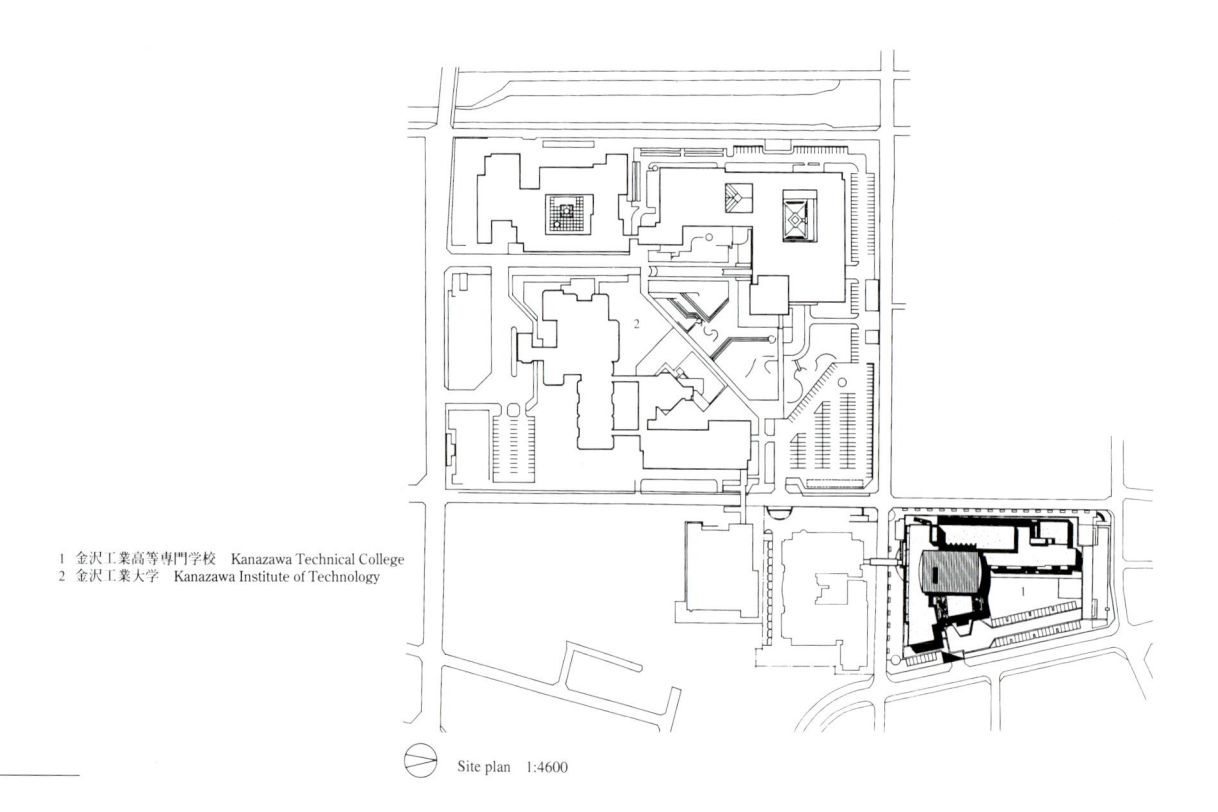

1　金沢工業高等専門学校　Kanazawa Technical College
2　金沢工業大学　Kanazawa Institute of Technology

Site plan　1:4600

北側外観　North facade

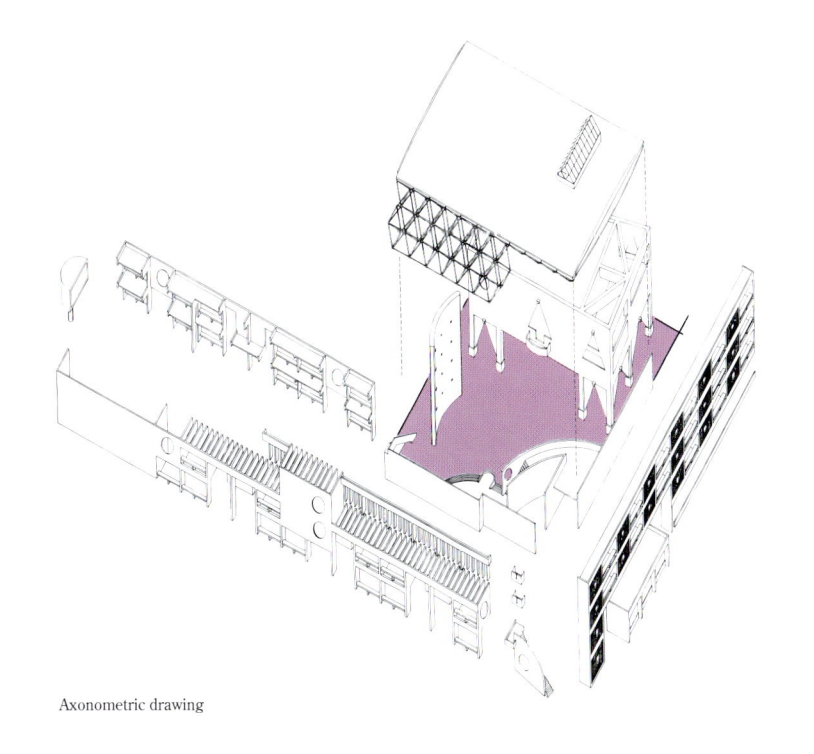

Axonometric drawing

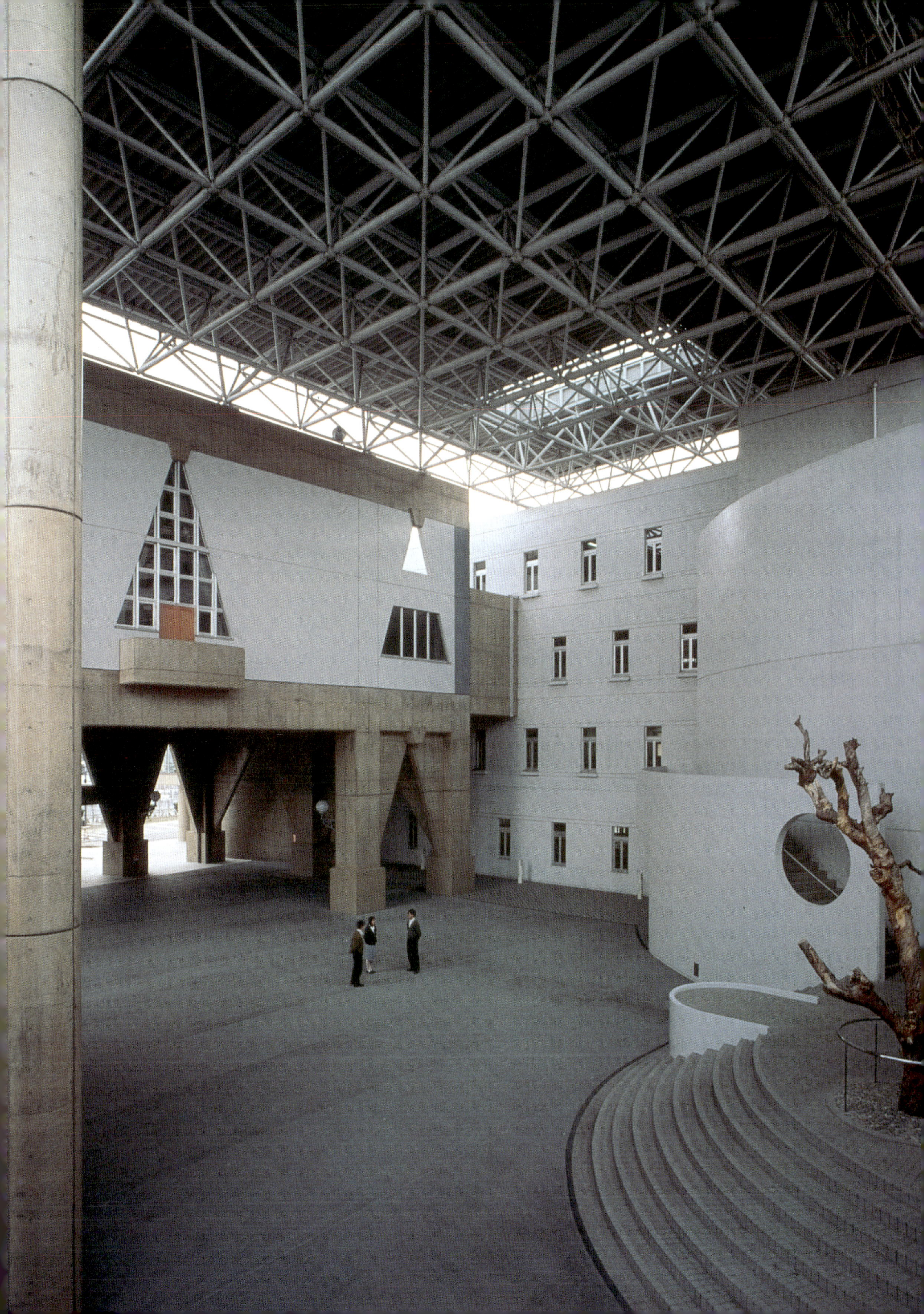

2階ホールへ通じる階段より広場を見る　Looking at the plaza from the stairway leading to 2nd floor hall

ピロティ　Pilotis

◀広場　Plaza

北東側外観　Northeast facade

鳥瞰　Bird's eye view

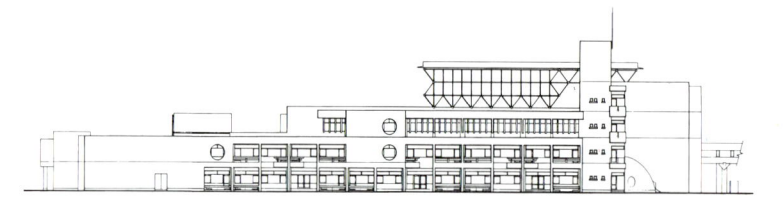

West elevation　1:1200

East elevation　1:1200

エントランスゲート、アプローチ　Entrance gate, approach

車寄せよりピロティ、広場を見る　Looking at the pilotis and plaza from the porch

西側外観　West facade 　　　　西側環境緩衝装置　Buffer device on the west side

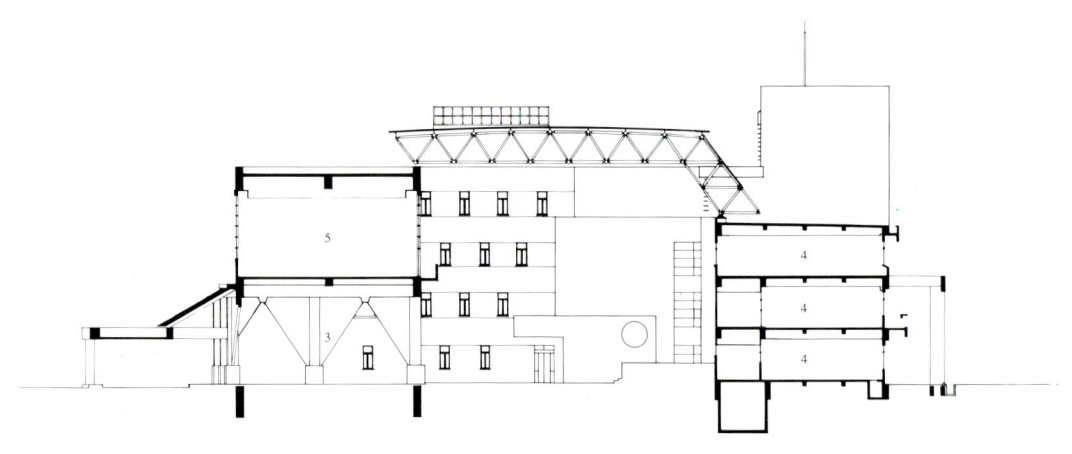

Section　1:600

3　ピロティ　Pilotis
4　実験室　Laboratory
5　合同講義室　Joint lecture hall

4th floor plan

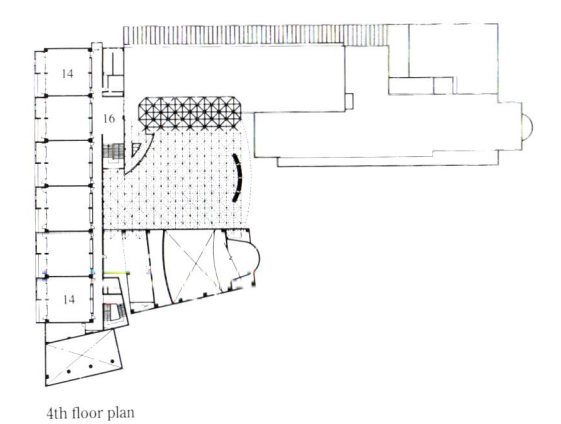

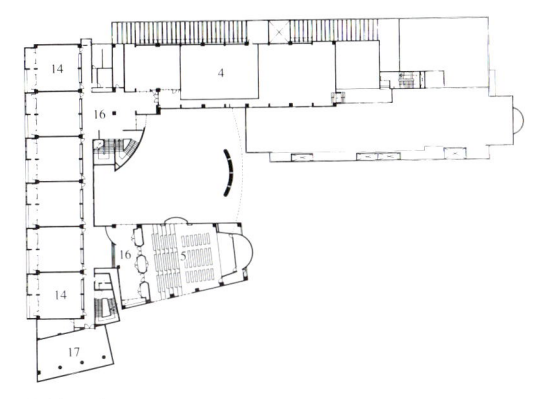

3rd floor plan

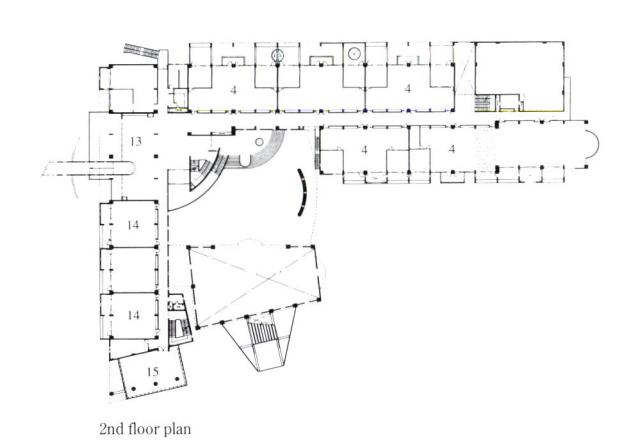

2nd floor plan

1st floor plan 1:1600

3階 合同講義室　3rd floor, joint lecture hall

工業高等専門学校は学制の中で難しい位置にいる。本校も大学との施設共用によって各部門の高いレベルを維持する一方で、自律した存在であるとの意志も強い。また、本校の立地する北陸は降雨、降積雪が大きいゆえに通常の庭園広場の役立つ期間が短い。大屋根の架かった屋内広場はこうした工大学園の中での自律と連担の関係の表現であり、四季折々多目的に役立ち、かつ日常動線が交差し、学生と教職員が交流する学園広場の形成装置である。

Technical colleges hold a difficult position in the Japanese educational system. Kanazawa Technical College is no exception; it tries to maintain a high educational standard by sharing the facilities with the adjacent university while asserting its autonomy. Because of characteristic heavy rain and snow, ordinary open-air spaces are often unusable. The indoor space covered with a large roof is called an indoor plaza, and is used for a variety of activities throughout the year. The plaza is where the traffic lines of daily activities cross and serves as a meeting place for students and faculty.

所在地　　石川県金沢市
設計　　　水野一郎・田中光＋金沢計画研究所
施工　　　池田建設
竣工　　　1991年6月
敷地面積　11,608.47m²
建築面積　4,635.21m²
延床面積　9,960.50m²
階数　　　地上4階
構造　　　鉄筋コンクリート造、一部鉄骨スペースフレーム
撮影　　　新建築社

Location: Kanazawa-city, Ishikawa
Architect: Ichiro Mizuno, Hikaru Tanaka + Kanazawa Planning Research
General contractor: Ikeda Construction Co.,Ltd.
Completion date: June 1991
Site area: 124,952.41sq.ft.
Building area: 49,892.94sq.ft.
Total floor area: 107,213.82sq.ft.
Number of floors: 4 floors above ground
Structure: Reinforced concrete structure and steel frame
Photographer: Shinkenchiku-sha・Co.,Ltd.

4　実験室　　Laboratory
5　合同講義室　Joint lecture hall
6　広場　　　Plaza
7　会議室　　Conference room
8　学生会館　Student hall
9　教員室　　Faculty office
10　主事室　　Director's office
11　事務室　　Office
12　校長室　　Principal's office
13　ラウンジ　Lounge
14　講義室　　Lecture room
15　ギャラリー　Gallery
16　ホール　　Hall
17　音楽室　　Music room

慶應義塾大学湘南藤沢キャンパス
KEIO UNIVERSITY SHONAN FUJISAWA CAMPUS

槇総合計画事務所
MAKI AND ASSOCIATES

野外劇場よりキャンパスを見る　Looking at the campus from the open-air theater

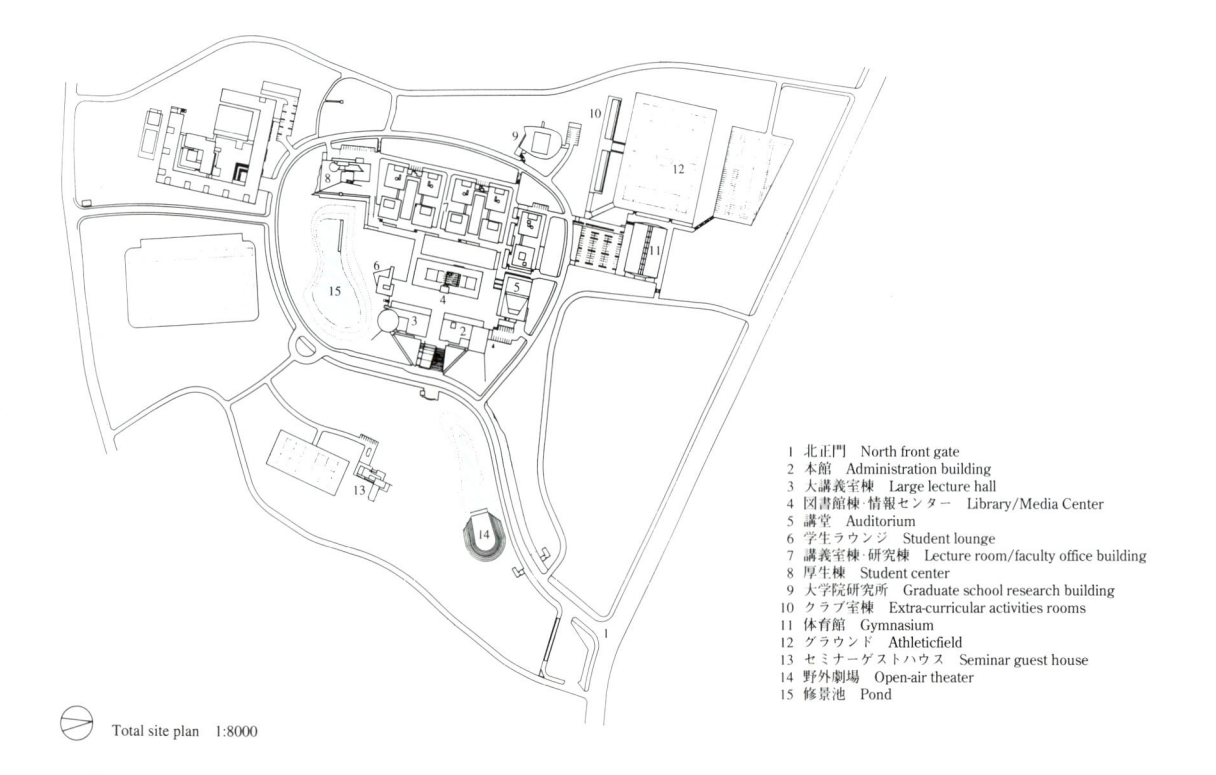

Total site plan　1:8000

1　北正門　North front gate
2　本館　Administration building
3　大講義室棟　Large lecture hall
4　図書館棟・情報センター　Library/Media Center
5　講堂　Auditorium
6　学生ラウンジ　Student lounge
7　講義室棟・研究棟　Lecture room/faculty office building
8　厚生棟　Student center
9　大学院研究所　Graduate school research building
10　クラブ室棟　Extra-curricular activities rooms
11　体育館　Gymnasium
12　グラウンド　Athleticfield
13　セミナーゲストハウス　Seminar guest house
14　野外劇場　Open-air theater
15　修景池　Pond

アプローチ道路側の外観　右に本館、左に大講義室棟　Looking at the university facades from the approach, administration building on the right, large lecture hall on the left

東側ループ道路より修景池を取り囲む建物群を見る　Looking at the buildings surrounding pond from loop road on the east

中庭より情報センター奥に本館のアーケードを見る　Looking at the administration building arcade behind Media Center from the courtyard

ストリートより本館を見る　左に講堂が見える　Looking at the administration building from walkway; auditorium on the left

本館と大講義室の間の広場より情報センターを見る　Looking at the Media Center from the plaza between administration building and large lecture hall

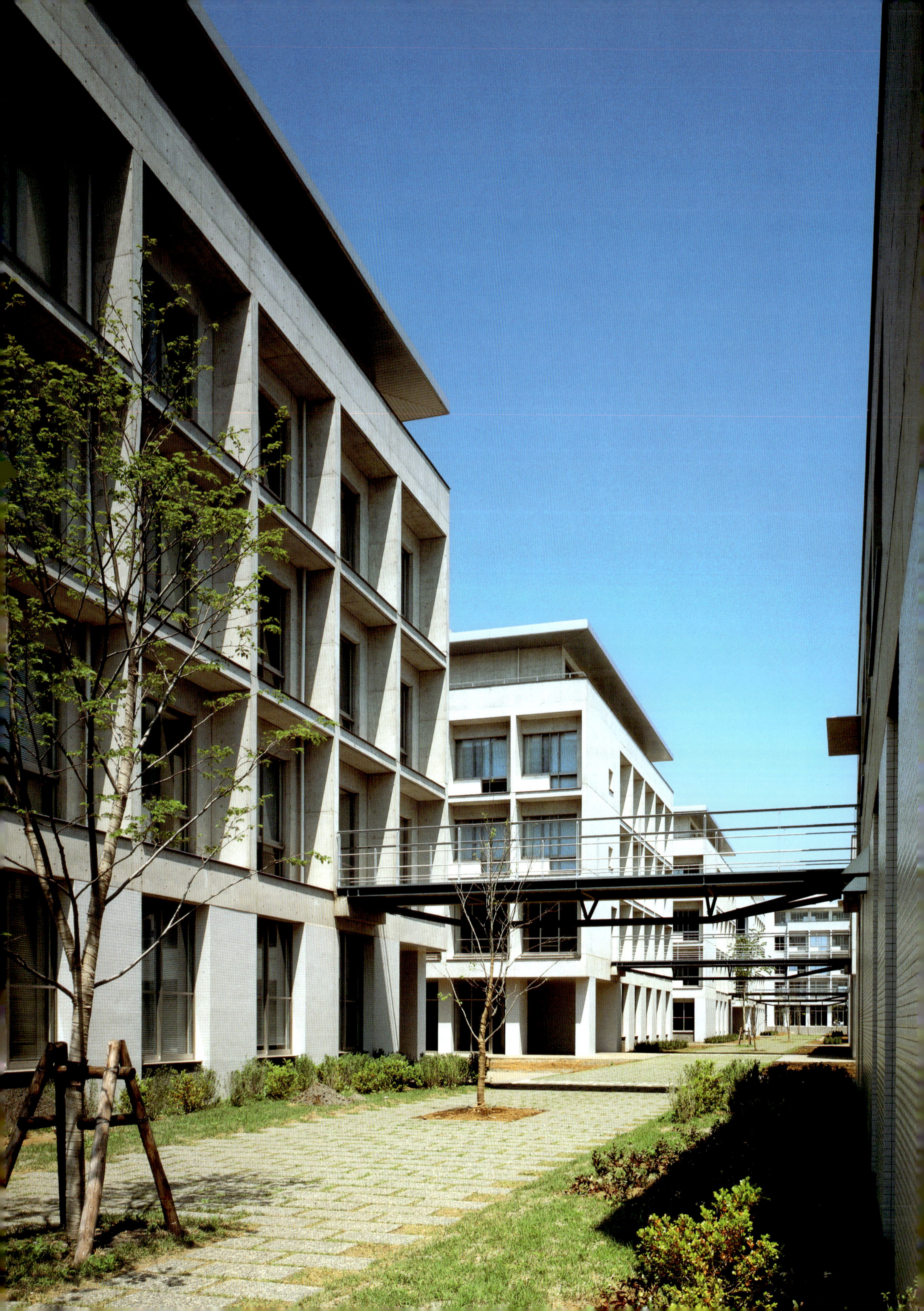

研究棟・講義室棟群 南東側外観　Southeast facades of faculty office building and lecture room building

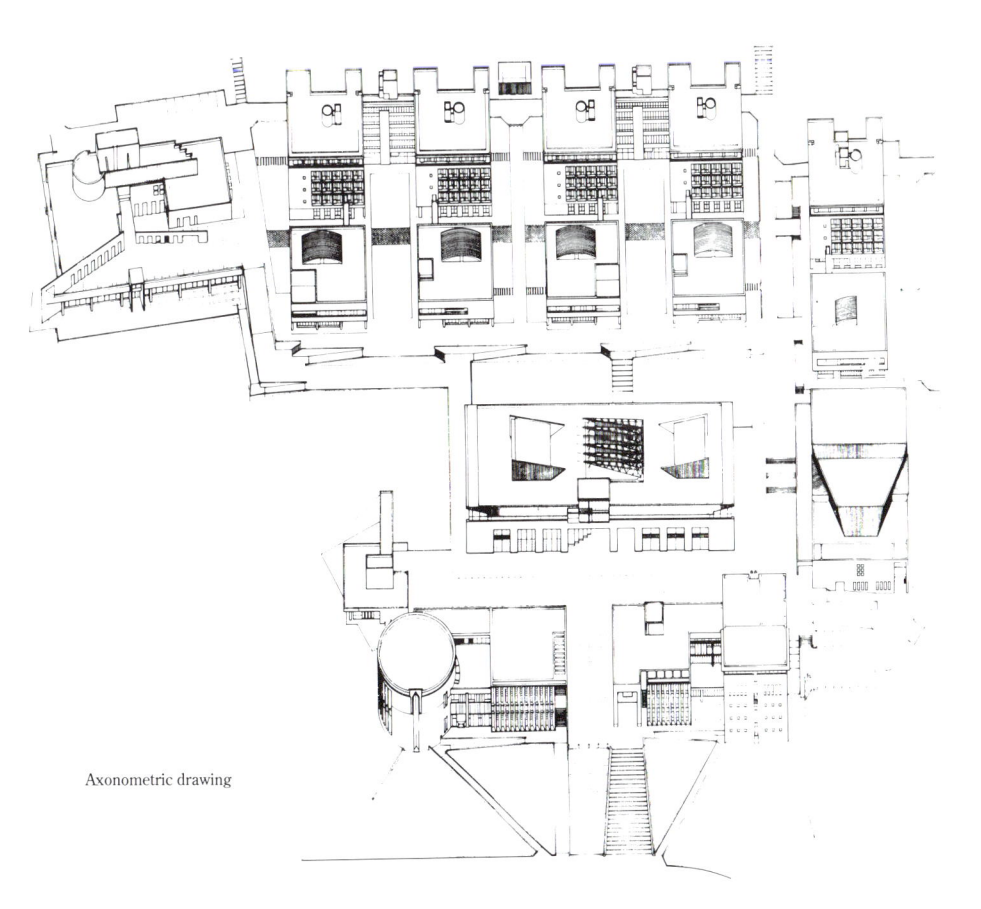

Axonometric drawing

◀研究棟と講義室棟の間のストリート
Walkway between faculty office building and lecture room building

163

大講義室棟ホールのスロープ　Ramp in the large lecture hall

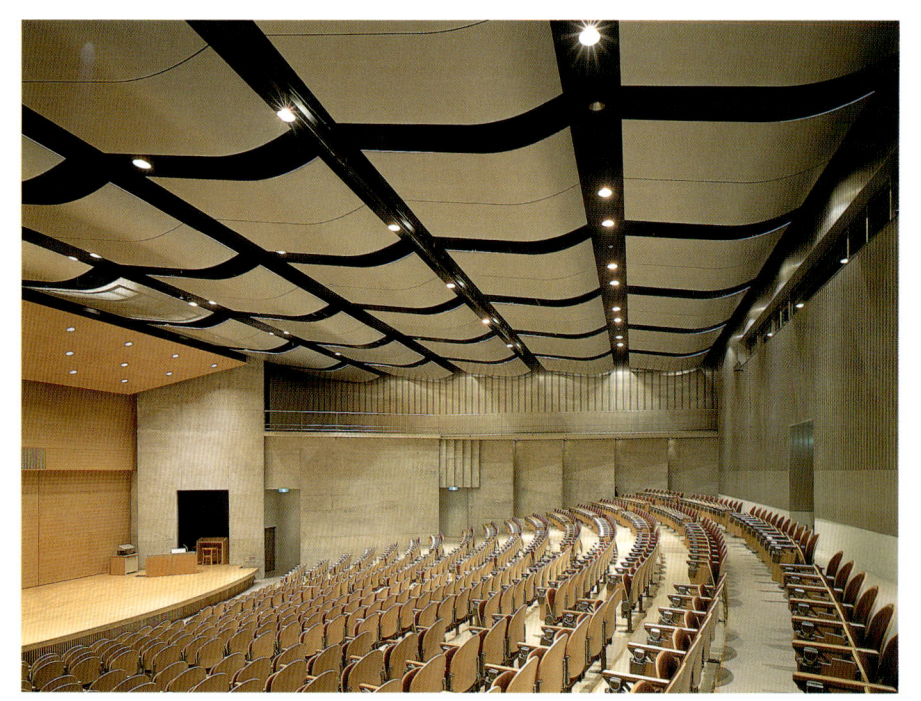

講堂　Auditorium

体育館 アリーナ　Gymnasium arena

2nd floor plan

2 本館	Administration building
3 大講義室棟	Large lecture hall
4 図書館棟・情報センター	Library/Media Center
5 講堂	Auditorium
6 学生ラウンジ	Student lounge
7 講義室棟・研究棟	Lecture room/faculty office building
8 厚生棟	Student center
16 ホール	Hall
17 ロビー	Lobby
18 大講義室	Large lecture hall
19 レファレンスコーナー	Reference area
20 研究個室	Faculty office
21 事務室	Office
22 教員控室	Faculty lounge
23 AVラウンジ	AV lounge
24 ワークステーションラウンジ	Work station lounge
25 ワークステーションルーム	Work station room
26 リサーチエリア	Research area
27 大型映像装置室	AV equipment
28 国際交流センター	International Exchange Center
29 保健センター	Health Center
30 研究者閲覧室	Reading room for researchers
31 教職員レストラン	Faculty dining room
32 喫茶ラウンジ	Tea room/lounge
33 ショップ	School shop
34 特別教室	Special classroom
35 小講義室	Small lecture room
36 中講義室	Lecture room
37 共同研究室	Laboratory for joint research

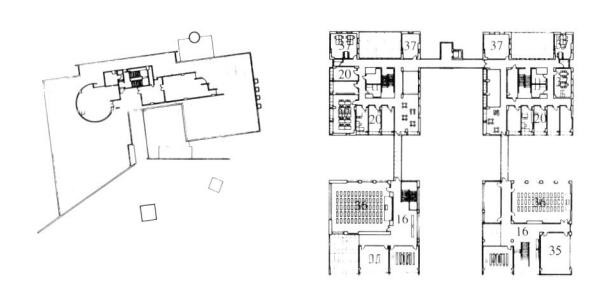

1st floor plan 1:1800

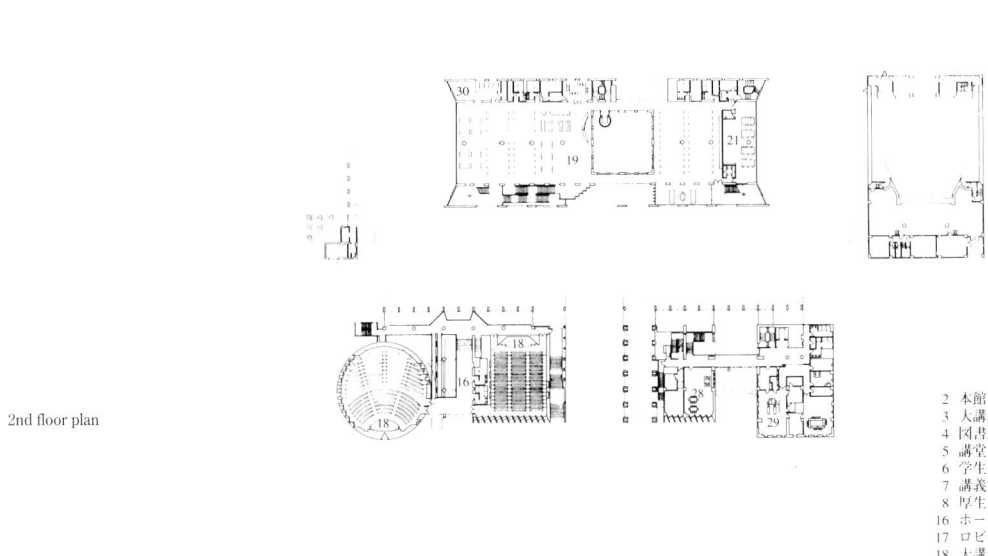

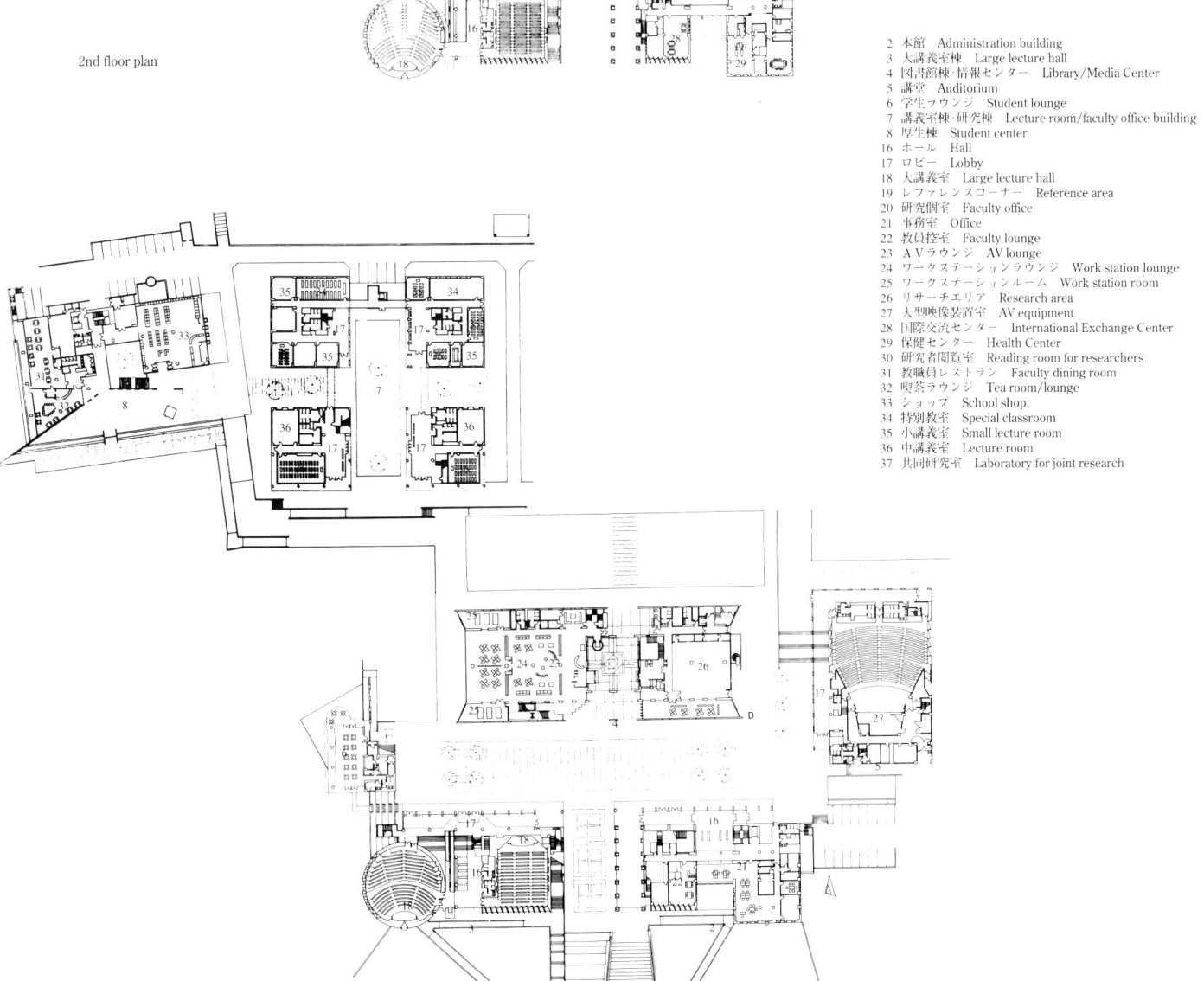

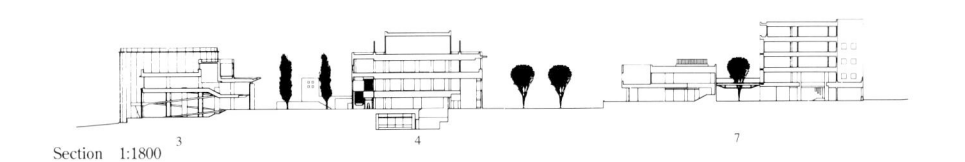

Section 1:1800

165

本館前より大学院研究所を見る　Looking at the graduate school research center from the administration building

エントランスホール外観　Entrance hall

北東側外観　Northeast facade

南東側外観　Southeast facade

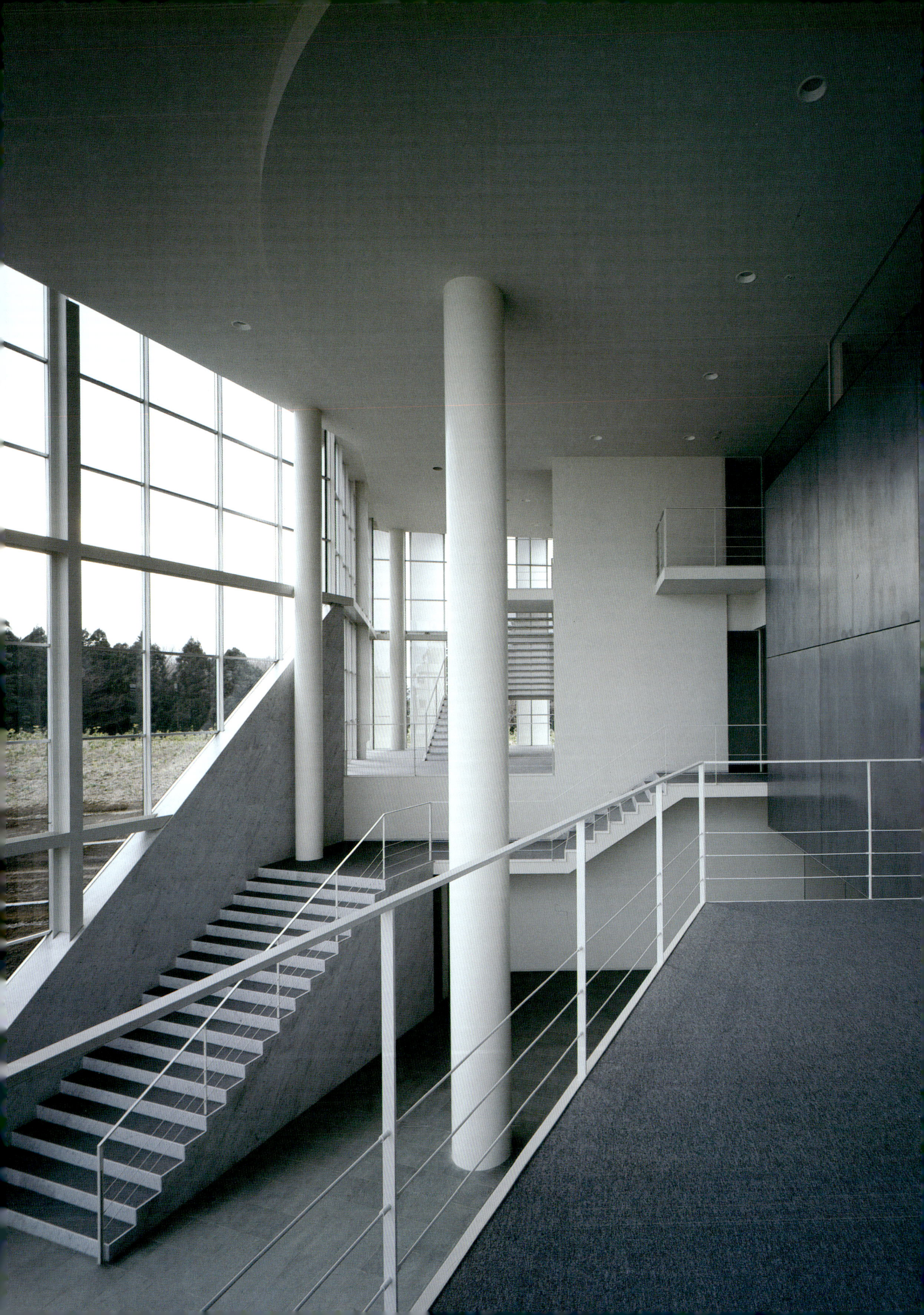

共同研究室よりルーバーを見る　Brise-soleil seen from inside

6	ラウンジ　Lounge
21	事務室　Office
37	共同研究室　Laboratory for joint research
38	エントランスホール　Entrance hall
39	講義室　Lecture room
40	会議室　Conference room
41	研究室　Laboratory

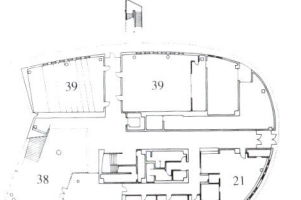

Graduate school research center: 1st floor plan　1:1300

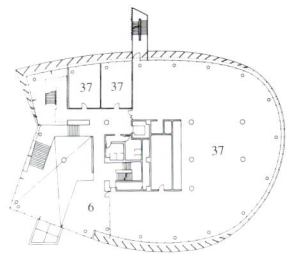

2nd floor plan

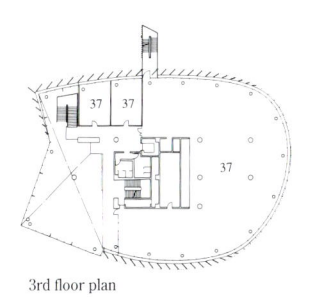

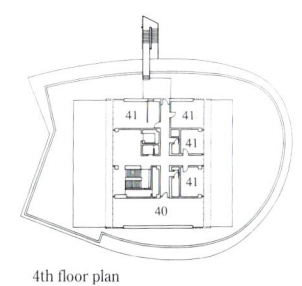

3rd floor plan

4th floor plan

本校は藤沢市郊外の丘に計画され、約10万坪におよぶ敷地とその周辺にはまだ緑が多く残っている。マスタープランの策定に当たっては、既存の緑と自然地形のなだらかな起伏をできるだけ活かしてゾーニングを行い、場所の潜在的な特性を重視している。大学の施設群は高台に集約し、構内道路、修景池、野外劇場、グラウンドなどは谷筋の低地に配置している。歩くにつれて視線の高さや方向が自然に変化し、緑を背景としながら建築群が複合的に見え隠れすることになる。このように新たなランドスケープがキャンパスの風景を基底で支えている。大学の中心ゾーンは"ひとつの都市"のように個々の建築が独立して立ちながらも、プラザ、街路、小広場によって互いに有機的につなげられている。一棟の規模と高さを抑え、接地性を高めることによって都市のにぎわいが生み出される。特に外部と連続した共有スペースはインフォーマルなコミュニケーションの場として重視しており、行き交う人々の流れを踏まえ広場や街路のネットワークに沿って設けられている。透明で開放的なロビーやラウンジでは、重層する都市的な風景と田園の緑を眺めながら学生たちがゆったりとたたずむシーンが展開されることになる。

The grounds stretch out for approximately 330,000m² (3,370,000sq.ft.) on a verdant hill outside Fujisawa City. The zoning was determined based on the policy to preserve existing vegetation and to take full advantage of the gently undulating terrain and its potential merits. University buildings are built on the hill while campus roads, a pond, an open-air theater, and an athletic field are sited on the lowland along the valley. As visitors proceed on foot, the height and direction of the views change and the campus buildings unfold one after another against the background of luxuriant nature. The campus scenery is underlined by the newly created landscapes. The core forms a "city" where each building maintains its independence and yet is organically linked with others via plazas, lanes and small open spaces. Their size and the height are restricted to a certain level to give an impression of being close to the ground and to create an atmosphere of bustling urban streets. Indoor common spaces connecting with the outdoor area have particular significance as a forum of informal communication; the common spaces are dotted along the pedestrian network. Lobbies and lounges are transparent and offer open spaces where students can comfortably relax watching the multi-layered urbane scenes and the lush nature.

所在地　神奈川県藤沢市
設計　槇総合計画事務所
施工　東急建設・清水建設・鹿島・大成建設JV.　安藤建設・大林組・錢高組JV.　錢高組・大林組・日本国土開発JV.　大成建設・竹中工務店・フジタ・三井建設JV.　清水建設・大成建設JV.　大林組・錢高組・日本国土開発JV.　戸田建設・鹿島・錢高JV.　日本国土開発・大成建設・フジタJV.　日本国土開発・清水建設JV.　東京急行電鉄
竣工　第1期：1990年3月　第2期：1991年3月　第3期：1992年3月　第4期：1994年3月
敷地面積　313,009.30m²（中・高等部を含む）
建築面積　17,226.40m²
延床面積　42,882.70m²
階数　本館：地上5階、地下1階　大講義室棟：地上3階、地下1階　情報センター：地上4階、地下1階　講堂、ラウンジ：地上2階　厚生棟：地上2階、地下1階　講義室棟・研究棟：地上5階、塔屋1階　体育館：地上3階　クラブ室棟：地上2階　大学院研究所：地上4階　セミナーゲストハウス：地上2階
構造　本館：鉄筋コンクリート造、鉄骨造　大講義室棟：鉄筋コンクリート造、鉄骨鉄筋コンクリート造　情報センター：鉄筋コンクリート造　講堂：鉄筋コンクリート造、鉄骨造　ラウンジ、厚生棟、講義室棟・研究棟：鉄筋コンクリート造　体育館：鉄筋コンクリート造、鉄骨造　クラブ室棟、大学院研究所、セミナーゲストハウス：鉄筋コンクリート造
撮影　北嶋俊治／158-164　ナカサ&パートナーズ／166-169

Location:　Fujisawa-city, Kanagawa
Architect:　Maki and Associates
General contractor:　Joint venture of Tokyu Construction, Shimizu, Kajima and Taisei　Joint venture of Ando Construction, Obayashi and Zenidaka　Joint venture of Zenidaka, Obayashi and JDC　Joint venture of Taisei, Takenaka, Fujita and Mitsui　Joint venture of Shimizu and Taisei　Joint venture of Obayashi, Zenitaka and JDC　Joint venture of Toda, Kajima and Zenidaka　Joint venture of JDC, Taisei and Fujita　Joint venture of JDC and Shimizu　Tokyu Electric Railway Co.,Ltd.
Completion date:　Phase I: March 1990　phase II: March 1991　phase III: March 1992　phase IV: March 1994
Site area:　3,369,200.80sq.ft. (including junior and senior high school areas)
Building area:　185,423.24sq.ft.
Total floor area:　461,585.09sq.ft.
Number of floors:　Administration building: 5 floors above ground, 1 floor below ground　large lecture hall: 3 floors above ground, 1 floor below ground　Media Center: 4 floors above ground, 1 floor below ground　auditorium and student lounge: 2 floors above ground　student center: 2 floors above ground, 1 floor below ground　lecture room/faculty office building: 5 floors above ground, tower on the 1st floor　gymnasium: 3 floors above ground　extra-curricular activities rooms: 2 floors above ground　graduate school research center: 4 floors above ground　seminar guest house: 2 floors above ground
Structure:　Administration building: reinforced concrete structure and steel structure　large lecture hall: reinforced concrete structure and steel framed concrete structure　Media Center: reinforced concrete structure　auditorium: reinforced concrete structure and steel structure　student lounge, student center and lecture room/faculty office building: reinforced concrete structure　gymnasium: reinforced concrete structure and steel structure　extra-curricular activities rooms, graduate school research center and seminar guest house: reinforced concrete structure
Photographer:　Toshiharu Kitajima / 158-164　Nacása & Partners / 166-169

◀エントランスホール　Entrance hall

東京造形大学
TOKYO UNIVERSITY OF ART AND DESIGN

磯崎新アトリエ
ARATA ISOZAKI & ASSOCIATES

鳥瞰 Bird's eye view

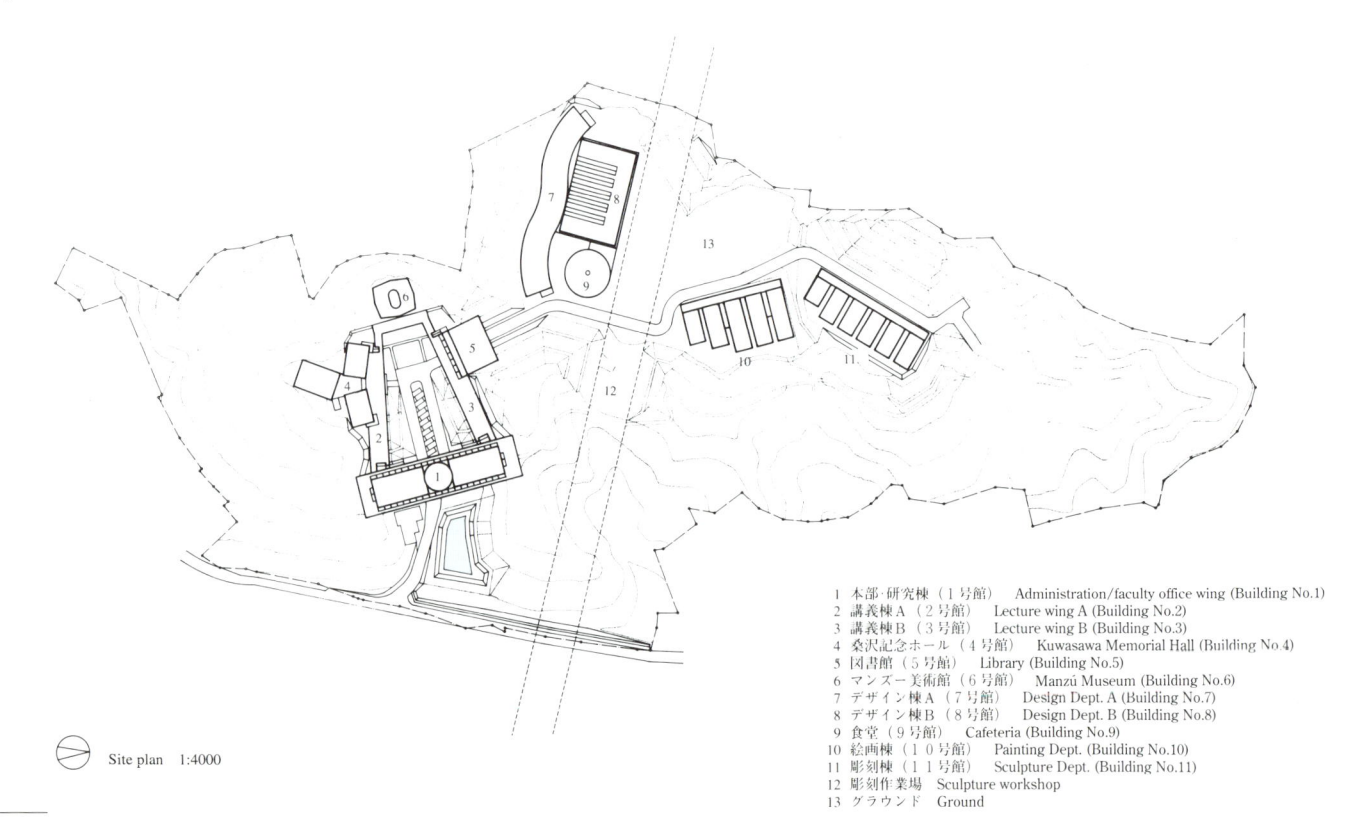

Site plan 1:4000

1 本部・研究棟（１号館）　Administration/faculty office wing (Building No.1)
2 講義棟A（２号館）　Lecture wing A (Building No.2)
3 講義棟B（３号館）　Lecture wing B (Building No.3)
4 桑沢記念ホール（４号館）　Kuwasawa Memorial Hall (Building No.4)
5 図書館（５号館）　Library (Building No.5)
6 マンズー美術館（６号館）　Manzú Museum (Building No.6)
7 デザイン棟A（７号館）　Design Dept. A (Building No.7)
8 デザイン棟B（８号館）　Design Dept. B (Building No.8)
9 食堂（９号館）　Cafeteria (Building No.9)
10 絵画棟（１０号館）　Painting Dept. (Building No.10)
11 彫刻棟（１１号館）　Sculpture Dept. (Building No.11)
12 彫刻作業場　Sculpture workshop
13 グラウンド　Ground

アプローチより本部・研究棟を見る　Looking at the administration/faculty office wing from the approach

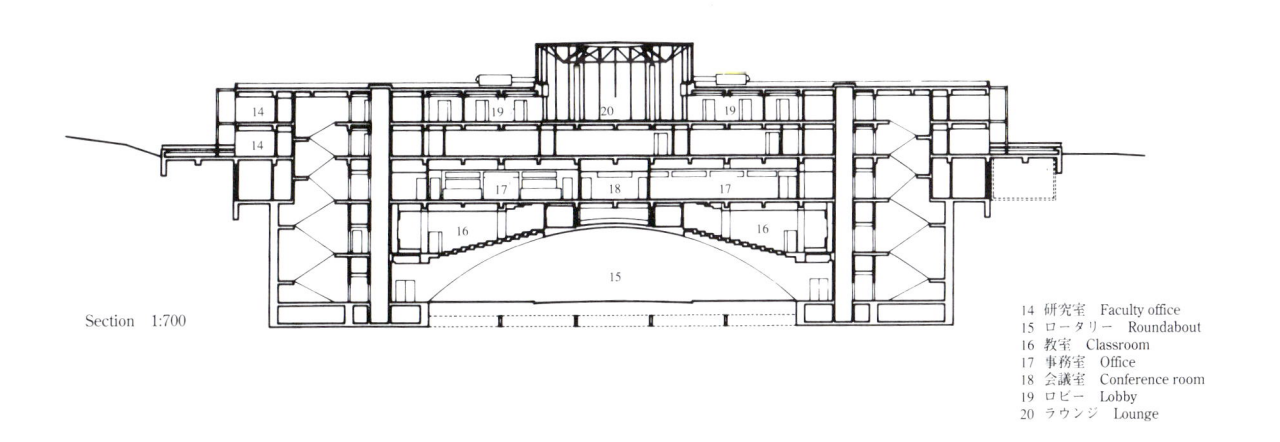

Section 1:700

14 研究室　Faculty office
15 ロータリー　Roundabout
16 教室　Classroom
17 事務室　Office
18 会議室　Conference room
19 ロビー　Lobby
20 ラウンジ　Lounge

東側より正面にマンズー美術館、両サイドに講義棟を見る　Looking from east at the Manzú Museum and lecture wings

講義棟A 北側外観　North facade of lecture wing A

桑沢記念ホール 山側外観　Kuwasawa Memorial Hall, facade

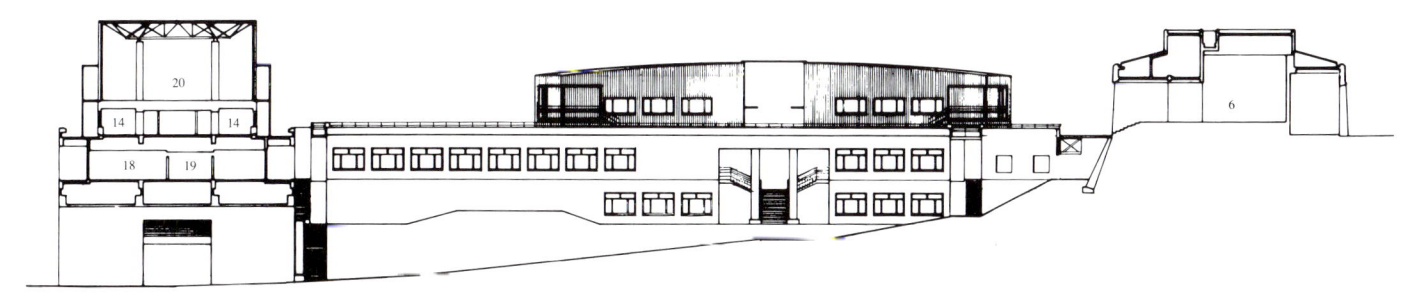

Section 1:700

2nd floor plan

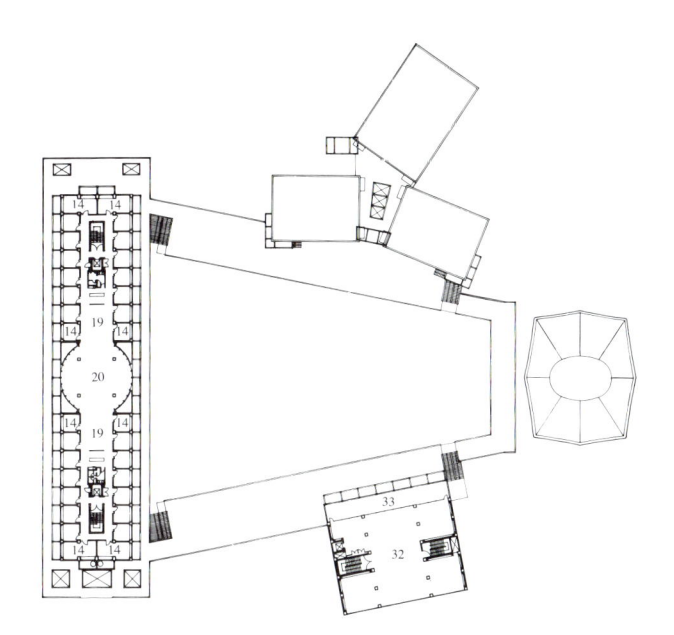

4th floor plan

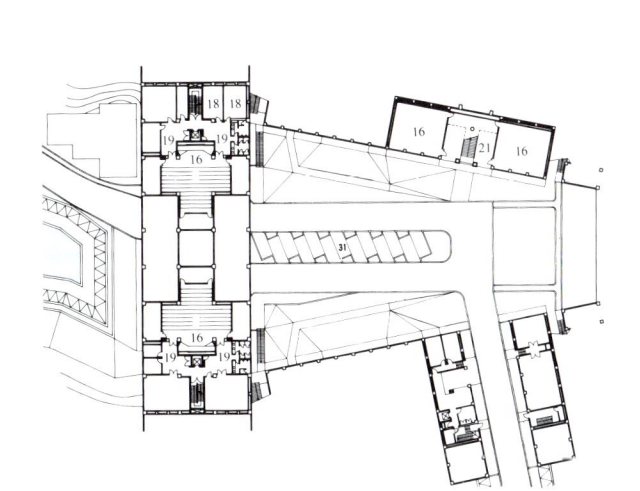

1st floor plan

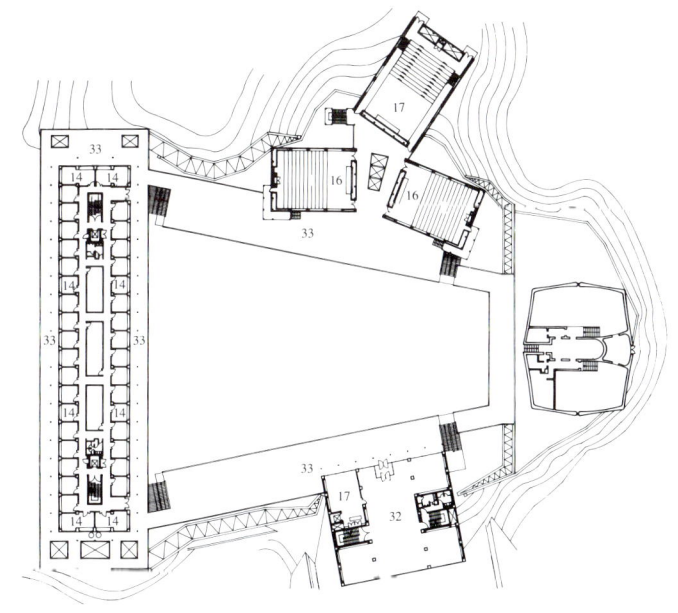

3rd floor plan

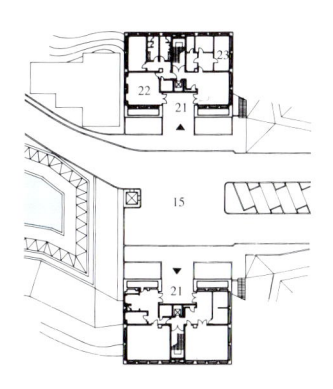

Building No.1〜6: basement floor plan 1:1500

6 マンズー美術館（6号館） Manzú Museum (Building No.6)
14 研究室   Faculty office
15 ロータリー Roundabout
16 教室   Classroom
17 事務室 Office
18 会議室 Conference room
19 ロビー Lobby
20 ラウンジ Lounge
21 エントランス Entrance
22 医務室 Infirmary
23 中央管理室 Central administration office
24 学長室 President's office
25 理事長室 Director's office
26 理事室 Director's room
27 閉架書庫 Closed-shelf library
28 保存書庫 Archive
29 館長室 Chief librarian's room
30 視聴覚室 Audio-visual room
31 視聴覚資料室 Audio-visual library
32 閉架書庫・閲覧室 Closed-shelf library reading room
33 屋上テラス Rooftop terrace

デザイン棟A 南側外観　Design Dept. A, south facade

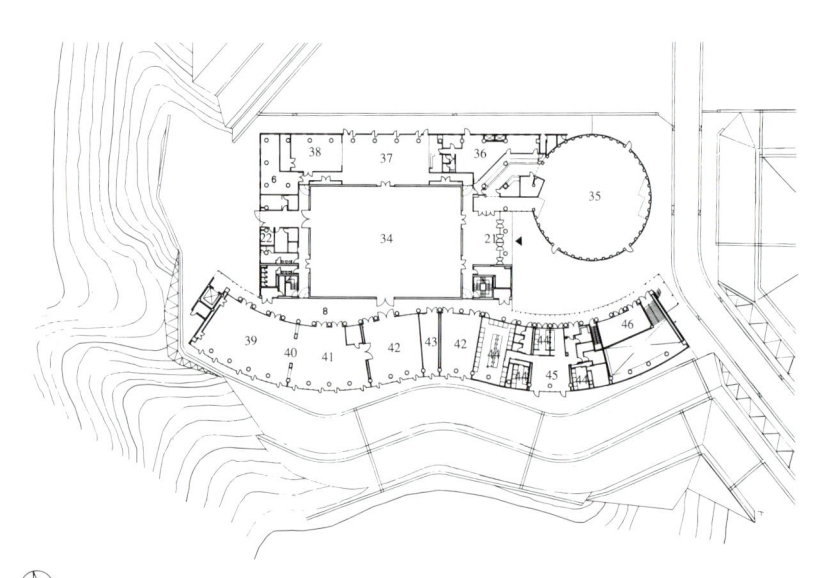

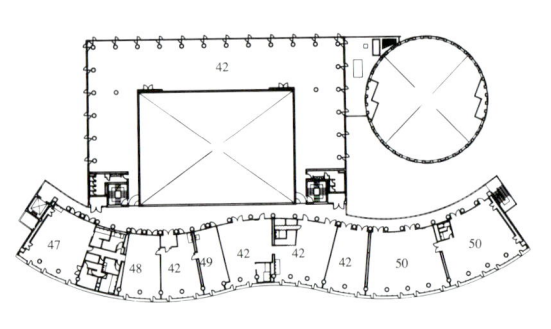

Building No.7〜9: 1st floor plan　1:1500

2nd floor plan

デザイン棟A 右は食堂外観 Design Dept. A, cafeteria on the right

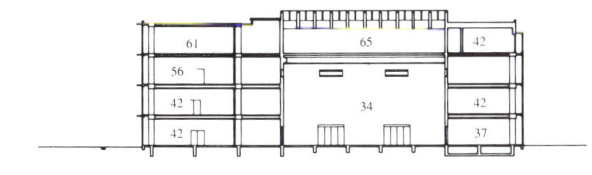

Building No.7〜8: section 1:1000

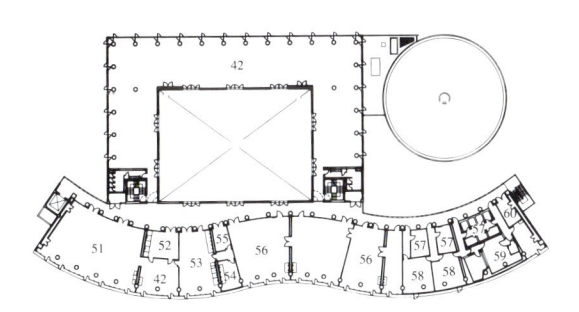

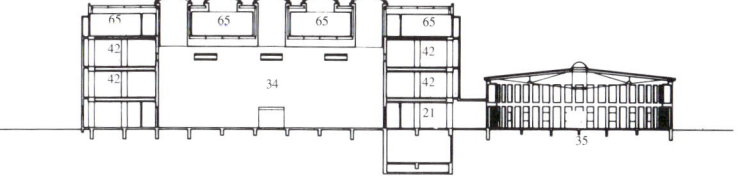

Building No.8〜9: section 1:1000

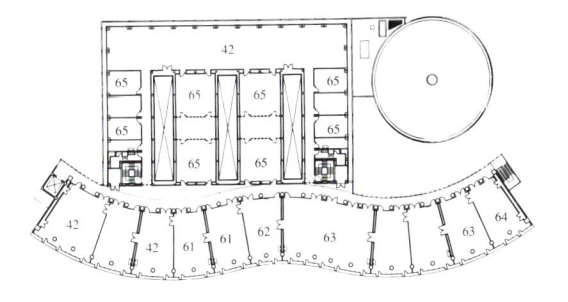

3rd floor plan

4th floor plan

21 エントランス Entrance	44 暗室 Darkroom	56 蝋纈室 Batik dyeing workshop
22 医務室 Infirmary	45 仕上室 Finishing room	57 編集室 Film cutting room
34 体育館 Gymnasium	46 小スタジオ Small studio	58 試写室 Projection room
35 学生食堂 Cafeteria	47 オフセット印刷室 Offset printing room	59 録音スタジオ Recording studio
36 厨房 Kitchen	48 写植印字室 Phototype setting room	60 複写室 Reproduction studio
37 学生ホール Student hall	49 活版印刷室 Typographic printing room	61 製図室 Drawing studio
38 売店 Shop	50 技術センター Technical Center	62 測定室 Measurement lab.
39 木材加工室 Wood workshop	51 捺染室 Textile printing workshop	63 実験室 Laboratory
40 粘土・石膏・合成樹脂加工室 Clay/gypsum/synthetic resin workshop	52 染料調合室 Dye mixing lab.	64 ニューメディアラボラトリー New media lab.
41 金属・プラスチック加工室 Metal/plastics workshop	53 染色室 Dyeing workshop	65 プレゼンテーションルーム Presentation room
42 作業室 Workshop	54 製版現像室 Plate-making/developing lab.	
43 保管室 Repository	55 製版撮影室 Plate-making/photographing lab.	

175

絵画棟 西側外観　Painting Dept., west facade

彫刻棟 東側外観　Sculpture Dept., east facade

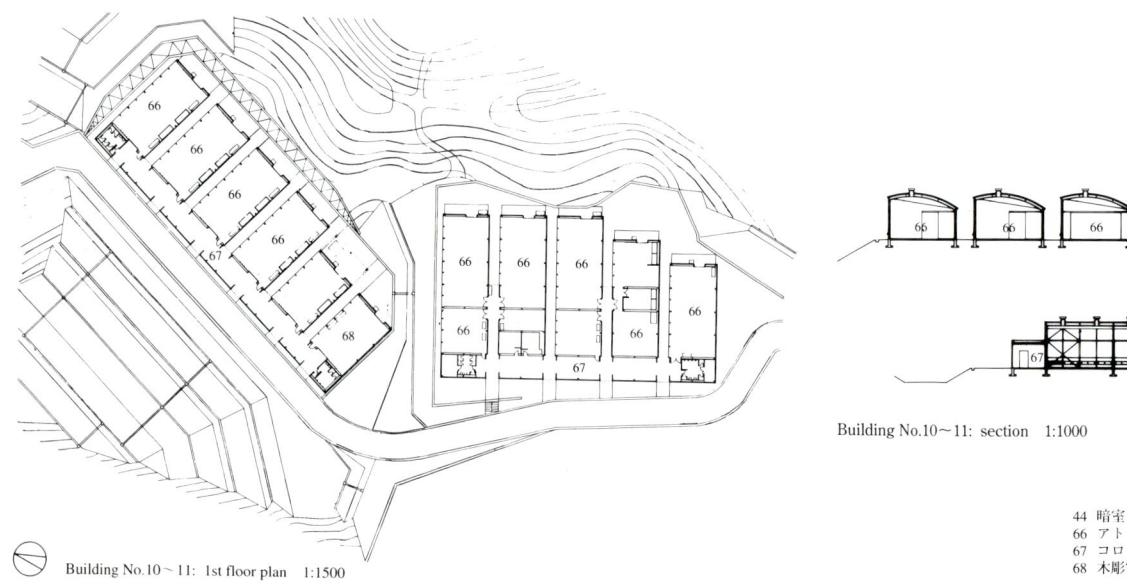

Building No.10〜11: 1st floor plan　1:1500

Building No.10〜11: section　1:1000

44　暗室　Darkroom
66　アトリエ　Atelier
67　コロネード　Colonnade
68　木彫室　Wood carving workshop

本部・研究棟 4階中央のラウンジ　4th floor lounge in the administration/faculty office wing

桑沢記念ホールの大教室　Lecture hall in the Kuwasawa Memorial Hall

デザイン棟A 体育館　Design Dept., gymnasium

絵画棟、彫刻棟のアトリエ　Studios in the Painting and Sculpture Dept.

大学機能を3つの施設群に分けた。それぞれ、管理室、小教室を台形に配し、その上に研究室、大教室、図書館、美術館を含めた"中軸施設群"、デザイン実習室、食堂、ワークステーション(学生への開放スペース)で体育室を囲むように構成されている"スタジオ群"、絵画、彫刻のアトリエが採光のためのコートヤードを挟んで並置し連続している"アトリエ群"である。それらの施設群を沢すじに分散配置し、スカイラインを構成する尾根線を破壊せず、できる限り既存の緑を残し、それぞれの施設は視点の動きにより継起的に出現するキャンパスとなった。

The university functions are divided into three groups of facilities. The administration offices and small classrooms are arranged in a trapezoid. Above them are arranged "core facilities" such as faculty offices, large classrooms, a library and a museum. "Studio wing" contains design workshops, a cafeteria and spaces opened to students and surrounds the physical exercise room. Another "atelier wing" contains painting and sculpture studios, lining on both sides of and getting light from a courtyard. These wings are scattered along the valley without disturbing the ridge line that constitutes the campus skyline. The existing vegetation is preserved as much as possible, and the campus buildings successively come into and out of sight as the line of vision shifts.

所在地	東京都八王子市
設計	磯崎新アトリエ
施工	大林組・田中建設・東京造形大学八王子JV.
竣工	1993年2月
敷地面積	86,062.65m²
建築面積	1〜5号館：4,213.55m²　6号館：514.30m²
	7〜9号館：3,970.90m²　10〜11号館：2,723.53m²
延床面積	1〜5号館：10,121.50m²　6号館：555.33m²
	7〜9号館：12,615.79m²　10〜11号館：2,723.53m²
階数	地上4階、地下1階　6号館：地上2階
	10〜11号館：地上1階
構造	鉄筋コンクリート造、鉄骨鉄筋コンクリート造、鉄骨造
撮影	新建築社／170-171,172下,174-175,177-178
	高瀬良夫／172上中,176

Location: Hachioji-city, Tokyo
Architect: Arata Isozaki & Associates
General contractor: Joint venture of Obayashi, Tanaka Construction and Tokyo University of Art and Design, Hachioji
Completion date: February 1993
Site area: 926,369.75sq.ft.
Building area: Building No.1〜5: 45,354.23sq.ft.
Building No.6: 5,535.87sq.ft.　Building No.7〜9: 42,742.37sq.ft.
Building No.10〜11: 29,315.80sq.ft.
Total floor area: Building No.1〜5: 108,946.81sq.ft.
Building No.6: 5,977.52sq.ft.　Building No.7〜9: 135,795.10sq.ft.
Building No.10〜11: 29,315.80sq.ft.
Number of floors: 4 floors above ground, 1 floor below ground
Building No.6: 2 floors above ground
Building No.10〜11: 1 floor above ground
Structure: Reinforced concrete structure, steel framed reinforced concrete structure and steel structure
Photographer: Shinkenchiku-sha・Co.,Ltd. / 170-171, 172: bottom, 174-175, 177-178　Yoshio Takase / 172: top, middle, 176

東京都立大学
TOKYO METROPOLITAN UNIVERSITY

日本設計
NIHON SEKKEI, INC.

鳥瞰　Bird's eye view

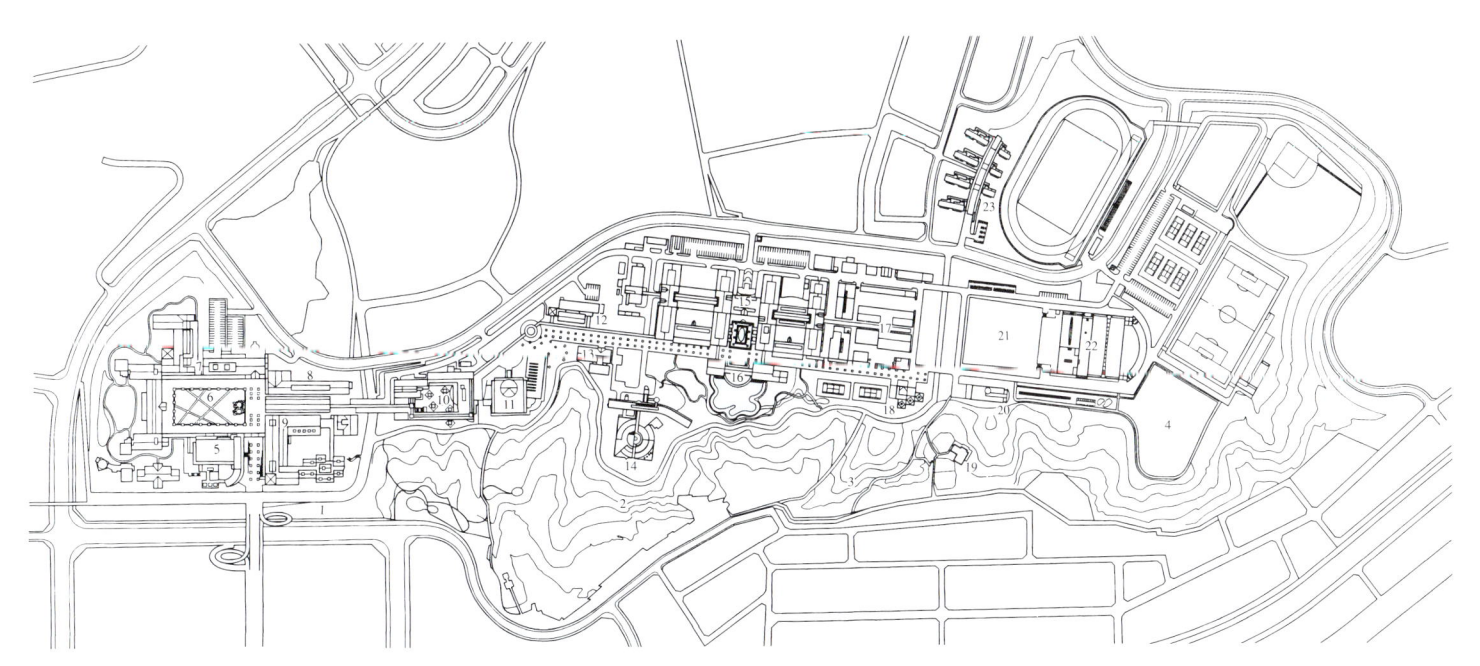

Site plan　1:8000

1　本部・文系ゾーン　Administration/Humanities zone
2　交流ゾーン　Public area
3　理工系ゾーン　Science/Engineering zone
4　スポーツゾーン　Sports zone
5　講堂　Auditorium
6　大学広場　University plaza
7　本部・文系3学部棟　Administration/Humanities Departments
8　学生部棟　Student Affairs Management Dept.
9　教養部教室棟　Liberal Arts Dept. classrooms
10　学生ホール　Student hall
11　図書館　Library
12　情報処理施設　Data processing facilities
13　牧野標本館・自然史研究棟　Makino Museum of Specimens/Natural History Dept.
14　国際交流会館　International Exchange Hall
15　理・工学部本館　Main building for Science/Engineering Dept.
16　理・工教室棟　Science/Engineering Dept. classrooms
17　工学部実験棟　Engineering Dept. laboratory
18　カフェテリア館　Cafeteria
19　植物実験棟　Botanical lab.
20　体育研究棟　Physical Education Dept.
21　運動広場　Athletic field
22　体育館　Gymnasium
23　学生寮　School dormitory

大学広場　右奥に人文学部　University plaza, Humanities Dept. on the right at the back

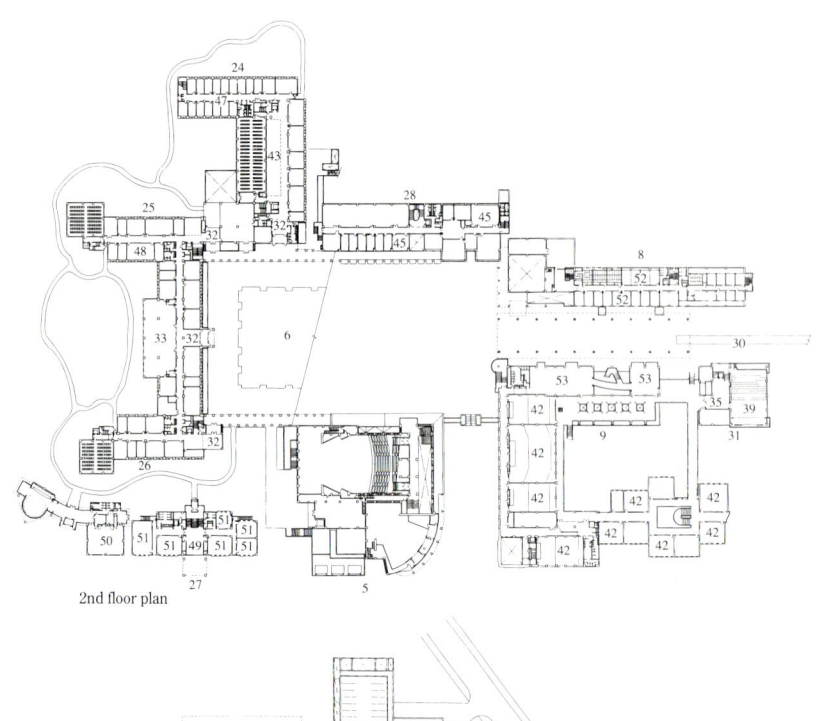

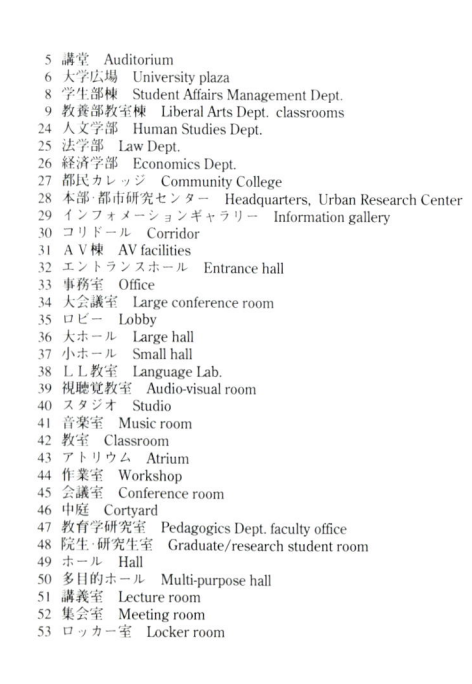

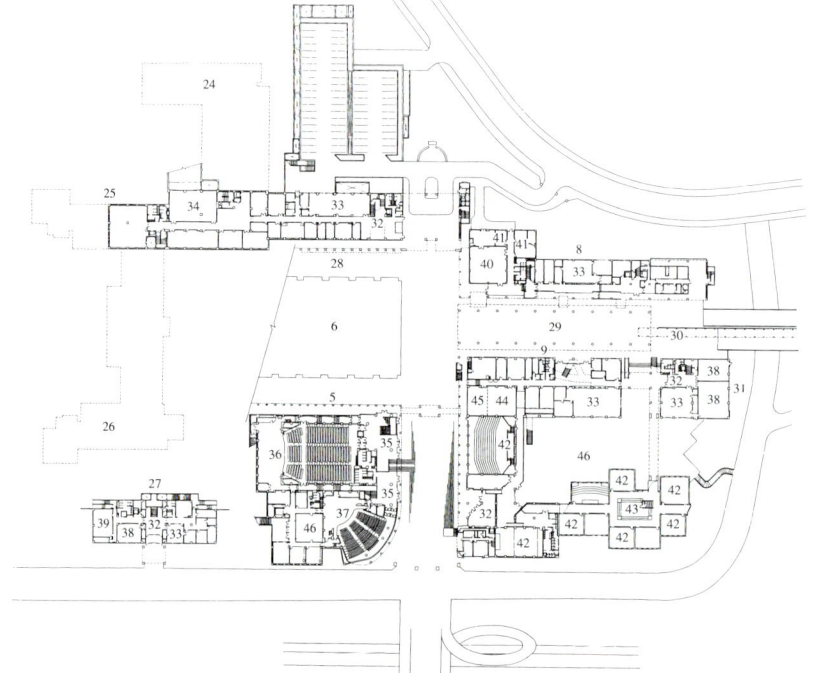

2nd floor plan

5 講堂　Auditorium
6 大学広場　University plaza
8 学生部棟　Student Affairs Management Dept.
9 教養部教室棟　Liberal Arts Dept. classrooms
24 人文学部　Human Studies Dept.
25 法学部　Law Dept.
26 経済学部　Economics Dept.
27 都民カレッジ　Community College
28 本部・都市研究センター　Headquarters, Urban Research Center
29 インフォメーションギャラリー　Information gallery
30 コリドール　Corridor
31 ＡＶ棟　AV facilities
32 エントランスホール　Entrance hall
33 事務室　Office
34 大会議室　Large conference room
35 ロビー　Lobby
36 大ホール　Large hall
37 小ホール　Small hall
38 ＬＬ教室　Language Lab.
39 視聴覚教室　Audio-visual room
40 スタジオ　Studio
41 音楽室　Music room
42 教室　Classroom
43 アトリウム　Atrium
44 作業室　Workshop
45 会議室　Conference room
46 中庭　Cortyard
47 教育学研究室　Pedagogics Dept. faculty office
48 院生・研究生室　Graduate/research student room
49 ホール　Hall
50 多目的ホール　Multi-purpose hall
51 講義室　Lecture room
52 集会室　Meeting room
53 ロッカー室　Locker room

180　大学

インフォメーションギャラリー　Information gallery 　　　中庭より教養学部教室棟コーナーを見る　Looking at the Liberal Arts Dept. from the courtyard

E/W section　1:1800

7　本部・文系3学部棟　Administration/Humanities Departments
8　学生部棟　Student Affairs Management Dept.
32　エントランスホール　Entrance hall
33　事務室　Office

人文学部アトリウム　Atrium in the Liberal Arts Dept.

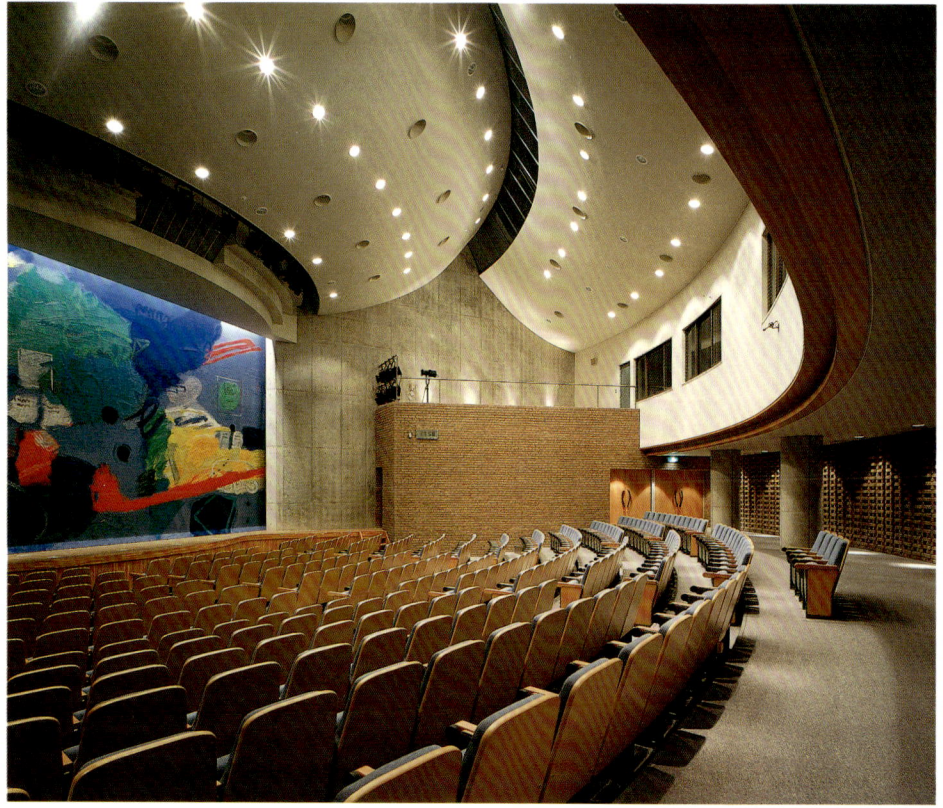

講堂小ホール　Auditorium, small hall

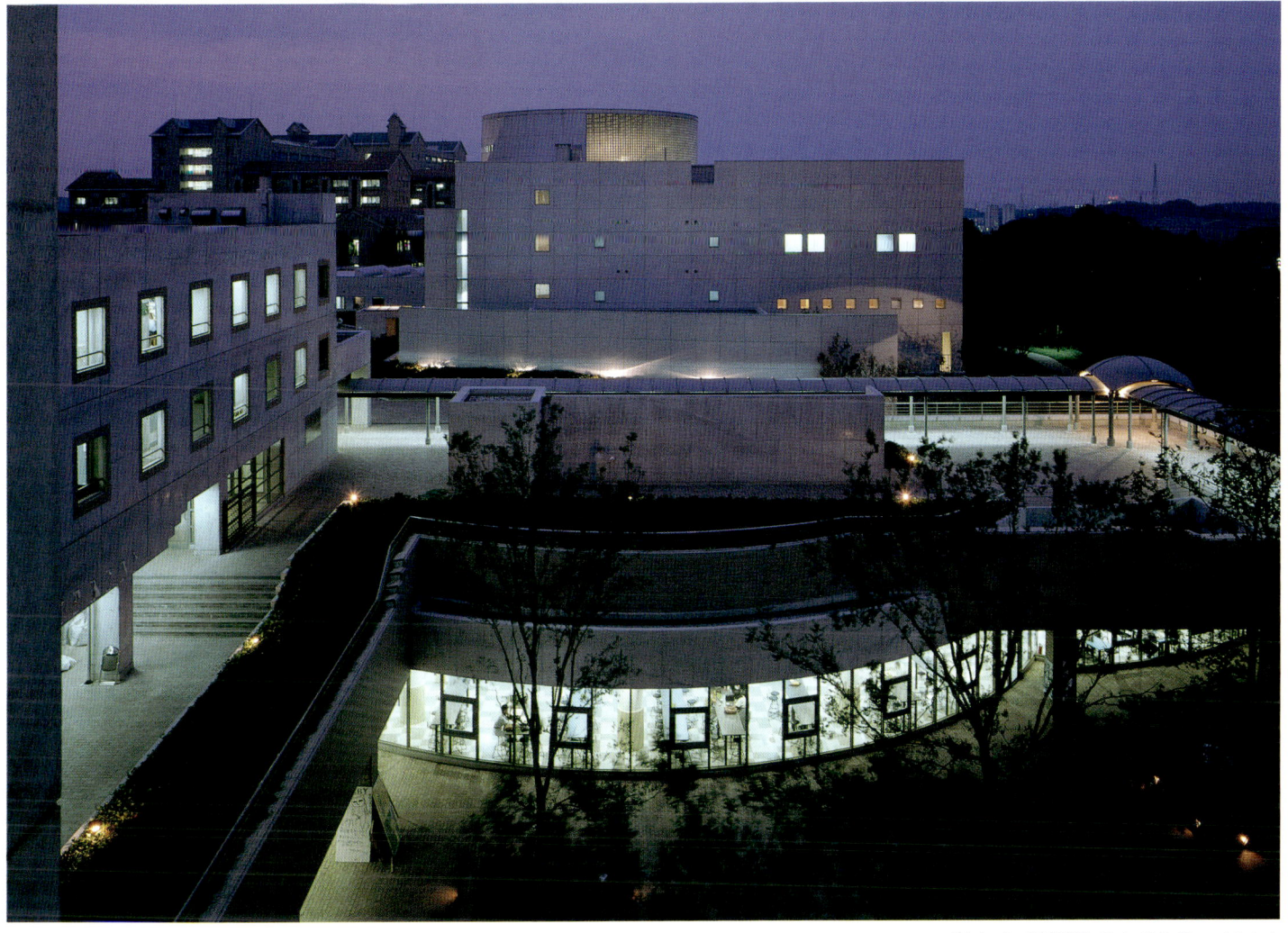

学生ホール　奥に図書館　Student hall, library at the back

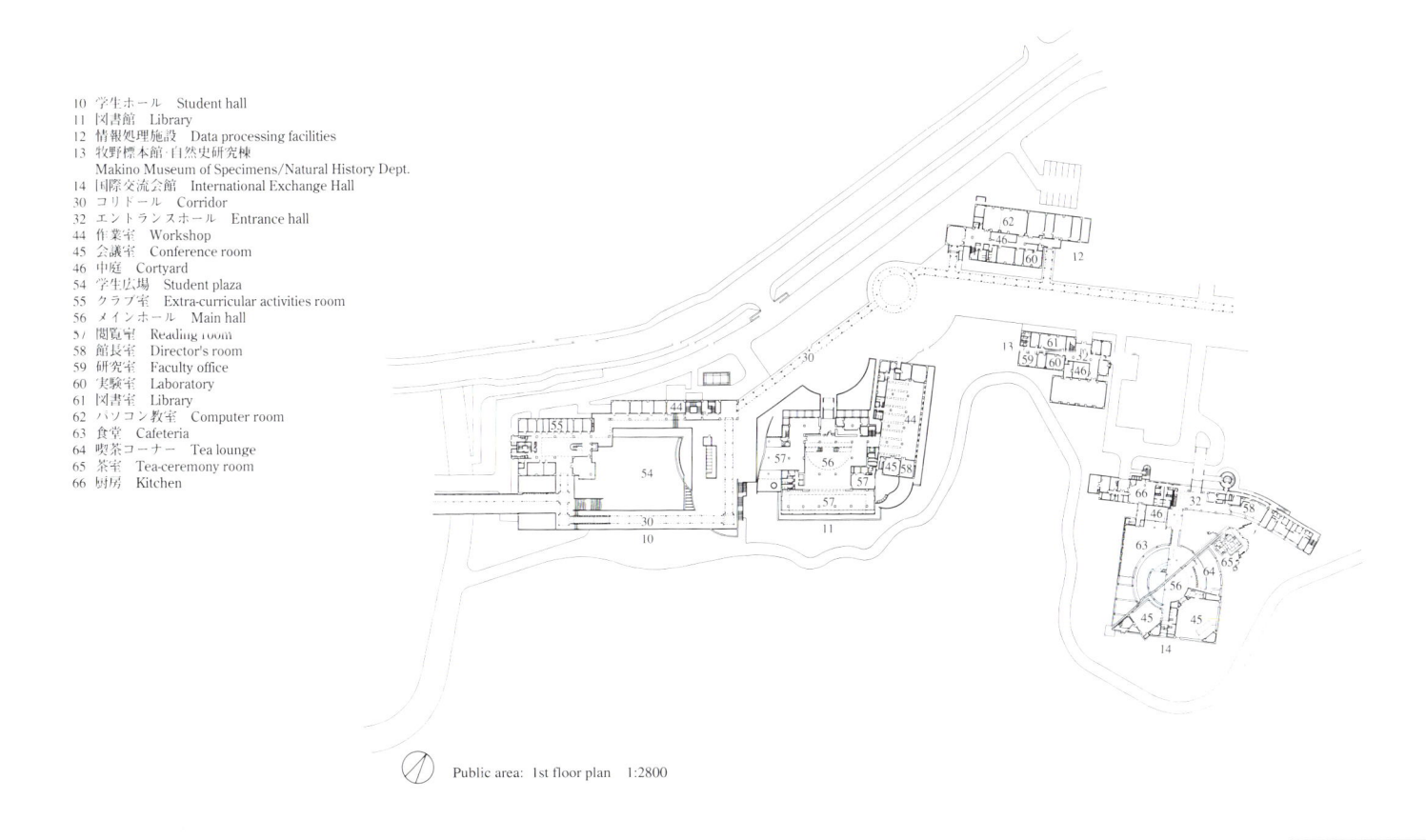

10 学生ホール　Student hall
11 図書館　Library
12 情報処理施設　Data processing facilities
13 牧野標本館·自然史研究棟
　　Makino Museum of Specimens/Natural History Dept.
14 国際交流会館　International Exchange Hall
30 コリドール　Corridor
32 エントランスホール　Entrance hall
44 作業室　Workshop
45 会議室　Conference room
46 中庭　Cortyard
54 学生広場　Student plaza
55 クラブ室　Extra-curricular activities room
56 メインホール　Main hall
57 閲覧室　Reading room
58 館長室　Director's room
59 研究室　Faculty office
60 実験室　Laboratory
61 図書室　Library
62 パソコン教室　Computer room
63 食堂　Cafeteria
64 喫茶コーナー　Tea lounge
65 茶室　Tea-ceremony room
66 厨房　Kitchen

Public area: 1st floor plan　1:2800

183

東側より理・工モールと富士の眺め　Mall in front of the Science/Engineering Dept., with the view of Mt. Fuji

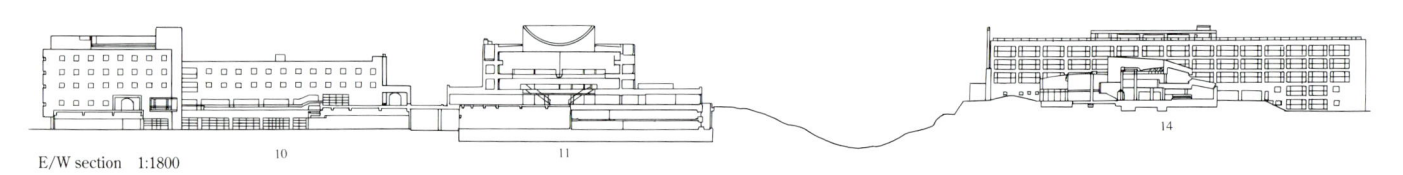

E/W section　1:1800

10　学生ホール　Student hall
11　図書館　Library
14　国際交流会館　International Exchange Hall

多摩の貴重な自然植生とされる松木日向緑地の保全は、施設配置に優先し、雨水還元等設計の基本とされた。また教育研究にも活用されることで育成されるよう努めた。キャンパスが街であること、街並みの重要な要素であることから地域に開かれ、連続する環境の創造を目指した。施設群は4つのゾーンに分け、広場、モールでつないでいる。丘陵地の緑となじみ、変化あるスカイラインを構成するため、主要な施設には赤瓦の屋根を葺き、壁面を分割した。

Preservation of the Matsuki-Hinata Greenbelt abundant with the precious vernacular flora of Tama area was given the top priority in the planning. Recycling of rain water and use of the Greenbelt for educational and academic purposes are examples of measures taken in an effort to preserve and nurture the Greenbelt. Linkage and continuity with the surrounding communities are the key design concept on the recognition that the campus is a town in itself and an important element of the neighborhood. The facilities are arranged in four different zones that are connected by plazas and malls. Red roof tiles are used on main buildings to accentuate the skyline against the background vegetation of the hill, and the wall surfaces are divided to give diversity to the scene.

学生ホール 食堂　Student hall, cafeteria

所在地　東京都八王子市
設計　日本設計　大谷研究室（基本計画）　第一工房（図書館、国際交流館、カフェテリア館、体育研究棟、体育館、学生寮の基本・実施設計、監理）
施工　本部・文系ゾーン：青木建設・浅沼組・日本国土開発・富士工・立石建設JV.　理工系ゾーン：飛島建設・三井建設・佐藤工業・東海興業・大日本土木・三建協JV.　図書館・学生ホール：鴻池組・大豊建設・伊藤組JV.　情報処理施設・牧野標本館・国際交流会館：五洋建設・福田組・西東京協JV.　体育館・学生寮：長谷工・地崎工業・南建協JV.
竣工　1991年3月
敷地面積　427,293.00m²
建築面積　56,921.71m²
延床面積　146,572.44m²
階数　地上9階、地下1階
構造　鉄骨鉄筋コンクリート造、鉄筋コンクリート造、鉄骨造
撮影　新建築社／179,181左　川澄建築写真事務所／180,181右,182　彰国社　和木通／183-185

Location: Hachioji-city, Tokyo
Architect: Nihon Sekkei, Inc.　Sachio Otani & Associates (conceptual design)　Daiichi-Kobo Associates (general design, execution design and supervising: library, International Exchange Hall, cafeteria, Physical Education Dept., gymnasium and school dormitory)
General contractor: Administration/Humanities zone: joint venture of Aoki, Asanuma-gumi, JDC, Fujikou and Tateishi　Science/Engineering zone: joint venture of Tobishima, Mitsui, Sato Kogyo, Tokai Kogyo, Dainihon and Sankenkyo　library and student hall: joint venture of Konoike, Taihou and Ito-gumi　data processing facilities, Makino Museum of Specimens and International Exchange Hall: joint venture of Penta-Ocean Construction, Fukuda-gumi, Nishitokyokyo　gymnasium and school dormitory: joint venture of Haseko, Chizaki Kogyo and Nankenkyo
Completion date: March 1991
Site area: 4,599,339.10sq.ft.
Building area: 612,699.59sq.ft.
Total floor area: 1,577,691.09sq.ft.
Number of floors: 9 floors above ground, 1 floor below ground
Structure: Steel framed reinforced concrete structure, reinforced concrete structure and steel structure
Photographer: Shinkenchiku-sha・Co.,Ltd. / 179, 181: left
Kawasumi Architectural Photograph Office / 180, 181: right, 182
Toru Waki　The Shokokusha Publishing Co.,Ltd. / 183-185

Science/Engineering zone: 1st floor plan　1:2800

18　カフェテリア館　Cafeteria
32　エントランスホール　Entrance hall
35　ロビー　Lobby
43　アトリウム　Atrium
46　中庭　Cortyard
51　講義室　Lecture room
60　実験室　Laboratory
63　食堂　Cafeteria
67　理・工教室棟　Science/Engineering Dept. classrooms
68　理・工モール　Mall in front of Science/Engineering Dept.
69　機械・精密実験棟　Machinery/Precision Machine lab.
70　機械実験棟　Machinery lab.
71　建築実験棟　Architecture lab.
72　機械・建築実験棟　Machinery/Architecture lab.
73　土木実験棟　Civil engineering lab.
74　電気・電子情報実験棟　Electric/electric data processing lab.
75　理工広場　Science/Engineering plaza
76　実習室　Practice room
77　資料室　Reference room

東北芸術工科大学
TOHOKU UNIVERSITY OF ART & DESIGN

本間利雄設計事務所＋地域環境計画研究室
TOSHIO HOMMA & ASSOCIATES, CO.,LTD.

鳥瞰　Bird's eye view

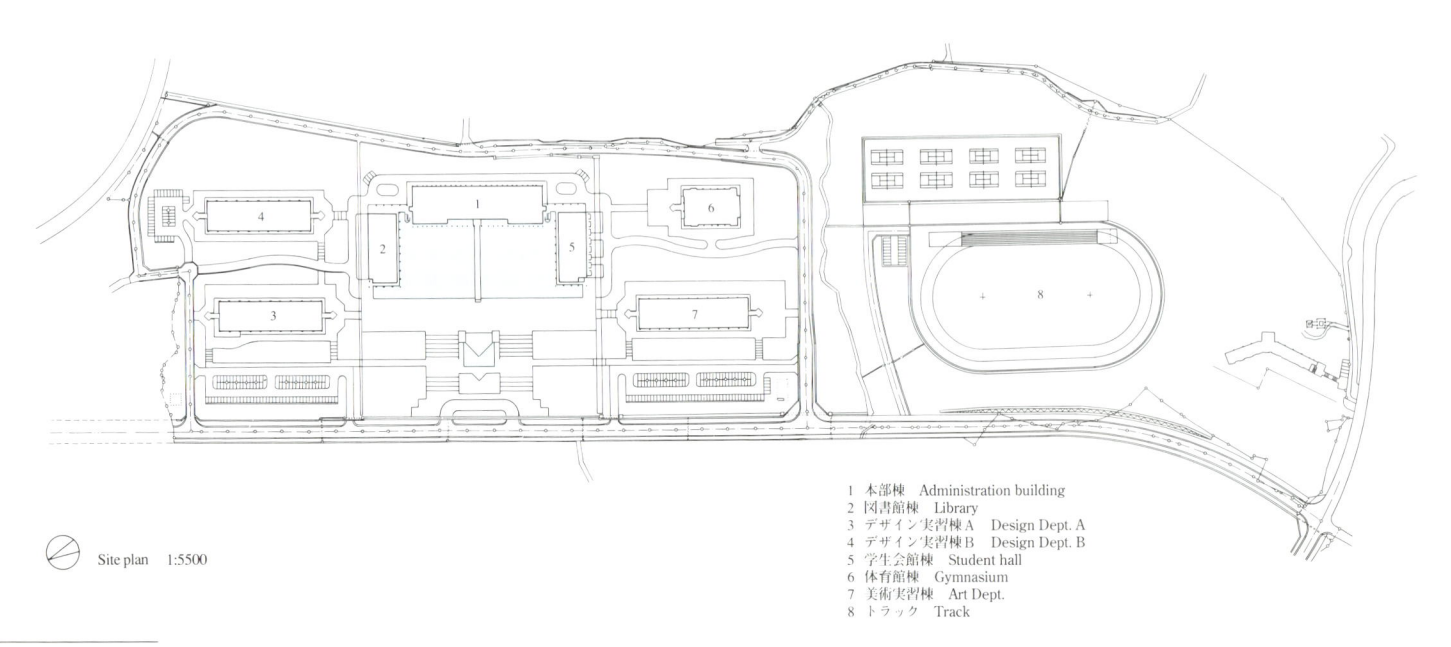

Site plan　1:5500

1　本部棟　　　　　Administration building
2　図書館棟　　　　Library
3　デザイン実習棟A　Design Dept. A
4　デザイン実習棟B　Design Dept. B
5　学生会館棟　　　Student hall
6　体育館棟　　　　Gymnasium
7　美術実習棟　　　Art Dept.
8　トラック　　　　Track

西側外観　West facade

本部棟西側を北側より見る　Looking from the north at west facade of administration building

本部棟正面外観　Facade of administration building

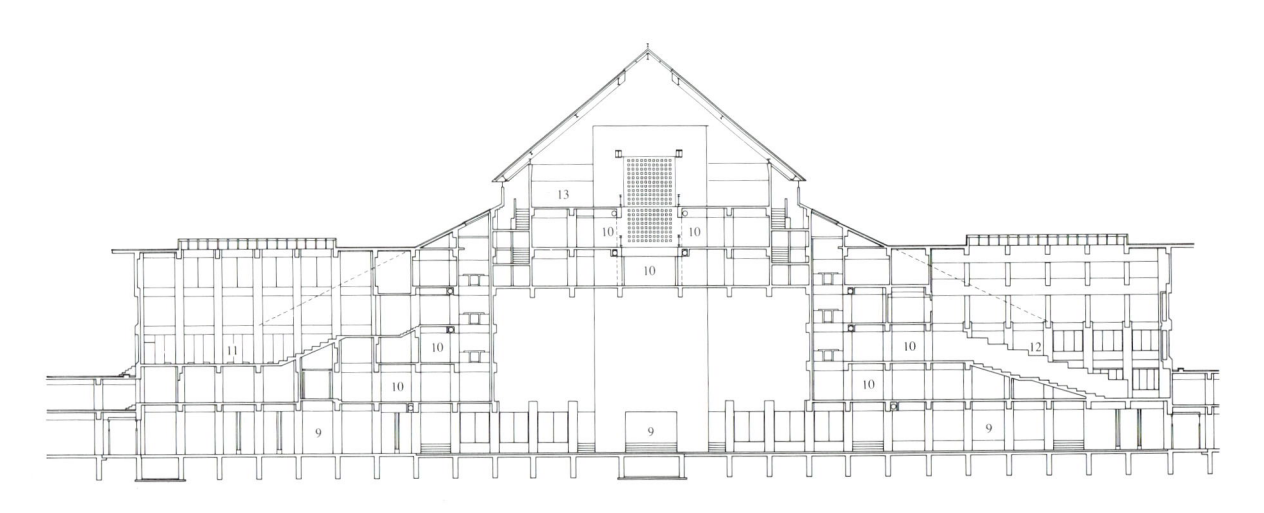

Administration building: section　1:700

9　ロビー　Lobby
10　ホール　Hall
11　講義室　Lecture room
12　階段教室　Lecture theater
13　ギャラリー　Gallery

学生会館と本部棟の間の見返し　Passage between student hall and administration building

本部棟ロビーよりラウンジ越しに見る　Looking from the lobby in the administration building across lounge

本部棟7階ベランダより実習棟、体育館棟を見る　Looking at the Art Dept. and gymnasium from 7th floor veranda in the administration building

体育館越しに美術実習棟東側外観を見る　Looking at the east facade of the Art Dept. behind gymnasium

本部棟 7 階 ベランダ   7th floor veranda in the administration building

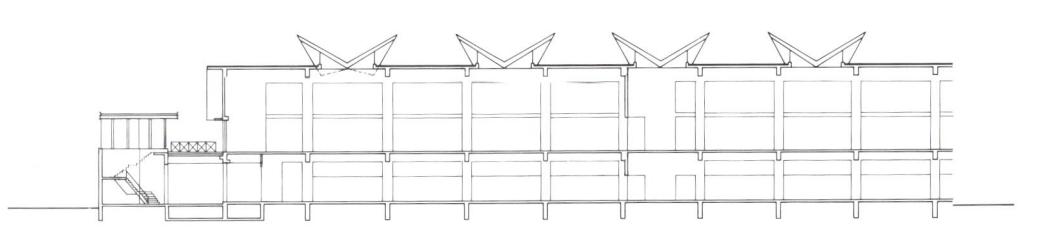

Art Dept.: section   1:700

本部棟1階 ロビーと闇の吹抜　1st floor lobby and dark air-well in the administration building

本部棟2階 光の吹抜見上げ　Looking up at the light air-well from 2nd floor of the administration building

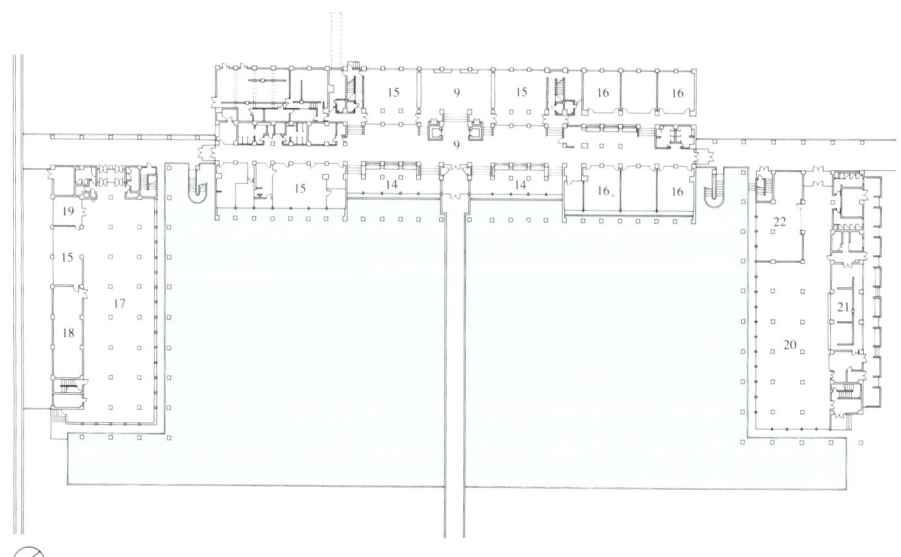

Administration building/Library/Student hall: 1st floor plan　1:1500

本部棟7階 ギャラリー　7th floor gallery in the administration building

美術実習棟2階 廊下　2nd floor corridor in the Art Dept.

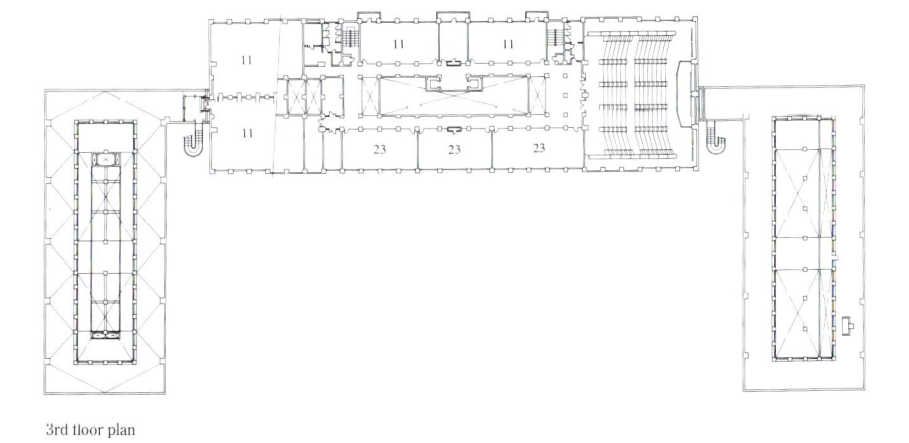

3rd floor plan

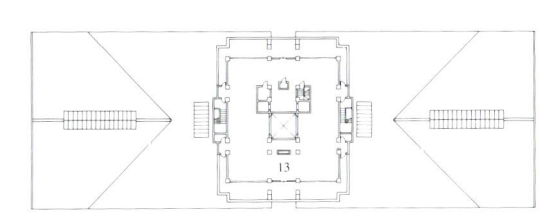

7th floor plan

9　ロビー　Lobby
11　講義室　Lecture room
12　階段教室　Lecture theater
13　ギャラリー　Gallery
14　ラウンジ　Lounge
15　事務室　Office
16　小講義室　Small lecture room
17　図書室　Library
18　閉架書庫　Closed-shelf library
19　AVルーム　Audio-visual room
20　食堂　Cafeteria
21　厨房　Kitchen
22　売店　Shop
23　コンピューター室　Computer room

本部棟2〜3階 講義室　Lecture room in 2nd and 3rd floors of administration building

実習棟外部階段の内部　Inside of stairway outside Art Dept.

池越しに正面外観 夜景　Front facade viewed from across pond at night

本校は"公設民営"の芸術工科系大学である。地域の新しいシンボルとして、東北・山形の雄大なランドスケープの要素のひとつになるよう、背後の蔵王の山並みから市街地越しに西の彼方の山並みへとつながる空間軸を強く意識し、切妻の大屋根が特徴の本部棟と正面の人口池を中心に、敷地の高低差を生かした施設配置とした。縄文的な力強さ、さらに精神鍛練の場のイメージから、内外ともコンクリート打ち放しを主体に木質の仕上げを介在させ、バナキュラーな中にも人間味ある空間とした。

The university was constructed by the public sector and is run by the private sector. As a new symbol of the community amid the magnificent landscape, the buildings are constructed along the spatial axis that extends from the Zao Mountains through the streets of Yamagata City toward the distant mountains on the west. The administration wing with the impressive high gabled roof and the artificial lake are the core elements, and the entire layout is planned to take advantage of differences in the ground level. To create an image of arena for ascetic mental trainings, the interior as well as the exterior is finished mainly with exposed concrete. Wood finishes are also used to give warm touches and vernacular robustness of the archaic Jomon (Neolithic straw-patterned) culture.

所在地　山形市
設計　本間利雄設計事務所＋地域環境計画研究室
施工　本部棟・図書館棟・学生会館棟：清水建設・鴻池組・千歳建設JV.　デザイン実習棟：山形建設・小野建設JV.
美術実習棟・体育館：市村工務店・東南建設JV.
竣工　1992年8月
敷地面積　194,551.82m²
建築面積　14,879.63m²
延床面積　30,366.41m²
階数　本部棟：地上7階、塔屋1階　図書館棟・学生会館棟：地上2階　美術実習棟・デザイン実習棟：地上2階
体育館：地上2階
構造　本部棟・図書館棟・学生会館棟：鉄筋コンクリート造、一部鉄骨造　美術実習棟・デザイン実習棟：鉄筋コンクリート造
体育館：鉄筋コンクリート造、鉄骨造
撮影　須賀信夫／186　木寺安彦／187-189,190上,191,192,193右,194-195　菅雅昭／190下,193左

Location: Yamagata-city, Yamagata
Architect: Toshio Homma & Associates, Co.,Ltd.
General contractor: Administration building, library and student hall: Joint venture of Shimizu, Konoike and Chitose
Design Dept.: Joint venture of Yamagata and Ono
Art Dept. and gymnasium: Joint venture of Ichimura and Tonan
Completion date: August 1992
Site area: 2,094,136.30sq.ft.
Building area: 160,162.84sq.ft.
Total floor area: 326,861.00sq.ft.
Number of floors: Administration building, library and student hall: 7 floors above ground, tower on the 1st floor　library and student hall: 2 floors above ground　Art Dept. and Design Dept.: 2 floors above ground　gymnasium: 2 floors above ground
Structure: Administration building, library and student hall: reinforced concrete structureand and steel structure
Art Dept. and Design Dept.: reinforced concrete structure
gymnasium: reinforced concrete structure and steel structure
Photographer: Nobuo Suga / 186　Yasuhiko Kidera / 187-189, 190: top, 191, 192, 193: right, 194-195
Masaaki Kan / 190: bottom, 193: left

明治学院大学 本館
MEIJI GAKUIN UNIVERSITY MAIN HALL

内井昭蔵建築設計事務所
S. UCHII ARCHITECT & ASSOCIATES

南側全景　Overall view of the south side

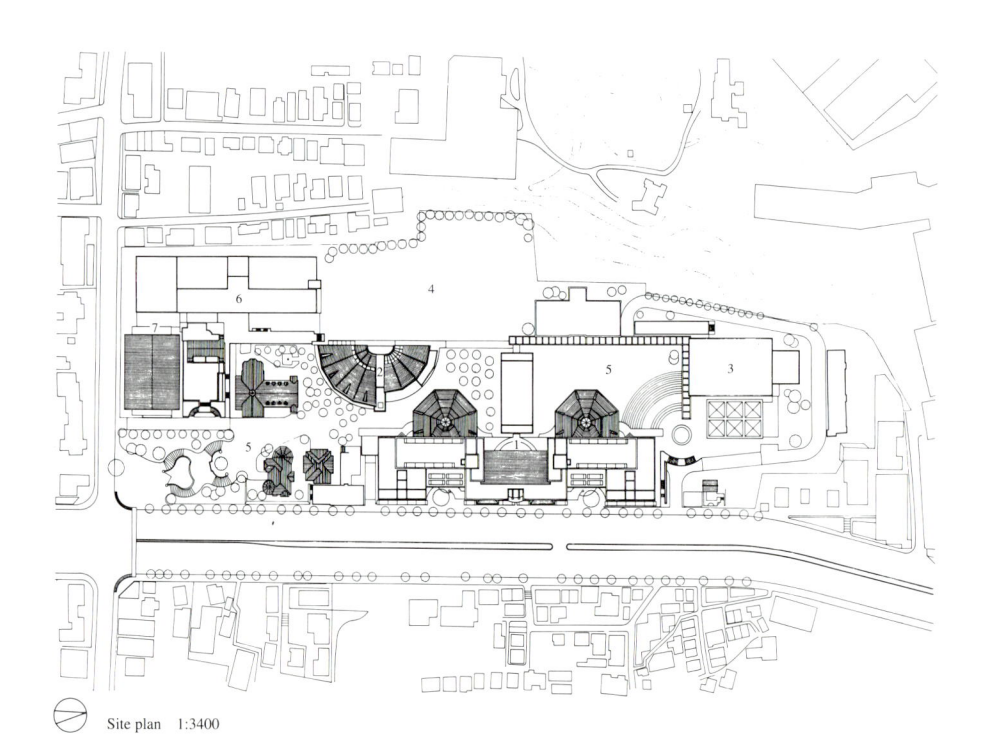

1　本館　　　Main hall
2　校舎　　　School building
3　体育館　　Gymnasium
4　グラウンド　Playground
5　広場　　　Plaza
6　高校校舎　High school building
7　高校体育館　High school gymnasium

Site plan　1:3400

広場廻り 東側全景　East facade, plaza

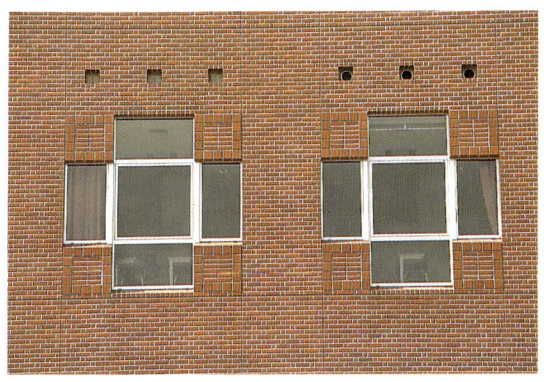

教室外観 壁面ディテール　Classroom, exterior wall detail

南東側外観 上層部壁面ディテール　Southwest facade, exterior wall detail on upper floors

東側より屋上テラスを見る　Looking at the rooftop terrace from east

東側外観 ディテール　East facade, detail

キャンパス側全景　Looking at the main hall from the campus

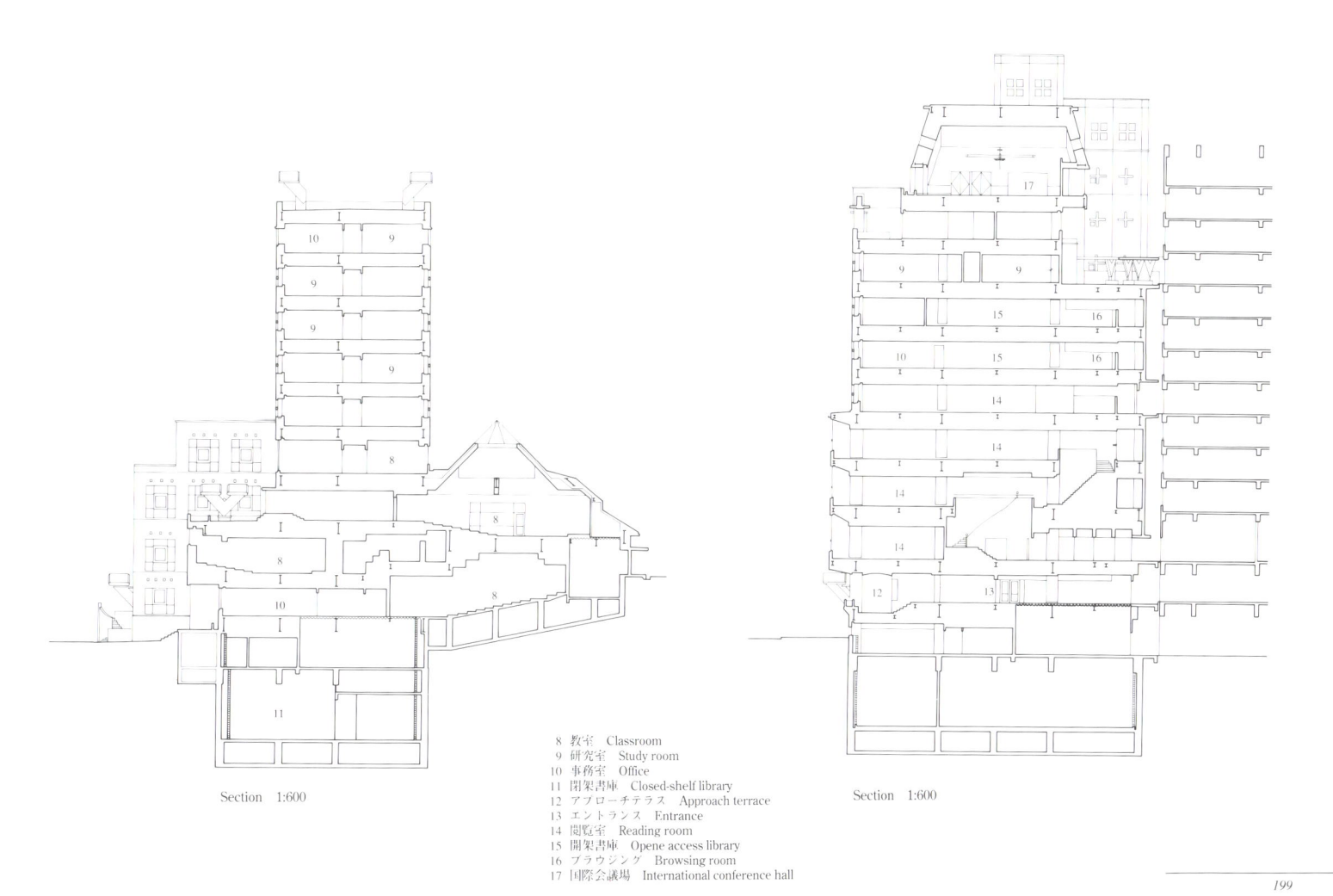

Section 1:600

Section 1:600

8 教室　Classroom
9 研究室　Study room
10 事務室　Office
11 閉架書庫　Closed-shelf library
12 アプローチテラス　Approach terrace
13 エントランス　Entrance
14 閲覧室　Reading room
15 開架書庫　Opene access library
16 ブラウジング　Browsing room
17 国際会議場　International conference hall

アプローチテラス 右、エントランス　Approach terrace, entrance on the right

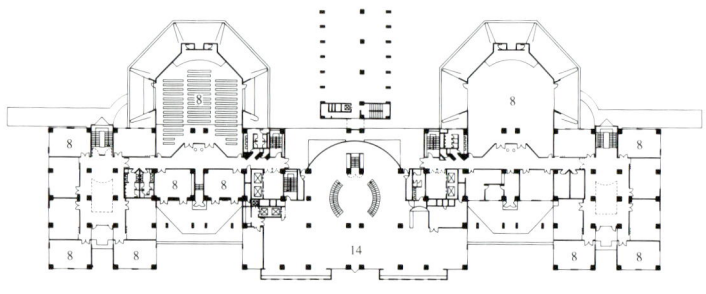

3rd floor plan

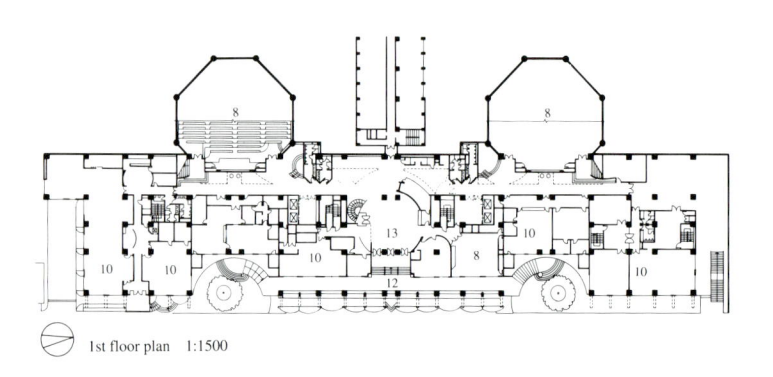

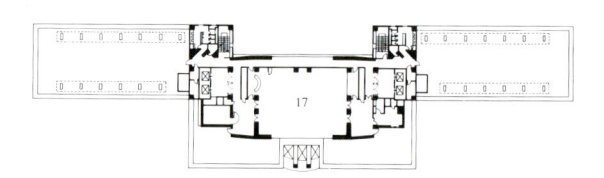

10th floor plan

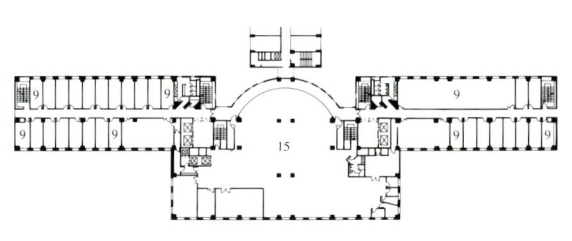

1st floor plan　1:1500

8th floor plan

- 8　教室　Classroom
- 9　研究室　Study room
- 10　事務室　Office
- 12　アプローチテラス　Approach terrace
- 13　エントランス　Entrance
- 14　閲覧室　Reading room
- 15　開架書庫　Open access library
- 17　国際会議場　International conference hall

2階図書館 エントランス　2nd floor, library entrance

2階回廊、ロビー　2nd floor colonnade, lobby

10階 国際会議場　10th floor, international conference hall

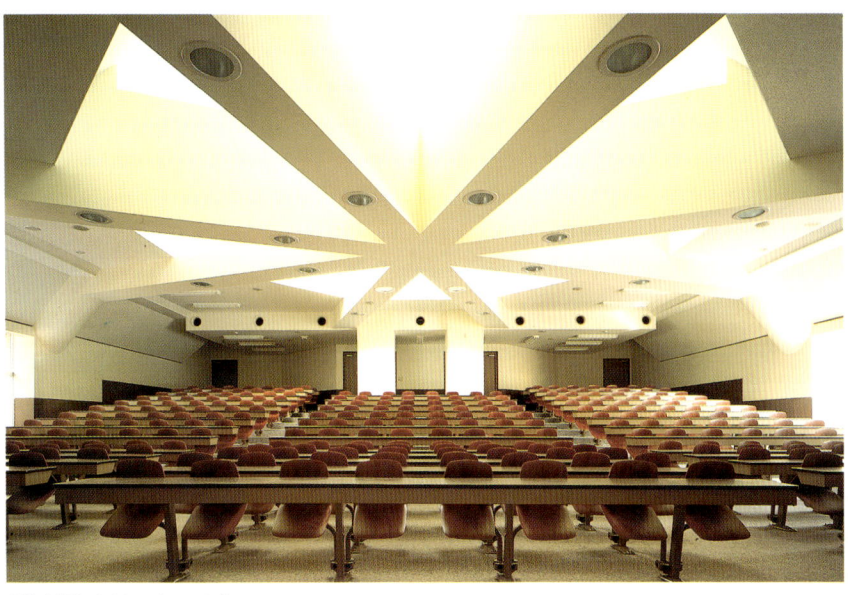

3階 大教室　3rd floor, lecture hall

本館は図書館、教室、研究室、会議場、事務室など大学の主要な機能を内包する複合的な建築である。その基本理念はキリスト教精神に基づく教育理念を反映し、人間的教育の場として大学を生活空間と考えることであり、図書館を中心に各ゾーンが相互に連続し、広場と回廊による新しい秩序と構成を生み出している。また都市や地域環境と有機的に連続した開かれた都心型大学であり、都市の景観上も開口部の彫塑的な彫りの深さやレンガとコンクリートの構成により柔らかさを与えるファサードを提案し、伝統を次代に受け継いだ明治学院の新しい象徴となる形態と空間をつくり出している。

This is a university complex containing cardinal functions of a university such as a library, classrooms, faculty offices, conference rooms and administration offices. To reflect the basic philosophy which is based on the Christianity, the university is considered as a space of disciplining for humane life. With the library at the core, various functions are linked with each other by open spaces and colonnades, creating orderly framework for the university life. It also functions as an urban type university open to the community. The clear-cut openings and use of bricks and concrete give the facade warmth and the image of relief work, creating a new form and space that symbolizes the school that passes on the tradition to the next generations.

所在地　　東京都港区
設計　　　内井昭蔵建築設計事務所
施工　　　明治学院白金校地再開発工事JV.
竣工　　　1993年3月
敷地面積　37,445.18m²
建築面積　3,106.77m²
延床面積　23,081.91m²
階数　　　地上10階、地下2階
構造　　　鉄骨鉄筋コンクリート造
撮影　　　堀内広治／196,197上,198下,199-201
　　　　　ナカサ＆パートナーズ／197下,198上　　冨田治／202

Location: Minato-ward, Tokyo
Architect: S. Uchii Architect & Associates
General contractor: Joint venture of Meiji Gakuin Shirokane Campus Project
Completion date: March 1993
Site area: 403,056.17sq.ft.
Building area: 33,440.96sq.ft.
Total floor area: 248,451.37sq.ft.
Number of floors: 10 floors above ground, 2 floors below ground
Structure: Steel framed reinforced concrete structure
Photographer: Koji Horiuchi / 196, 197: top, 198: bottom, 199-201
Nacása & Partners Inc. / 197: bottom, 198: top
Osamu Tomita / 202

専門学校　Technical Colleges

ヒコ・みづのジュエリーカレッジ
HIKO・MIZUNO COLLEGE OF JEWELRY

吉柳満アトリエ
MITSURU KIRYU ATELIER

北東側外観　Northeast facade

エントランス部分見上げ　Looking up at the entrance

屋上広場　Rooftop plaza

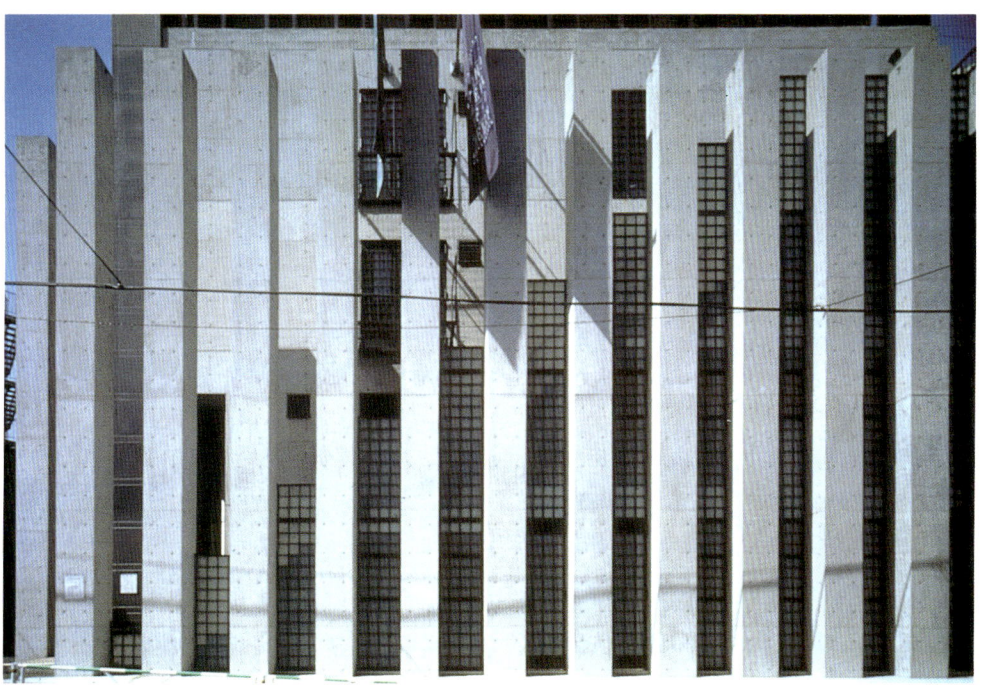

北東側下部外観　Lower northeast facade

1階 ギャラリー内部　Inside 1st floor gallery

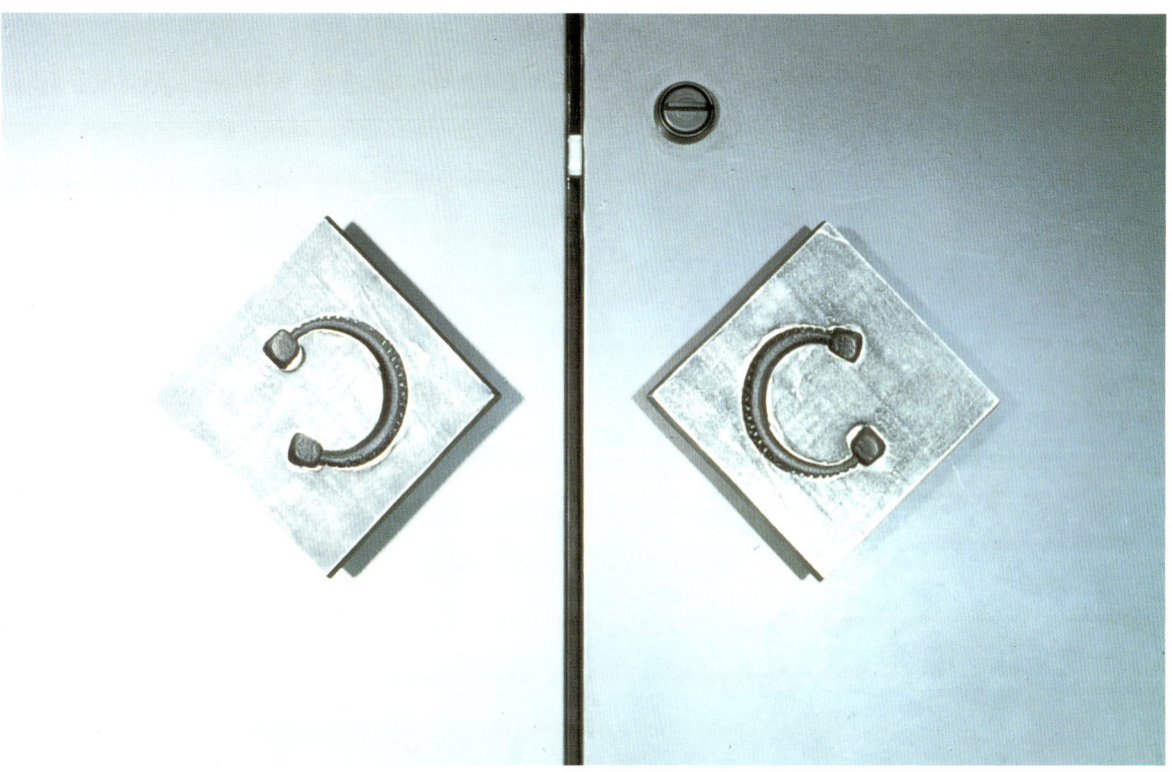

各室ドアノブ　Door knobs

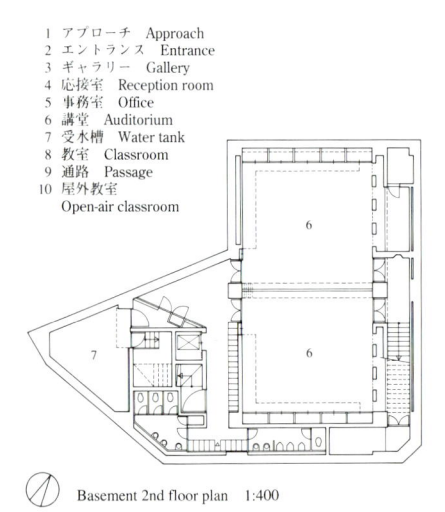

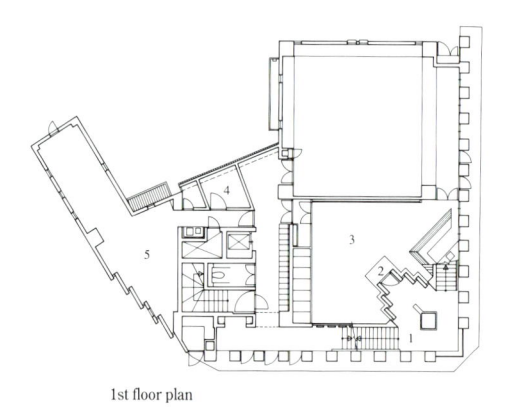

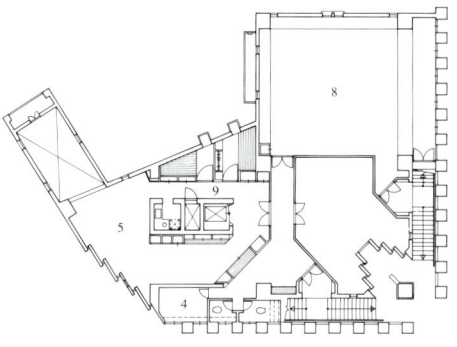

1 アプローチ　Approach
2 エントランス　Entrance
3 ギャラリー　Gallery
4 応接室　Reception room
5 事務室　Office
6 講堂　Auditorium
7 受水槽　Water tank
8 教室　Classroom
9 通路　Passage
10 屋外教室　Open-air classroom

Basement 2nd floor plan　1:400

1st floor plan

2nd floor plan

教室　Classroom

地下2階 講堂　Basement 2nd floor, auditorium

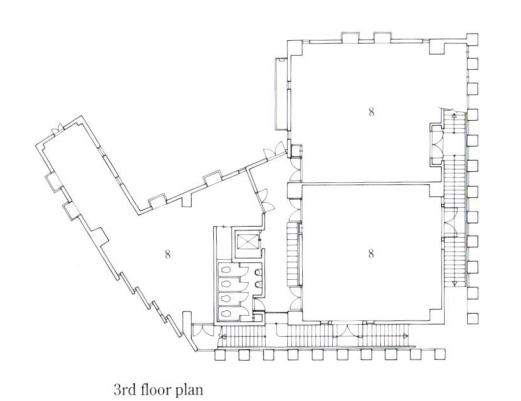

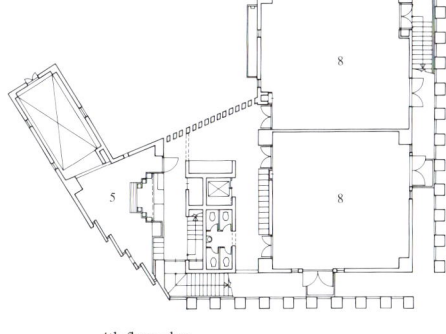

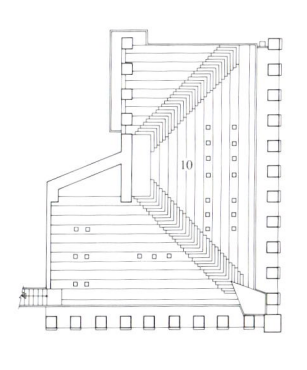

3rd floor plan

4th floor plan

Roof plan

北側外観見上げ夜景　Looking up at the north facade at night

本校は民営のジュエリーデザインの専門学校であるため、特に将来的な人口の変化による生徒の増減に対して、ジュエリーデザインの需要の拡大に様々な発信ができるような学校であること、時代の変化にも対応できる建築デザインが求められた。建物内部は、学ぶというより創造的意識の高揚を感じるような、プロのアトリエを創るイメージでデザインされた。法規の制限のため切り取られた屋上は段状にデザインされ、屋外教室、休息スペース、デザイン展等のイベントの発信空間となる。都心の外部環境からの自立と機能を明示する列柱は、各階各室へのアプローチとなる屋外階段を支え、時代の変化によってこの建物の使用機能が変わっても、対応可能な自立も意図している。

This is a private technical college of jewelry design. Flexibility was the key concept to cope with the future increase/decrease in the number of students and demand for jewelry design as well as the change of the times. The interior is finished as a workshop of professional craftsmen, rather than as a space for learning, to inspire the creativity of students. The rooftop space which is sloped due to regulatory restrictions is tiered and used as an outdoor classroom, a space for relaxation and a space for exhibition and other events. The columns that stand in lines explicitly symbolize independence from the urban surroundings and support the outside stairways that act as the approach to the inside. The building can easily be accommodated to various functions to meet the changes in needs.

所在地	東京都渋谷区
設計	吉柳満アトリエ
施工	加賀田組
竣工	1992年3月
敷地面積	330.89m²
建築面積	249.81m²
延床面積	1,312.32m²
階数	地上5階、地下2階
構造	鉄骨鉄筋コンクリート造、鉄筋コンクリート造
撮影	新建築社／204-205,206上,207

Location: Shibuya-ward, Tokyo
Architect: Mitsuru Kiryu Atelier
General contractor: Kagata-gumi
Completion date: March 1992
Site area: 3,561.67sq.ft.
Building area: 2,688.93sq.ft.
Total floor area: 14,125.68sq.ft.
Number of floors: 5 floors above ground, 2 floors below ground
Structure: Steel framed reinforced concrete structure and reinforced concrete structure
Photographer: Shinkenchiku-sha・Co.,Ltd. / 204-205, 206: top, 207

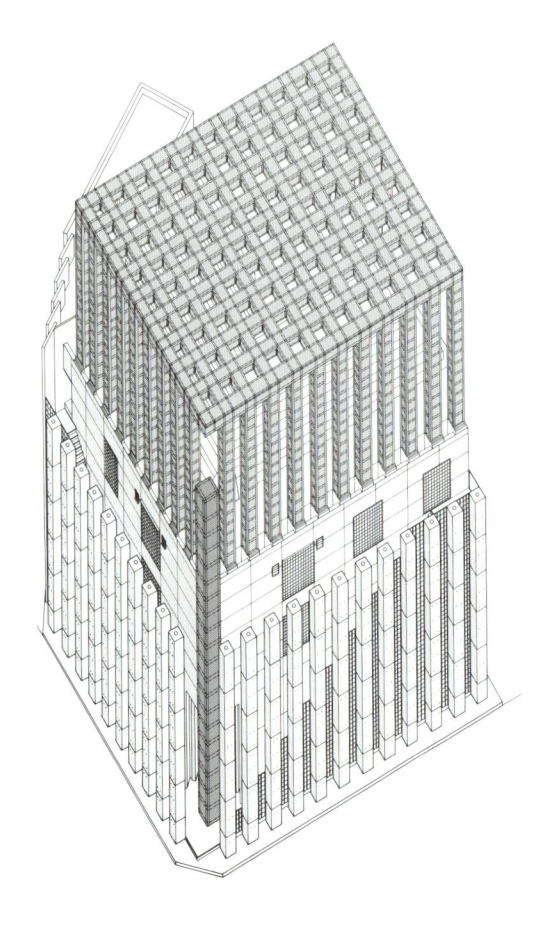

Axonometric drawing

早稲田ゼミナール所沢校 1988
WASEDA SEMINAR IN TOKOROZAWA

富永譲＋フォルムシステム設計研究所
YUZURU TOMINAGA + FORM SYSTEM INSTITUTE

駅舎越しに東側外観を見る　Looking at the east facade over station building

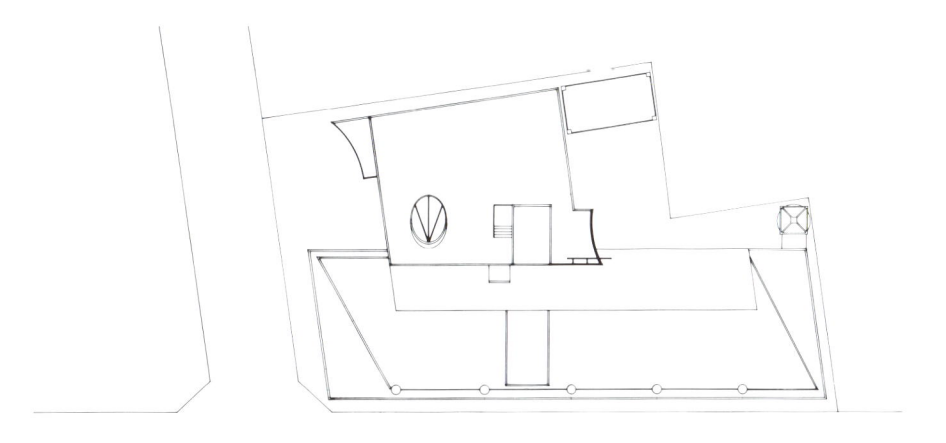

Site plan　1:500

北側外観見上げ　Looking up at the north facade

北側全景　Overall view of the north side

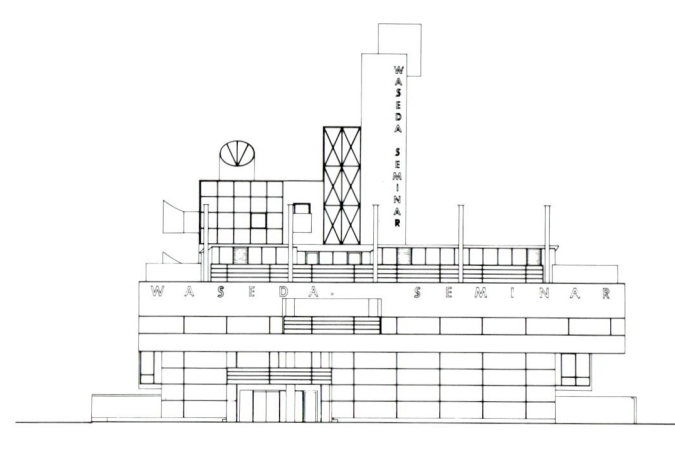

N/E elevation　1:500

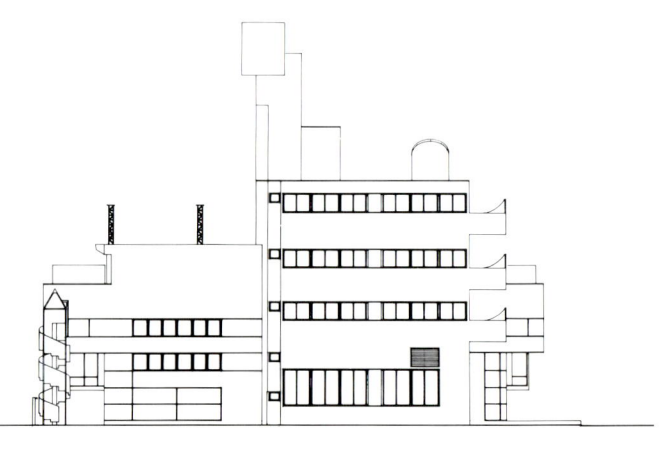

N/W elevation　1:500

東側外観見上げ　Looking up at the east facade

エントランスへのアプローチ
Approach to the entrance

2階ブリッジより1階ロビーを見る　Looking down at the lobby from the bridge on the 2nd floor

北側ロビー外観 夜景　North facade of the lobby at night

1階ロビー吹抜を見る　Lookind at the air-well in 1st floor lobby ▶

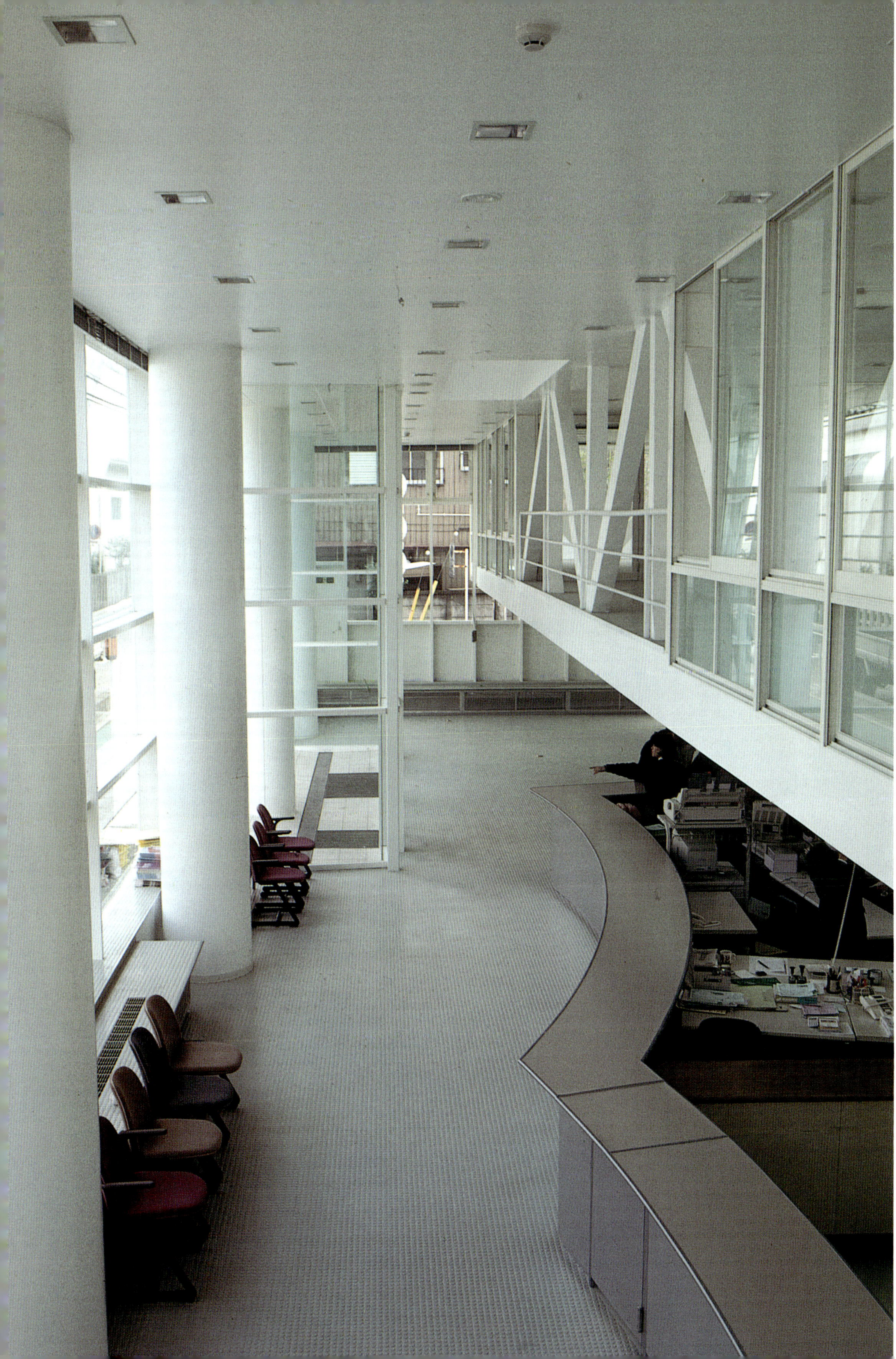

営業中

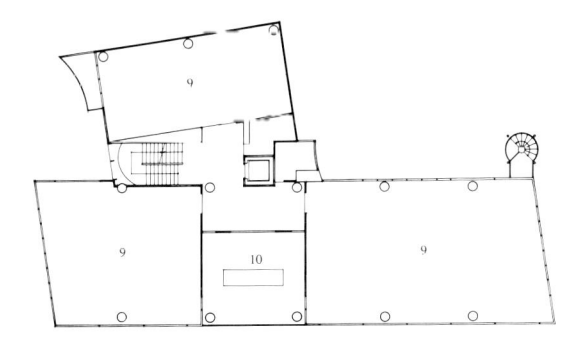

3rd floor plan

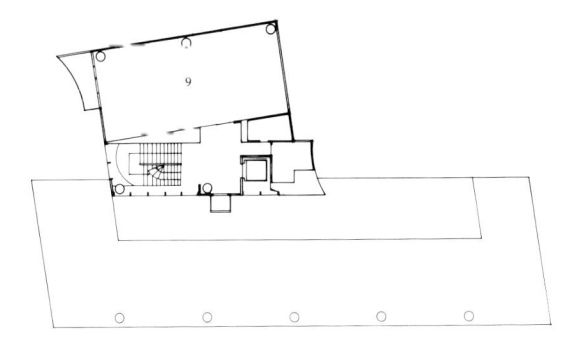

5th floor plan

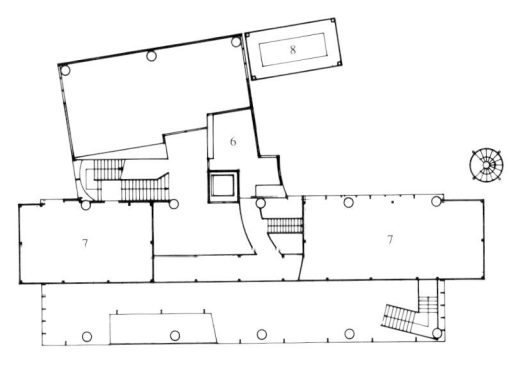

2nd floor plan

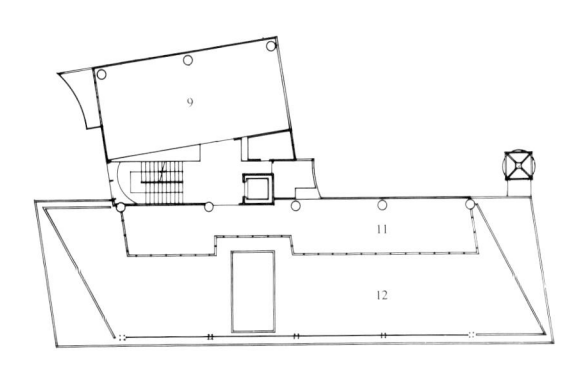

4th floor plan

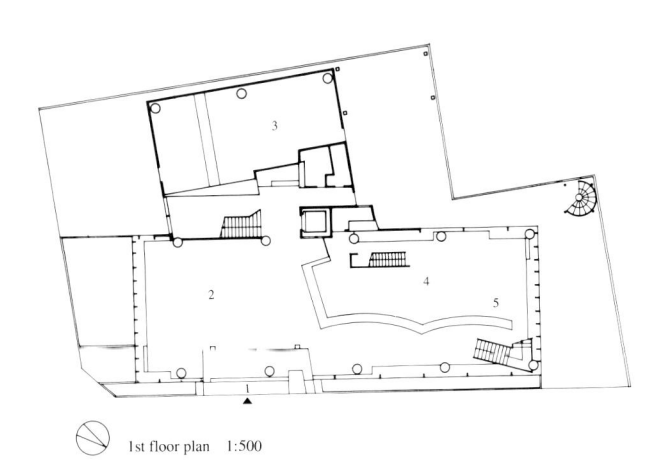

1st floor plan 1:500

Axonometric drawing

1 エントランス　Entrance
2 ロビー　Lobby
3 カフェテリア　Cafeteria
4 事務室　Office
5 相談コーナー　Guidance area
6 校長室　Principal's office
7 サロン　Salon
8 受水槽　Water tank
9 教室　Classroom
10 光庭　Light court
11 図書室　Library
12 屋外テラス

◀ カフェテリア前よりエントランスを見る　Looking at the entrance from the cafeteria

階段トップライト見上げ　Looking up at the stairway top-light

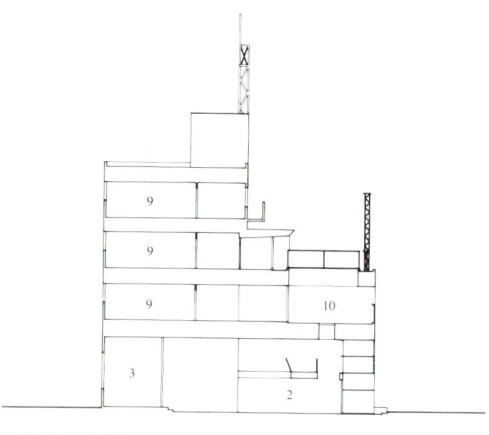

Section 1:500

1　ロビー　Lobby
3　カフェテリア　Cafeteria
9　教室　Classroom
12　光庭　Light court

エレベーターホールより階段を見る　Looking at the stairs from the elevator hall

私鉄の駅舎に隣接した敷地に建つ、大学入試を控えた若い学生が利用するための施設である。若者にとって快適に勉学ができ、一日が過ごせる場を規則的な鉄骨架構によって設定した。空間は線路に沿って平行に、層状に構成されている。それは空港の待合ロビーや船のデッキや橋や工場の内部空間に近づいていった。それらは現代の私たち都市の住民の一日の生活の記憶の主要な部分を占めるようになった、魅力ある環境のひとつであり、無性格な教育の環境を、そうした異質な心理的連想作用へと連れ出すことによって活性化することをねらったものである。

This is a preparatory school for university examinations built adjacent to a train station. Steel frame construction is employed to create a comfortable space for young students to study and spend the day. The school buildings are lined parallel to the railway and give students an impression of being in the waiting lounge of an airport, on the ship deck, on a bridge or in an industrial plant. These are non-ordinary spaces which attract the mind of urban people, and the psychological association that would be induced by the design would invigorate the students in otherwise and inherently non-descriptive educational environment.

4階図書室　4th floor, library

所在地　　埼玉県所沢市
設計　　　富永譲＋フォルムシステム設計研究所
施工　　　工新建設
竣工　　　1989年3月
敷地面積　701.11m²
建築面積　461.40m²
延床面積　1,352.08m²
階数　　　地上5階
構造　　　鉄骨造
撮影　　　富永譲

Location: Tokorozawa-city, Saitama
Architect: Yuzuru Tominaga + Form System Institute
General contractor: Koshin Construction Co.,Ltd.
Completion date: March 1989
Site area: 7,546.68sq.ft.
Building area: 4,966.46sq.ft.
Total floor area: 14,553.65sq.ft.
Number of floors: 5 floors above ground
Structure: Steel structure
Photographer: Yuzuru Tominaga

インデックス　Index

作品名／Project Name

あいく幼稚園, ANNEX	岩本秀三設計事務所	10-13
淡路町立岩屋中学校	Team Zoo いるか設計集団	68-73
育英学院サレジオ小・中学校	藤木隆男建築研究所	118-125
出石町立弘道小学校	Team Zoo いるか設計集団＋神戸大学 重村研究室	28-34
板橋さざなみ幼稚園 アネック	遠藤建築スタジオ　遠藤吉生	14-17
稲城市立城山小学校	船越徹＋アルコム	35-41
内子町立大瀬中学校	原広司＋アトリエ・ファイ建築研究所	74-83
OPEN-AIR KINDERGARTEN	宮本佳明＋アトリエ第5建築界	18-21
小国町立西里小学校	木島安史＋ＹＡＳ都市研究所	42-46
角館町立西長野小学校	渡辺豊和建築工房	47-53
金沢工業高等専門学校	水野一郎・田中光＋金沢計画研究所	150-157
金山町立金山中学校	木曽三岳奥村設計所・東京芸術大学益子研究室　奥村昭雄　益子義弘	84-90
熊本県立東稜高等学校	木島安史＋ＹＡＳ都市研究所	110-116
慶應義塾湘南藤沢中等部・高等部	谷口建築設計研究所　谷口吉生	126-133
慶應義塾大学湘南藤沢キャンパス	槇総合計画事務所	158-169
新宿区立落合中学校	船越徹＋アルコム	91-97
千里国際学園	長島孝一＋ＡＵＲ	134-141
つくば市立竹園西小学校	原広司＋アトリエ・ファイ建築研究所	54-59
東金市立嶺南幼稚園	篠原聡子＋空間研究所	22-26
東京造形大学	磯崎新アトリエ	170-178
東京都立大学	日本設計	179-185
東北芸術工科大学	本間利雄設計事務所＋地域環境計画研究室	186-195
中之口村立中之口西小学校	石本建築事務所	60-66
ヒコ・みづのジュエリーカレッジ	吉柳満アトリエ	204-208
三春町中郷学校	鈴木恂＋ＡＭＳ	142-148
三春町立桜中学校	香山アトリエ／環境造形研究所	98-103
睦学園 神戸国際中学校	竹中工務店	104-109
明治学院大学 本館	内井昭蔵建築設計事務所	196-202
早稲田ゼミナール所沢校1988	富永譲＋フォルムシステム設計研究所	209-216
AIKU KINDERGARTEN	HIDEMI IWAMOTO ARCHITECT & ASSOCIATES	10-13
HIKO・MIZUNO COLLEGE OF JEWELRY	MITSURU KIRYU ATELIER	204-208
ITABASHI SAZANAMI KINDERGARTEN ANNEX	Yoshitaka Endo　ENDO ARCHITECT STUDIO	14-17
IWAYA JUNIOR HIGH SCHOOL	TEAM ZOO ATELIER IRUKA CO.,LTD.	68-73
KANAZAWA TECHNICAL COLLEGE	ICHIRO MIZUNO, HIKARU TANAKA + KANAZAWA PLANNING RESEARCH	150-157
KANEYAMA JUNIOR HIGH SCHOOL	Akio Okumura　Yoshihiro Masko　KISO MITAKE OKUMURA DESIGN ACTIVITIES,TOKYO NATIONAL UNIVERSITY OF FINE ARTS AND MUSIC / MASKO LABORATORY	84-90
KEIO SHONAN-FUJISAWA JUNIOR & SENIOR HIGH SCHOOL	Yoshio Taniguchi　TANIGUCHI AND ASSOCIATES	126-133
KEIO UNIVERSITY SHONAN FUJISAWA CAMPUS	MAKI AND ASSOCIATES	158-169
KOBE INTERNATIONAL JUNIOR HIGH SCHOOL	TAKENAKA CORP.	104-109
KODO ELEMENTARY SCHOOL	TEAM ZOO ATELIER IRUKA CO.,LTD. + KOBE UNIVERSITY SHIGEMURA INSTITUTE	28-34
MEIJI GAKUIN UNIVERSITY MAIN HALL	S. UCHII ARCHITECT & ASSOCIATES	196-202
NAKANOKUCHI-NISHI PRIMARY SCHOOL	ISHIMOTO ARCHITECTURAL & ENGINEERING FIRM, INC.	60-66
NAKASATO COMMUNITY SCHOOL, MIHARU	MAKOTO SUZUKI + AMS ARCHITECTS	142-148
NISHINAGANO PRIMARY SCHOOL	WATANABE TOYOKAZU KENCHIKU KOBO	47-53
NISHIZATO PRIMARY SCHOOL, OGUNI	YASUFUMI KIJIMA + YAS & URBANISTS	42-46
OCHIAI JUNIOR HIGH SCHOOL	TOHRU FUNAKOSHI + ARCOM R&D, ARCHITECTS	91-97
OPEN-AIR KINDERGARTEN	KATSUHIRO MIYAMOTO + ATELIER CINQUIÉME	18-21
OSE MIDDLE SCHOOL	HIROSHI HARA + ATELIER Φ	74-83
REINAN PUBLIC KINDERGARTEN	SATOKO SHINOHARA + SPATIAL DESIGN STUDIO	22-26
SAKURA JUNIOR HIGH SCHOOL	KŌYAMA ATELIER	98-103
SALESIANS OF DON BOSCO SALESIO PRIMARY AND JUNIOR HIGH SCHOOL	FUJIKI TAKAO ATELIER, INC.	118-125
SENRI INTERNATIONAL SCHOOL	KOICHI NAGASHIMA + AUR ARCHITECTURE・URBAN DESIGN ・RESEARCH・CONSULTANTS CO.,LTD.	134-141
SHIROYAMA ELEMENTARY SCHOOL	TOHRU FUNAKOSHI + ARCOM R&D, ARCHITECTS	35-41
TAKEZONO-NISHI PRIMARY SCHOOL TSUKUBA	HIROSHI HARA + ATELIER Φ	54-59
TOHOKU UNIVERSITY OF ART & DESIGN	TOSHIO HOMMA & ASSOCIATES, CO.,LTD.	186-195
TOKYO METROPOLITAN UNIVERSITY	NIHON SEKKEI, INC.	179-185
TOKYO UNIVERSITY OF ART AND DESIGN	ARATA ISOZAKI & ASSOCIATES	170-178
TORYO HIGH SCHOOL, KUMAMOTO	YASUFUMI KIJIMA + YAS & URBANISTS	110-116
WASEDA SEMINAR IN TOKOROZAWA	YUZURU TOMINAGA + FORM SYSTEM INSTITUTE	209-216

建築事務所名／Architectural Firm

石本建築事務所	中之口村立中之口西小学校	60-66
磯崎新アトリエ	東京造形大学	170-178
岩本秀三設計事務所	あいく幼稚園, ANNEX	10-13
内井昭蔵建築設計事務所	明治学院大学 本館	196-202
遠藤建築スタジオ　遠藤吉生	板橋さざなみ幼稚園 アネックス	14-17
木島安史＋ＹＡＳ都市研究所	小国町立西里小学校	42-46
	熊本県立東稜高等学校	110-116
木曽二丘奥村設計所・東京芸術大学益子研究室　奥村昭雄　益子義弘	金山町立金山中学校	84-90
吉柳満アトリエ	ヒコ・みづのジュエリーカレッジ	204-208
香山アトリエ／環境造形研究所	三春町立桜中学校	98-103
篠原聡子＋空間研究所	東金市立嶺南幼稚園	22-26
鈴木恂＋ＡＭＳ	三春町中郷学校	142-148
竹中工務店	睦学園 神戸国際中学校	104-109
谷口建築設計研究所　谷口吉生	慶應義塾湘南藤沢中等部・高等部	126-133
Team Zoo いるか設計集団	淡路町立岩屋中学校	68-73
Team Zoo いるか設計集団＋神戸大学 重村研究室	出石町立弘道小学校	28-34
富永譲＋フォルムシステム設計研究所	早稲田ゼミナール所沢校1988	209-216
長島孝一＋ＡＵＲ	千里国際学園	134-141
日本設計	東京都立大学	179-185
原広司＋アトリエ・ファイ建築研究所	内子町立大瀬中学校	74-83
	つくば市立竹園西小学校	54-59
藤木隆男建築研究所	育英学院サレジオ小・中学校	118-125
船越徹＋アルコム	稲城市立城山小学校	35-41
	新宿区立落合中学校	91-97
本間利雄設計事務所＋地域環境計画研究室	東北芸術工科大学	186-195
槇総合計画事務所	慶應義塾大学湘南藤沢キャンパス	158-169
水野一郎・田中光＋金沢計画研究所	金沢工業高等専門学校	150-157
宮本佳明＋アトリエ第5建築界	OPEN-AIR KINDERGARTEN	18-21
渡辺豊和建築工房	角館町立西長野小学校	47-53

ARATA ISOZAKI & ASSOCIATES	TOKYO UNIVERSITY OF ART AND DESIGN	170-178
Yoshitaka Endo　ENDO ARCHITECT STUDIO	ITABASHI SAZANAMI KINDERGARTEN ANNEX	14-17
FUJIKI TAKAO ATELIER, INC.	SALESIANS OF DON BOSCO SALESIO PRIMARY AND JUNIOR HIGH SCHOOL	118-125
HIDEMI IWAMOTO ARCHITECT & ASSOCIATES	AIKU KINDERGARTEN	10-13
HIROSHI HARA + ATELIER Φ	OSE MIDDLE SCHOOL	74-83
	TAKEZONO-NISHI PRIMARY SCHOOL TSUKUBA	54-59
ICHIRO MIZUNO, HIKARU TANAKA + KANAZAWA PLANNING RESEARCH	KANAZAWA TECHNICAL COLLEGE	150-157
ISHIMOTO ARCHITECTURAL & ENGINEERING FIRM, INC.	NAKANOKUCHI-NISHI PRIMARY SCHOOL	60-66
KATSUHIRO MIYAMOTO + ATELIER CINQUIÉME	OPEN-AIR KINDERGARTEN	18-21
Akio Okumura　Yoshihiro Masko　KISO MITAKE OKUMURA DESIGN ACTIVITIES,TOKYO NATIONAL UNIVERSITY OF FINE ARTS AND MUSIC / MASKO LABORATORY	KANEYAMA JUNIOR HIGH SCHOOL	84-90
KŌYAMA ATELIER	SAKURA JUNIOR HIGH SCHOOL	98-103
KOICHI NAGASHIMA + AUR ARCHITECTURE・URBAN DESIGN・RESEARCH・CONSULTANTS CO.,LTD.	SENRI INTERNATIONAL SCHOOL	134-141
MAKI AND ASSOCIATES	KEIO UNIVERSITY SHONAN FUJISAWA CAMPUS	158-169
MAKOTO SUZUKI + AMS ARCHITECTS	NAKASATO COMMUNITY SCHOOL, MIHARU	142-148
MITSURU KIRYU ATELIER	HIKO・MIZUNO COLLEGE OF JEWELRY	204-208
NIHON SEKKEI, INC.	TOKYO METROPOLITAN UNIVERSITY	179-185
SATOKO SHINOHARA + SPATIAL DESIGN STUDIO	REINAN PUBLIC KINDERGARTEN	22-26
S. UCHII ARCHITECT & ASSOCIATES	MEIJI GAKUIN UNIVERSITY MAIN HALL	196-202
TAKENAKA CORP.	KOBE INTERNATIONAL JUNIOR HIGH SCHOOL	104-109
Yoshio Taniguchi　TANIGUCHI AND ASSOCIATES	KEIO SHONAN-FUJISAWA JUNIOR & SENIOR HIGH SCHOOL	126-133
TEAM ZOO　ATELIER IRUKA CO.,LTD.	IWAYA JUNIOR HIGH SCHOOL	68-73
TEAM ZOO　ATELIER IRUKA CO.,LTD. + KOBE UNIVERSITY/ SHIGEMURA INSTITUTE	KODO ELEMENTARY SCHOOL	28-34
TOHRU FUNAKOSHI + ARCOM R&D, ARCHITECTS	OCHIAI JUNIOR HIGH SCHOOL	91-97
	SHIROYAMA ELEMENTARY SCHOOL	35-41
TOSHIO HOMMA & ASSOCIATES, CO.,LTD.	TOHOKU UNIVERSITY OF ART & DESIGN	186-195
WATANABE TOYOKAZU KENCHIKU KOBO	NISHINAGANO PRIMARY SCHOOL	47-53
YASUFUMI KIJIMA + YAS & URBANISTS	NISHIZATO PRIMARY SCHOOL, OGUNI	42-46
	TORYO HIGH SCHOOL, KUMAMOTO	110-116
YUZURU TOMINAGA + FORM SYSTEM INSTITUTE	WASEDA SEMINAR IN TOKOROZAWA	209-216

所在地／Location

淡路町立岩屋中学校	〒656-24 兵庫県津名郡淡路町岩屋2875	0799-72-5512
育英学院サレジオ小・中学校	〒187 東京都小平市上水南町4-7-1	0423-21-0312
出石町立弘道小学校	〒668-02 兵庫県出石郡出石町東條寺町345	0796-52-2105
板橋さざなみ幼稚園 アネックス	〒724 広島県東広島市西条町寺家金平山	0824-22-3788
稲城市立城山小学校	〒206 東京都稲城市向陽台6-17	0423-79-0700
内子町立大瀬中学校	〒791-33 愛媛県喜多郡内子町大瀬本町1	0893-47-1141
小国町立西里小学校	〒869-25 熊本県阿蘇郡小国町西里972	0967-46-2123
角館町立西長野小学校	〒014-04 秋田県仙北郡角館町西長野中泊402	0187-53-2094
金沢工業高等専門学校	〒921 石川県金沢市久安2-270	0762-48-1100
金山町立金山中学校	〒999-54 山形県最上郡金山町金山久保641	0233-52-2905
熊本県立東稜高等学校	〒862 熊本県熊本市健軍町小峯2614-1	096-369-1008
慶應義塾湘南藤沢中等部・高等部	〒252 神奈川県藤沢市遠藤5466	0466-47-5111
慶應義塾大学湘南藤沢キャンパス	〒252 神奈川県藤沢市遠藤5322	0466-47-5111
淨念寺学園　あいく幼稚園, ANNEX	〒729-26 広島県豊田郡安浦町安登393-5	0823-84-5860
新宿区立落合中学校	〒161 東京都新宿区下落合2-24-6	03-3565-0701
千里国際学園	〒562 大阪府箕面市小野原西4-4-16	0727-27-5090
宝塚武庫山幼稚園（OPEN-AIR KINDERGARTEN）	〒665 兵庫県宝塚市武庫山1-1-17	0797-23-0200
つくば市立竹園西小学校	〒305 茨城県つくば市竹園2-19-2	0298-51-7975
東金市立嶺南幼稚園	〒283 千葉県東金市堀上947-2	0475-54-1479
東京造形大学	〒192 東京都八王子市宇津貫町1556	0426-37-8111
東京都立大学	〒192-03 東京都八王子市南大沢1-1	0426-77-1111
東北芸術工科大学	〒990 山形県山形市上桜田200	0236-27-2000
中之口村立中之口西小学校	〒950-13 新潟県西蒲原郡中之口村打越244	025-375-3015
水野学園 専門学校 ヒコ・みづのジュエリーカレッジ	〒150 東京都渋谷区神宮前5-29-2	03-3499-0300
三春町中郷学校	〒977 福島県田村郡三春町柴原神久保235	0247-62-3091
三春町立桜中学校	〒977 福島県田村郡三春町鷹ノ巣瀬山132	0247-62-3090
睦学園 神戸国際中学校	〒654 兵庫県神戸市須磨区高倉台7-21-1	078-731-4665
明治学院大学 本館	〒108 東京都港区白金台1-2-37	03-5421-5111
早稲田ゼミナール所沢校1988	〒359 埼玉県所沢市喜多町16-4	0429-28-6711

AIKU KINDERGARTEN	393-5 Ato, Yasuura-town, Toyota-county, HIROSHIMA 729-26	0823-84-5860
HIKO・MIZUNO COLLEGE OF JEWELRY	5-29-2 Jingumae, Shibuya-ward, TOKYO 150	03-3499-0300
ITABASHI SAZANAMI KINDERGARTEN ANNEX	Kanahirayama, Jike, Saijo-cho, Higashihiroshima-city, HIROSHIMA 724	0824-22-3788
IWAYA JUNIOR HIGH SCHOOL	2875 Iwaya, Awaji-town, Tsuna-county, HYOGO 656-24	0799-72-5512
KANAZAWA TECHNICAL COLLEGE	2-270 Hisayasu, Kanazawa-city, ISHIKAWA 921	0762-48-1100
KANEYAMA JUNIOR HIGH SCHOOL	641 Kubo, Kaneyama, Kaneyama-town, Mogami-county, YAMAGATA 999-54	0233-52-2905
KEIO SHONAN-FUJISAWA JUNIOR & SENIOR HIGH SCHOOL	5466 Endo, Fujisawa-city, KANAGAWA 252	0466-47-5111
KEIO UNIVERSITY SHONAN FUJISAWA CAMPUS	5322 Endo, Fujisawa-city, KANAGAWA 252	0466-47-5111
KOBE INTERNATIONAL JUNIOR HIGH SCHOOL	7-21-1 Takakuradai, Suma-ward, Kobe-city, HYOGO 654	078-731-4665
KODO ELEMENTARY SCHOOL	345 Tojotera-machi, Izushi-town, Izushi-county, HYOGO 668-02	0796-52-2105
MEIJI GAKUIN UNIVERSITY MAIN HALL	1-2-37 Shirokanedai, Minato-ward, TOKYO 108	03-5421-5111
NAKANOKUCHI-NISHI PRIMARY SCHOOL	244 Uchikoshi, Nakanokuchi-village, Nishikanbara-county, NIIGATA 950-13	025-375-3015
NAKASATO COMMUNITY SCHOOL, MIHARU	235 Kamikubo, Shibahara, Miharu-town, Tamura-county, FUKUSHIMA 977	0247-62-3091
NISHINAGANO PRIMARY SCHOOL	402 Nakadomari, Nishinagano, Kakunodate-town, Senboku-county, AKITA 014-04	0187-53-2094
NISHIZATO PRIMARY SCHOOL, OGUNI	972 Nishizato, Oguni-town, Aso-county, KUMAMOTO 869-25	0967-46-2123
OCHIAI JUNIOR HIGH SCHOOL	2-24-6 Shimoochiai, Shinjuku-ward, TOKYO 161	03-3565-0701
OSE MIDDLE SCHOOL	1 Honcho, Ose, Uchiko-town, Kita-county, EHIME 791-33	0893-47-1141
REINAN PUBLIC KINDERGARTEN	947-2 Horiage, Togane-city, CHIBA 283	0475-54-1479
SAKURA JUNIOR HIGH SCHOOL	132 Seyama, Takanosu, Miharu-town, Tamura-county, FUKUSHIMA 977	0247-62-3090
SALESIANS OF DON BOSCO SALESIO PRIMARY AND JUNIOR HIGH SCHOOL	4-7-1 Jyosuiminami-cho, Kodaira-city, TOKYO 187	0423-21-0312
SENRI INTERNATIONAL SCHOOL	4-4-16 Onohara Nishi, Minoh-city, OSAKA 562	0727-27-5090
SHIROYAMA ELEMENTARY SCHOOL	6-17 Kohyoudai, Inagi-city, TOKYO 206	0423-79-0700
TAKARAZUKA MUKOYAMA KINDERGARTEN (OPEN-AIR KINDERGARTEN)	1-1-17 Mukoyama, Takarazuka-city, HYOGO 665	0797-23-0200
TAKEZONO-NISHI PRIMARY SCHOOL TSUKUBA	19-2 Takezono, Tsukuba-city, IBARAKI 305	0298-51-7975
TOHOKU UNIVERSITY OF ART & DESIGN	200 Kamisakurada, Yamagata-city, YAMAGATA 990	0236-27-2000
TOKYO METROPOLITAN UNIVERSITY	1-1 Minamiohsawa, Hachioji-city, TOKYO 192-03	0426-77-1111
TOKYO UNIVERSITY OF ART AND DESIGN	1556 Uzunuki-cho, Hachioji-city, TOKYO 192	0426-37-8111
TORYO HIGH SCHOOL, KUMAMOTO	2614-1 Omine, Kengun-machi, Kumamoto-city, KUMAMOTO 862	096-369-1008
WASEDA SEMINAR IN TOKOROZAWA	16-4 Kita-cho, Tokorozawa-city, SAITAMA 359	0429-28-6711

建築事務所アドレス／Architectural Firm's Address

アトリエ・ファイ建築研究所	〒150 東京都渋谷区猿楽町28-10	03-3464-8970
株式会社アルコム	〒107 東京都港区南青山4-15-8	03-3423-6331
株式会社石本建築事務所	〒102 東京都千代田区九段南4-6-12	03-3221-8921
株式会社磯崎新アトリエ	〒107 東京都港区赤坂9-6-17	03-3405-1526
Team Zoo 株式会社いるか設計集団	〒650 兵庫県神戸市中央区海岸通3-1-5-303	078-332-4902
岩本秀三設計事務所	〒737 広島県呉市中央3-1-17-204	0823-25-6633
内井昭蔵建築設計事務所	〒102 東京都千代田区六番町13-12	03-5275-0881
ＡＵＲ建築・都市・研究コンサルタント	〒106 東京都港区麻布十番2-3-5	03-3456-2731
遠藤建築スタジオ	〒730 広島県広島市中区国泰寺町1-8-20	082-240-6810
金沢計画研究所	〒921 石川県金沢市西泉1-66-1	0762-44-9222
木曽三岳奥村設計所・東京芸術大学益子研究室	〒176 東京都練馬区中村北3-16-19	03-3990-3934
吉柳満アトリエ	〒466 愛知県名古屋市昭和区滝川町47-48	052-836-1225
空間研究所	〒162 東京都新宿区天神町77	03-3266-9971
株式会社計画・環境建築 ＹＡＳ都市研究所	〒102 東京都千代田区麹町4-3-5	03-3230-4445
香山アトリエ／環境造形研究所	〒113 東京都文京区本郷3-44-2	03-3815-4702
鈴木恂＋ＡＭＳ	〒150 東京都渋谷区神宮前2-31-1	03-3497-1080
株式会社竹中工務店	〒541 大阪府大阪市中央区本町4-1-13	06-252-1201
谷口建築設計研究所	〒105 東京都港区虎ノ門4-1-40	03-3438-1506
富永譲＋フォルムシステム設計研究所	〒113 東京都文京区本郷4-12-16-611	03-3811-4159
株式会社日本設計	〒163-04 東京都新宿区西新宿2-1-1	03-5350-7111
藤木隆男建築研究所	〒153 東京都目黒区青葉台4-6-6	03-3466-1310
株式会社プライム	〒160 東京都新宿区新宿5-10-12-204	03-3354-8204
本間利雄設計事務所十地域環境計画研究室	〒990 山形県山形市小白川町4-13-12	0236-41-7711
槇総合計画事務所	〒103 東京都中央区日本橋3-6-2	03-3274-6681
宮本佳明＋アトリエ第5建築界	〒659 兵庫県芦屋市三条町6-28-302	0797-23-6985
渡辺豊和建築工房	〒541 大阪府大阪市中央区伏見町3-3-3	06-229-9833

ARATA ISOZAKI & ASSOCIATES	9-6-17 Akasaka, Minato-ward, TOKYO 107	03-3405-1526
ARCOM R&D	4-15-8 Minami Aoyama, Minato-ward, TOKYO 107	03-3423-6331
ATELIER Φ	28-10 Sarugaku-cho, Shibuya-ward, TOKYO 150	03-3464-8970
AUR ARCHITECTURE・URBAN DESIGN・RESEARCH・CONSULTANTS CO.,LTD.	2-3-5 Azabu Juban, Minato-ward, TOKYO 106	03-3456-2731
ENDO ARCHITECT STUDIO	1-8-20 Kokutaiji-machi, Naka-ward, Hiroshima-city, HIROSHIMA 730	082-240-6810
FUJIKI TAKAO ATELIER, INC. ARCHITECTS	4-6-6 Aobadai, Meguro-ward, TOKYO 153	03-3466-1310
HIDEMI IWAMOTO ARCHITECT & ASSOCIATES	3-1-17-204 Chuo, Kure-city, HIROSHIMA 737	0823-25-6633
ISHIMOTO ARCHITECTURAL & ENGINEERING FIRM, INC.	4-6-12 Kudan Minami, Chiyoda-ward, TOKYO 102	03-3221-8921
KANAZAWA PLANNING RESEARCH	1-66-1 Nishiizumi, Kanazawa-city, ISHIKAWA 921	0762-44-9222
KATSUHIRO MIYAMOTO + ATELIER CINQUIÉME	6-28-302 Sanjo-cho, Ashiya-city, HYOGO 659	0797-23-6985
KEIKAKU INC. / YAS & URBANISTS	4-3-5 Kohji-machi, Chiyoda-ward, TOKYO 102	03-3230-4445
KISO MITAKE OKUMURA DESIGN ACTIVITIES, TOKYO NATIONAL UNIVERSITY OF FINE ARTS AND MUSIC / MASKO LABORATORY	3-16-19 Nakamura Kita, Nerima-ward, TOKYO 176	03-3990-3934
KŌYAMA ATELIER	3-44-2 Hongo, Bunkyo-ward, TOKYO 113	03-3815-4702
MAKI AND ASSOCIATES	3-6-2 Nihonbashi, Chuo-ward, TOKYO 103	03-3274-6681
MAKOTO SUZUKI + AMS ARCHITECTS	2-31-1 Jingumae, Shibuya-ward, TOKYO 150	03-3497-1080
MITSURU KIRYU ATELIER	47-48 Takigawa-cho, Showa-ward, Nagoya-city, AICHI 466	052-836-1225
NIHON SEKKEI INC.	2-1-1 Nishi Shinjuku, Shinjuku-ward, TOKYO 163-04	03-5350-7111
PRIME INC. ARCHITECTURE & PLANNING	#204, 5-10-12 Shinjuku, Shinjuku-ward, TOKYO 160	03-3354-8204
SPATIAL DESIGN STUDIO	77 Tenjin-cho, Shinjuku-ward, TOKYO 162	03-3266-9971
S.UCHII ARCHITECT & ASSOCIATES	13-12 Rokuban-cho, Chiyoda-ward, TOKYO 102	03-5275-0881
TAKENAKA CORP.	4-1-13 Hommachi, Chuo-ward, Osaka-city, OSAKA 541	06-252-1201
TANIGUCHI AND ASSOCIATES	4-1-40 Toranomon, Minato-ward, TOKYO 105	03-3438-1506
TEAM ZOO ATELIER IRUKA CO.,LTD.	#303, 3-1-5 Kaigandori, Chuo-ward, Kobe-city, HYOGO 650	078-332-4902
TOSHIO HOMMA & ASSOCIATES, CO.,LTD.	4-13-12 Kojirakawa-machi, Yamagata-city, YAMAGATA 990	0236-41-7711
WATANABE TOYOKAZU KENCHIKU KOBO	3-3-3 Fushimi-cho, Chuo-ward, Osaka-city, OSAKA 541	06-229-9833
YUZURU TOMINAGA + FORM SYSTEM INSTITUTE	#611, 4-12-16 Hongo, Bunkyo-ward, TOKYO 113	03-3811-4159

フォトグラファーアドレス／Photographer's Address

アカサカスタジオ（山本伸生）	〒810 福岡県福岡市中央区今泉1-9-12-402	092-714-7809
有限会社アラ井建築写真事務所（荒井政夫）	〒113 東京都文京区湯島2-4-3-906	03-3815-7733
アトリエ木寺（木寺安彦）	〒158 東京都世田谷区中町4-25-13-202	03-3703-5744
上田明	〒431-13 静岡県引佐郡細江町気賀693	053-474-9261
大橋富夫	〒203 東京都東久留米市下里2-2-4	0424-74-5057
岡田泰治	〒182 東京都調布市調布ヶ丘2-29-1-103	0424-81-9298
加藤嘉六	〒168 東京都杉並区高井戸東3-14-11-6	03-3302-4460
川澄建築写真事務所	〒162 東京都新宿区余丁町9-5	03-3341-7886
有限会社川元写真事務所（川元斉）	〒542 大阪府大阪市中央区南船場4-9-2	06-244-0506
北嶋俊治	〒160 東京都新宿区荒木町23	03-3354-2203
プロフォート クシロ（久代正人）	〒950 新潟県新潟市蒲原町3-24	025-245-7843
甲陽園写真スタジオ（生田将人）	〒662 兵庫県西宮市甲陽園本庄町9-18	0798-72-0694
小林研二写真事務所	〒112 東京都文京区春日2-10-19-901	03-5802-4828
株式会社サン・プロジェクト（中田眞澄）	〒160 東京都新宿区新宿2-7-3-509	03-3352-3850
株式会社彰国社	〒160 東京都新宿区坂町25	03-3359-3231
株式会社新建築社	〒113 東京都文京区湯島2-31-2	03-3811-7101
株式会社新写真工房（堀内広治）	〒164 東京都中野区本町1-5-5-102	03-3373-2476
虹や（須賀信夫）	〒990 山形県山形市小荷駄町7-55	0236-41-2448
鈴木悠撮影事務所	〒160 東京都新宿区歌舞伎町2-3-23-602	03-3200-5092
スタジオ村井（村井修）	〒164 東京都中野区弥生町2-41-10	03-3381-2497
株式会社テクニカル・アート（柴田泰夫）	〒160 東京都新宿区新宿6-27-10	03-3203-3573
テクニ・スタッフ（岡本公二）	〒814 福岡県福岡市早良区百道浜4-17-2	092-823-1150
冨田治	〒167 東京都杉並区上荻2-21-25-402	03-5310-4344
ナカサ＆パートナーズ	〒106 東京都港区南麻布3-5-5	03-3444-2922
ナガミネスタジオ	〒165 東京都中野区江原町1-30-8	03-3951-6569
古館克明	〒153 東京都目黒区青葉台3-18-10-202	03-3464-8073
レトリア（高瀬良夫）	〒151 東京都渋谷区千駄ヶ谷3-12-14	03-3403-0977
渡邊和俊	〒107 東京都港区南青山2-8-27-604	03-3402-7072

AKASAKA STUDIO（Sinsey Yamamoto）	#402, 1-9-12 Imaizumi, Chuo-ward, Fukuoka-city, FUKUOKA 810	092-714-7809
ARAI ARCHIPHOTO（Masao Arai）	#906, 2-4-3 Yushima, Bunkyo-ward, TOKYO 113	03-3815-7733
ATELIER KIDERA（Yasuhiko Kidera）	#202, 4-25-13 Nakamachi, Setagaya-ward, TOKYO 158	03-3703-5744
Furudate Katsuaki	#202, 3-18-10 Aobadai, Meguro-ward, TOKYO 153	03-3464-8073
Karoku Kato	3-14-11-6 Takaido Higashi, Suginami-ward, TOKYO 168	03-3302-4460
KAWAMOTO PHOTO OFFICE（Hitoshi Kawamoto）	4-9-2 Minami Senba, Chuo-ward, Osaka-city, OSAKA 542	406-244-0506
KAWASUMI ARCHITECTURAL PHOTOGRAPH OFFICE	9-5 Yocho-machi, Shinjuku-ward, TOKYO 162	03-3341-7886
Toshiharu Kitajima	23 Araki-cho, Shinjuku-ward, TOKYO 160	03-3354-2203
KOBAYASHI KENJI PHOTOGRAPH OFFICE	#901, 2-10-19 Kasuga, Bunkyo-ward, TOKYO 112	03-5802-4828
KOYOEN PHOTO STUDIO（Masao Ikuta）	9-18 Honjo-cho, Koyoen, Nishinomiya-city, HYOGO 662	0798-72-0694
PROPHOTO KUSHIRO（Masato Kushiro）	3-24 Kanbara-cho, Niigata-city, NIIGATA 950	025-245-7843
NACÁSA & PARTNERS INC.	3-5-5 Minami Azabu, Minato-ward, TOKYO 106	03-3444-2922
NAGAMINE STUDIO	1-30-8 Ehara-cho, Nakano-ward, TOKYO 165	03-3951-6569
Tomio Ohashi	2-2-4 Shimosato, Higashikurume-city, TOKYO 203	0424-74-5057
Taiji Okada	2-29-1-103 Chotugaoka, Chotu-city, TOKYO 182	0424-81-9298
RETORIA（Yoshio Takase）	3-12-14 Sendagaya, Shibuya-ward, TOKYO 151	03-3403-0977
SHINKENCHIKU-SHA・CO.,LTD.	2-31-2 Yushima, Bunkyo-ward, TOKYO 113	03-3811-7101
SHIN-SHASHIN-KOBO INC.（Koji Horiuchi）	#102, 1-5-5 Honcho, Nakano-ward, TOKYO 164	03-3373-2476
THE SHOKOKUSHA PUBLISHING CO.,LTD.	25 Saka-machi, Shinjuku-ward, TOKYO 160	03-3359-3231
STUDIO MURAI（Osamu Murai）	2-41-10 Yayoi-cho, Nakano-ward, TOKYO 164	03-3381-2497
NIJIYA（Nobuo Suga）	7-55 Konida-machi, Yamagata-city, YAMAGATA 990	0236-41-2448
SUN PROJECT INC.（Masumi Nakada）	#509, 2-7-3 Shinjuku, Shinjuku-ward, TOKYO 160	03-3352-3850
TECHNICAL ART CORP.（Yasuo Shibata）	6-27-10 Shinjuku, Shinjuku-ward, TOKYO 160	03-3203-3573
TECHNI STAFF（Koji Okamoto）	4-17-2 Momojihama, Sawara-ward, Fukuoka-city, FUKUOKA 814	092-823-1150
Osamu Tomita	#402, 2-21-25 Kamiogi, Suginami-ward, TOKYO 167	03-5310-4344
Akira Ueda	693 Kiga, Hosoe-town, Inasa-county, SHIZUOKA 431-13	053-474-9261
Kazutoshi Watanabe	#604, 2-8-27 Minami Aoyama, Minato-ward, TOKYO 107	03-3402-7072
YUTAKA SUZUKI PHOTO ATELIER	#602, 2-3-23 Kabuki-cho, Shinjuku-ward, TOKYO 160	03-3200-5092

EDUCATIONAL FACILITIES
New Concepts in Architecture & Design

現代建築集成／教育施設

発行日
1994年 7月20日

定価
16,000円（本体15,534円）

編集・発行
株式会社メイセイ出版
東京都千代田区神田神保町3-11-1-203　〒101
Phone. 03(5276)1941　Fax. 03(5276)1966

監修
富永讓
（富永讓＋フォルムシステム設計研究所）

アートディレクション＆デザイン
井上則人
（いのうえでざいん）

デザイン
石田剛
（いのうえでざいん）

発売元
株式会社オーク出版サービス
東京都千代田区神田神保町1-49　〒101
Phone. 03-3291-7031　Fax. 03-3291-8576

印刷
日本写真印刷株式会社

Published by
MEISEI PUBLICATIONS

Supervised by
Yuzuru Tominaga
YUZURU TOMINAGA + FORM SYSTEM INSTITUTE

Designed by
Norito Inoue / Tsuyoshi Ishida
INOUE DESIGN

Printed by
NISSHA PRINTING CO.,LTD.

ISBN4-87246-293-9 C3052 P16000E
©1994 MEISEI PUBLICATIONS
本書の収容内容の無断掲載、複写、引用を禁じます。